ANCIENT INDIAN TRADITION & MYTHOLOGY

Translated by
A BOARD OF SCHOLARS

Edited by
Dr. G.P. BHATT

VOLUME 63

ANCIENT INDIAN TRADITION AND MYTHOLOGY SERIES

[PURĀṆAS IN TRANSLATION]

Volumes Released

ŚIVA 1-4
LIṄGA 5-6
BHĀGAVATA 7-11
GARUḌA 12-14
NĀRADA 15-19
KŪRMA 20-21
BRAHMĀṆḌA 22-26
AGNI 27-30
VARĀHA 31-32
BRAHMA 33-36
VĀYU 37-38
PADMA 39-48
SKANDA, PARTS I-XXI, 49-69

Volumes Under Preparation

SKANDA, PARTS XXII-XXIII, 70-71
VĀMANA 72-73
BHAVIṢYA
BRAHMAVAIVARTA
DEVĪBHĀGAVATA
KĀLIKĀ
MĀRKAṆḌEYA
MATSYA
VIṢṆU
VIṢṆUDHARMOTTARA

THE SKANDA-PURĀṆA

Translated and Annotated by

Dr. G.V. TAGARE

PART XV

MOTILAL BANARSIDASS PUBLISHERS
PRIVATE LIMITED • DELHI

Reprint: Delhi, ***2010***
First Edition: Delhi, 2001

ISBN: 978-81-208-1837-8

MOTILAL BANARSIDASS
41 U.A. Bungalow Road, Jawahar Nagar, Delhi 110 007
8 Mahalaxmi Chamber, 22 Bhulabhai Desai Road, Mumbai 400 026
203 Royapettah High Road, Mylapore, Chennai 600 004
236, 9th Main III Block, Jayanagar, Bangalore 560 011
Sanas Plaza, 1302 Baji Rao Road, Pune 411 002
8 Camac Street, Kolkata 700 017
Ashok Rajpath, Patna 800 004
Chowk, Varanasi 221 001

UNESCO COLLECTION OF REPRESENTATIVE WORKS—*Indian Series*
This book has been accepted in the Indian Translation Series of the UNESCO Collection of Representative Works, jointly sponsored by the United Nations Educational, Scientific and Cultural Organization (UNESCO) and the Government of India

Printed in India
By Jainendra Prakash Jain at Shri Jainendra Press,
A-45 Naraina, Phase-I, New Delhi 110 028
and Published by Narendra Prakash Jain for
Motilal Banarsidass Publishers Private Limited,
Bungalow Road, Delhi 110 007

PUBLISHER'S NOTE

The purest gems lie hidden in the bottom of the ocean or in the depth of rocks. One has to dive into the ocean or delve into the rocks to find them out. Similarly, truth lies concealed in the language which with the passage of time has become obsolete. Man has to learn that language before he discovers that truth.

But he has neither the means nor the leisure to embark on that course. We have, therefore, planned to help him acquire knowledge by an easier course. We have started the series of Ancient Indian Tradition and Mythology in English Translation. Our goal is to universalize knowledge through the most popular international medium of expression. The publication of the Purāṇas in English Translation is a step towards that goal.

Acknowledgements

It is our pleasant duty to put on record our sincere thanks to Dr. R.N. Dandekar and the UNESCO authorities for their kind encouragement and valuable help in the publication of the volumes in this series.

CONTENTS

SKANDA-PURĀṆA
Book V: ĀVANTYA KHAṆḌA
Section III: REVĀ-KHAṆḌA

ABBREVIATIONS

Common and self-evident abbreviations such as Ch (s) Chapter(s), p page, pp pages, v verse, vv verses, Ftn Footnote, Hist. Ind. Philo. History of Indian Philosophy are not included in this list.

AGP	S.M. Ali's The Geography of Purāṇas, PPH, New Delhi, 1973
AIHT	Ancient Indian Historical Tradition, F.E. Pargiter, Motilal Banarsidass (MLBD), Delhi
AITM	Ancient Indian Tradition and Mythology Series, MLBD, Delhi
AP	Agni Purāṇa, Guru Mandal Edition (GM), Calcutta, 1957
AV	Atharva Veda, Svādhyāya Maṇḍal, Aundh
Bdp	Brahmāṇḍa Purāṇa, MLBD, Delhi, 1973
BG	Bhagavadgītā
BhP	Bhāgavata Purāṇa, Bhagavat Vidyapeeth, Ahmedabad
Br	Brāhmaṇa (preceded by name such as Śatapatha)
BsP	Bhaviṣya Purāṇa, Vishnu Shastri Bapat, Wai
BVP	Brahma Vaivarta Purāṇa, GM, 1955-57
CC	Caturvarga Cintāmaṇi by Hemādri
CVS	Caraṇa Vyūha Sūtra by Śaunaka, Com. by Mahdāsa
DB	Devi Bhāgavata, GM, 1960-61
De or GDAMI	The Geographical Dictionary of Ancient and Medieval India, N.L. De/Dey, Oriental Reprint, Delhi, 1971
DhS	Dharma Sūtra (preceded by the author's name such as Gautama)
GP	Garuḍa Purāṇa, ed. R.S. Bhattacharya, Chowkhamba, Varanasi, 1964
GS	Gṛhya Sūtra (preceded by the name of the author such as Āpastamba)
HD	History of Dharma Śāstra, P.V. Kane, G.O.S.
JP	Purāṇa (Journal of the Kashiraj Trust), Varanasi
KA	Kauṭilya Arthaśāstra
KP	Kūrma Purāṇa, Veṅkaṭeśvara Press Edn., Bombay; also Kashiraj Trust Edn., Varanasi, 1971

LP	Liṅga Purāṇa, GM, 1960; also MLBD, Delhi, 1981
Manu	Manusmṛti
Mbh	Mahābhārata, Gītā Press, Gorakhpur, VS 2014
MkP	Mārkaṇḍeya Purāṇa
MN	Mahābhārata Nāmānukramaṇī, Gītā Press, Gorakhpur, VS 2016
MtP	Matsya Purāṇa, GM, 1954
MW	M. Monier-Williams' Sanskrit-English Dictionary, MLBD, Delhi, 1976
NP	Nāradīya or Nārada Purāṇa, Veṅkaṭeśvara Press, Bombay
PdP	Padma Purāṇa, GM, 1957-59
PE	Purāṇic Encyclopaedia, V. Mani, English Version, MLBD, Delhi, 1975
PR or PRHRC	Purāṇic Records on Hindu Rites and Customs, R.C. Hazra, Calcutta, 1948
ṚV	Ṛg Veda, Svādhyāya Maṇḍal, Aundh
Śat Br	Śatapatha Brāhmaṇa
SC or SMC	Smṛti Candrikā by Devanna Bhaṭṭa
SkP	Skanda Purāṇa
SP	Śiva Purāṇa
VāP	Vāyu Purāṇa
VR	Vālmīki Rāmāyaṇa
VdP	Viṣṇudharmottara Purāṇa
VmP	Vāmana Purāṇa
VP	Viṣṇu Purāṇa
VrP	Varāha Purāṇa

SKANDA PURĀṆA

Book V: ĀVANTYA KHAṆḌA

Section III: REVĀ-KHAṆḌA

CHAPTER ONE HUNDRED ONE

The Greatness of Saṅkarṣaṇa Tīrtha

Śrī Mārkaṇḍeya said:

1-6. Thereafter, O great king, one should go to an extremely splendid Tīrtha on the northern bank of Narmadā in the centre of Yajñavāṭa (sacrificial hall), well-known on the earth as Saṅkarṣaṇa. It is destructive of sins. Formerly, O king, a penance was performed by Balabhadra there.

Devas are present there itself in the vicinity, O prince. Śambhu is stationed there along with Umā. Keśava too is present there.

By way of rendering help to all living beings, Śaṅkara, the destroyer of sins, has been installed there by Balabhadra with great devotion, O great king.

Subduing anger and all the sense-organs, a devotee should take his holy bath on the eleventh day in a bright fortnight (of a month). He should bathe Śiva with honey. One who devoutly performs Śrāddha unto the Pitṛs there itself goes to the highest region in accordance with the words of Balabhadra.

CHAPTER ONE HUNDRED TWO

The Glory of Manmatheśvara Tīrtha

Śrī Mārkaṇḍeya said:

1-7. Thereafter, a person should go to Manmatheśa Tīrtha bowed down to by all the Devas. Merely by taking holy bath, O king, the man will not see the world of Yama.

A woman having no child, who takes her holy bath there, O son of Pāṇḍu, obtains a son truthful and steadfast in his Vratas.

A man who takes the holy bath there, remains clean and mentally controlled and observes fast for a night, O king, obtains the benefit of (gifting) a thousand cows.

A king of Tīrthas fulfilling all desires like it will never be. One who observes fast for three nights, O king, shall obtain the benefit of (the Dāna of) a hundred thousand cows.

The devotee should make arrangements for dance. Parameśvara is pleased with the sounds of vocal and instrumental music and keeping awake at night.

Mahādeva called Manmatheśvara was seen by me at Eraṇḍī. Even if Yama be angry, he is not capable of doing anything. A good man sees everything good.

Śaṁbhu was installed by Kāma. Hence, O king, he is the bestower of cherished desires. Manmatheśvara is a flight of stairs extending from the earth to the heavenly path.

8-12. The speciality here, O son of Bharata, is in the performance of Śrāddha at dusk. By the gift of cooked food, O great king, an excellent benefit has been proclaimed.

Thus everything has been recounted to you due to your devotion, O descendant of Bharata. Manmatheśvara is well-known all over the ocean-bound earth. O excellent one among the sons of Pāṇḍu, (devotees) should make a gift of cows on the thirteenth lunar day in the bright half of the month of Caitra.

A devotee goes there with the sense-organs well-controlled, keeps awake at night before the deity, O excellent king, and devoutly offers light before the deity with ghee. The benefit thereof is the same whether the devotee is a woman or a man.

CHAPTER ONE HUNDRED THREE

The Greatness of the Confluence (Of Eraṇḍī and Narmadā)

Śrī Mārkaṇḍeya said:

1-8. Thereafter, O king, a person should go to the exalted confluence of Eraṇḍī. The account of this was heard formerly by me, O king, even as Śiva was recounting it.

Earlier Śaṅkara was asked this very question by Gaurī. O tiger among kings. The Lord spoke about it, (though) it is a very splendid, great secret.

Īśvara said:

Listen, O goddess, to this greatest of secrets not mentioned to anyone by me. There is an extremely splendid Tīrtha on the northern bank of Revā. O goddess; it destroys the sin of foeticide. It yields cherished desires and causes increase in the number of sons.

Pārvatī said:

Recount, O Mahādeva, the details of the extremely splendid Tīrtha. How is it destructive of the sin of foeticide? How does it accord cherished desires? How is it a guide to heaven?

Īśvara said:

O great goddess, there is a mental son of Brahmā named Atri. He is always engaged in Agnihotra. He adored Devas and guests. Seven Somasaṁsthas (variety of Soma Sacrifice) were performed by the Brāhmaṇa, O Pārvatī.

His wife, well-known by the name Anasūyā is endowed with all good qualities. She is a chaste lady always engaged in the duties and welfare of her Lord. In fact, her husband is her very vital breath. Thus they spent their days. They had neither a son nor a daughter.

Once, in the afternoon, O great goddess, O beautiful lady, they were comfortably seated talking about what had befallen them earlier, both happiness and misery.

Atri said:

9-16. O my beloved, (you are) a splendid, gentle lady of great beauty in all the limbs, richly endowed with learning and humility, having the eyes resembling petals of a lotus, with a face resembling the full moon, walking slowly with the weight of the huge hips! There is no other woman like you in all the three worlds consisting of mobile and immobile creatures.

It is cited by expounders of the Vedas that a woman is one

who gives sexual pleasure and a son. O beautiful lady, my happiness is that happiness which can be expected of a person without a son.

I have no son even as clever in all the rites as I am. O beautiful lady, even by his very birth a son saves his father about to fall into the Naraka named Put if he happens to be a great sinner.

Excellent sons redeem their grandfathers who being engaged in evil actions had fallen into terrible plights, even if they have gone to Vaitaraṇī.

One wins over the worlds through one's sons. One attains the highest goal through a grandson. Then through the grandson of the son one attains the eternal Brahman. There is no other kinsman on a par with a son whether in this world or in the other.

I am worried over this during day as well as midnight, nay always. My limbs are dried up like waters of a river during summer.

Anasūyā said:

17-20. O Brāhmaṇa, what you bewail I too grieve over; what gives you great anguish burns me within my mind.

Think about that rite whereby long-lived sons endowed with good qualities will be born and whereby Prajāpati (Brahmā himself) may be pleased.

Atri said:

O fair lady, penance has been performed by me, penance that is very difficult for anyone born under the Sun to do. I am now exhausted in my body as a result of observing Vratas, fasts, restraints and intake of mere vegetarian diet of greens. I am incapable of any further great Vrata. Hence I bewail myself. The secret of my heart has been divulged to you by me.

Anasūyā said:

21-33. A chaste lady enhances the sexual pleasure of her husband and makes the family flourish. She is the means of realizing the threefold aim of human life. Hence she deserves the praise of learned persons.

Japa, Tapas (penance), pilgrimage, adoration of Śiva, practice of Mantras and propitiation of deities – these six cause the downfall of women and Śūdras (if undertaken without the concurrence of a husband or a Brāhmaṇa priest).

Such a great defect is involved in the practice of a Vrata by women. This is what all the sages say as has been cited in the Vedas.

With your permission, O holy Brāhmaṇa, I shall perform even a very difficult penance. I shall propitiate the excellent Suras for the purpose of getting a son.

Atri said:

Well, well, O highly intelligent lady engaged in doing what pleases me! O fair lady, you have been commanded by me. Undertake a penance for the sake of a son so that I may be free from indebtedness to Devas, Pitṛs and human beings.

In all the three worlds, there is no kinsman on a par with one's own wife. Therefore, Devas proclaim that there is no other pleasure on a par with that of wife. If wife is pleasant-faced, sons too are pleasant-faced. If wife is averse, sons too turn away their faces. Hence all people including Devas, Asuras and human beings praise wife.

O lady of exalted Vratas, O highly intelligent lady, O lady of auspicious vision and Sattva quality! At my bidding do perform a penance quickly for the sake of a son.

Īśvara continued:

At the conclusion of these words of her husband, she prostrated before him with eight limbs touching the ground and said: "With your favour, O eminent Brāhmaṇa, I shall attain all the cherished desires."

That fawn-eyed lady of excellent complexion and graceful gait of a swan observed holy vows and came to River Narmadā, the divine river originating from Śiva's perspiration and capable of destroying all sins. Merely by perceiving her, masses of sins perish. Merely by taking the holy bath therein, one obtains the benefit of a horse-sacrifice.

O great goddess, those men with faith who drink her auspicious water (obtain great benefit). Drinking her water is on a par with drinking the Soma juice. No doubt need be entertained (about this).

34-44. Those who remember her (Narmadā) day and night even from a distance of hundreds of Yojanas, are liberated from all sins. They go to Rudraloka.

In the vicinity of Narmadā, within a pair of Yojanas are those two (? Rudraloka and Soma juice). O lady of excellent complexion, those who die there do not see Yama.

Then, O beautiful lady, the lady with wide eyes began to observe holy restraints on the northern bank at the auspicious confluence of Eraṇḍī, taking a diet of only vegetarian food (of mere greens). By means of auspicious Vratas and Stotras she propitiated the three Devas.

O great goddess, during summer she performed the penance within the five fires. During rainy season, she performed Cāndrāyaṇa Vrata with wet clothes on. When Hemanta (winter) set in, she remained in the midst of water always.

She took the holy bath in the morning; then performed the Sandhyā prayers; then she offered libations to Devas and Sages. After performing the adoration of Devas, she performed Homa in accordance with the injunctions. She worshipped the Vaiṣṇava worlds by means of Snāna (holy bath), Japa and Homa.

When a hundred years passed off thus, Rudra, Viṣṇu and Pitāmaha assumed the forms of Brāhmaṇas and came there, O my beloved, to the confluence of Eraṇḍī. They stood in front of her and began to recite Vedic passages.

Anasūyā discontinued her Japa, saw them carefully again and again, duly offered Argha, and remained standing.

The lady of wide eyes said: "Now my birth has become fruitful. Now my penance has become fruitful. By seeing Brāhmaṇas one is rid of all sins."

Then she circumambulated them and prostrated before them. She said: "I shall offer to you, O sages of purified souls, bulbuous roots, roots, fruits, greens and the sacred Nīvāra rice grains."

The Brāhmaṇas said:

45-51. O lady of excellent Vratas, we are satisfied with your wonderful penance and the truthfulness of the penance. Further, through seeing you all our desires are fulfilled.

We were rather curious to know why you have undertaken

the Vrata of sages. Were you performing the severe penance for the sake of heaven, salvation or for the sake of a son?

Anasūyā said:

Svarga is achieved through penance. The highest goal (Mokṣa) is attained through penance. Wealth and love can be acquired through penance. A son of very good qualities can be obtained through penance. O Brāhmaṇas, penance alone bestows the benefits of all cherished desires.

The Brāhmaṇas said:

You are a lady beautiful in every limb. You are slender, dark-complexioned, one having wide eyes and supple limbs. You have good physical form and the graceful gait of a swan. What have you to do with penance? Why do you subject yourself to sufferings?

Anasūyā said:

I notice the sign as though you are Rudra, Viṣṇu and Pitāmaha (Brahmā) himself in disguised forms.

Īśvara continued:

At the end of her speech they revealed their own forms. The Devas with the refulgence of a crore of suns stood there in their own forms.

52-62. O great goddess, there was Janārdana having four arms holding conch, discus and club, clad in yellow robes and having the complexion of an Atasī flower. Hari who had the vehicle of Garuḍa was accompanied by Śrī. The glorious Lord was standing in his own form with a beaming face.

O great goddess, Brahmā, the grandfather of the worlds, came to the banks of Narmadā, clad in yellow robes. He had four faces resembling lotus. He was riding on his swan. He had a rosary in his hand.

There was Maheśvara himself, the omnipresent Lord, riding on his bull. He had ten arms. His complexion was beautified by the holy ash smeared over the limbs; the Three-eyed Lord with five faces had matted hairs for a crown. The crescent moon adorned his head. The omnipresent Maheśvara appeared in this form.

On having a grand vision like this of the Devas, the chaste lady Anasūyā trembled and looked at them again and again.

Anasūyā said:

What are the features and functions of Viṣṇu, Rudra and Pitāmahā? I would rather listen to this. Do tell me entirely.

Brahmā said:

I am Brahmā, the rainy season. The waters are glorified (as my form). I have been declared as one having the form of clouds. I cause downpour of rain on the surface of the earth. During the twilight of dawn, when the Sun rises, I (develop) all the seeds. This is the cause. The great secret has been mentioned entirely.

Viṣṇu said:

Viṣṇu shall be Hemanta (winter). He has the form of the universe consisting of the mobile and immobile beings. He is for the protection of the entire universe. This is the excellent greatness of Viṣṇu.

Rudra said:

63-72. I have been declared the Summer season, the cause of the destruction of all living beings. O saintly lady, in the form of Rudra, I pull and drag the entire universe (within me).

Thus, O lady of great Vratas, the three Devas, Brahmā, Viṣṇu and Rudra, are the three *Sandhyās* (junctions, twilights?), three divisions of time (seasons) and three fires (Gārhapatya, Āhavanīya and Dakṣiṇa).

Similarly Brahmā, Viṣṇu and Rudra amalgamated into one Self. O fair lady, they shall grant you the boon, whatever is cherished in your mind.

Anasūyā said:

I am blessed, I am meritorious. I am praiseworthy and worthy of reverence always. If the three Devas are pleased, let them take pity on me, be present in this Tīrtha and be the bestowers of boons always.

Rudra said:

Let your words be true, O auspicious lady; what you have requested for will take place. What is named Eraṇḍī is the visible Māyā of Viṣṇu. Merely by perceiving it all the accumulation of sins can be destroyed. In the month of Caitra, one should observe fast for a day and a night after taking holy bath at the confluence of Eraṇḍī. He dispels the sin of Brāhmaṇa-slaughter. He should keep awake during the night and feed Brāhmaṇas in the morning in accordance with the injunctions. He should offer balls of rice duly. After circumambulation he should make gifts of gold, cloth, silver, cows and plots of land. Everything is proclaimed as having crore times the benefit. So said Svāyaṁbhuva.

73-79. The men who die at the splendid confluence of Eraṇḍī, O goddess, reside in the Rudraloka for a thousand Yugas.

After observing fast for a day and a night the devotee should recite the Vedic passages of Rudra numbering eleven and one and named too accordingly. He attains the greatest goal.

A seeker of learning acquires learning; a seeker of wealth obtains wealth; a seeker of sons gets sons and all desires cherished by him.

Even great sinners attain the great goal by taking the holy bath in the pure waters of Revā at the confluence of Eraṇḍī.

Anasūyā said:

Urged by my devotion, if all the three Devas are pleased, let Hari, Rudra and Pitāmaha become my sons.

Viṣṇu said:

This has never been heard by me that the venerable ones attain the status of sons. O splendid lady, I shall grant you sons possessing the valour of Devas, who will be handsome, equipped with good qualities, well-versed in the Vedas and capable of performing Yajñas.

Anasūyā said:

O Hari, what has been desired and requested for by me should be granted. My Putraiṣaṇā (desire for a son) should not be altered into something else.

Viṣṇu said:

80-87. Formerly in the course of a dialogue with Bhṛgu (I incurred the curse of) staying in the womb (and taking birth as a mortal). O splendid lady, I do not see a means of redemption from it. But remembering the earlier episode I think about it again and again.

After considering this the other (two) Devas, Pitāmaha and Maheśvara, said: "O lady of excellent countenance, we shall become your sons but not womb-born ones. O lady of great intellect, Devas do not take up residence in womb. We shall be the bestowers of boons on the worlds by our presence at the confluence, O fair lady, you will be visible Vaiṣṇavī Māyā of Eraṇḍī."

Saying thus the three Devas stationed themselves, O son of Kuntī, on the northern bank of Revā. After receiving the boons that honoured lady went to Mahendra Mountain.

In her performance of the penance the lady of splendid eyes wore the sacred thread. Gradually she became tired in her limbs. She became terrible in appearad with the hairs turned rough and dishevelled and the body emaciateel and pallid.

Her husband who was brilliant and glorious and occupied a slab of stone saw her and became delighted. She said, "Get up, get up".

Atri said:

Excellent! Excellent! O Anasūyā of great intellect and noble vows, you have obtained a boon that cannot be even thought of by Gālava and others.

Anasūyā said:

88-100. With your favour, O celestial sage, I have obtained a rare boon. Hence the Devas, Siddhas and pure sages praise (us).

Īśvara continued:

After saying this the honoured lady became highly delighted and looked at her beloved husband. That lady of splendid appearance too was looked at by him.

By this mutual seeing an auspicious halo took shape on the forehead. The sphere of halo was nine thousand Yojanas in extent and was full of rays. The circumference was three-fold and had the shape of Kadaṁbagolaka (buds of Kadamba tree bursting forth simultaneously). O goddess of Devas, there was a person of divine form in its centre. He had the colour of gold and was full of nectarine juice and the lustre of a crore of suns. He was Pitāmaha himself who became the first son of Anasūyā, well-known as Candramas (Moon) in the form of Soma, O Prince (?)[1]

In the course of Iṣṭāpūrta, O Maheśvarī, all his sixteen Kalās gather together successively Pratipat, Dvitīyā, Tṛtīyā, Caturthī, Pañcamī and the imperishable sixteenth Kalā (*obscure*). In his subtle form he is the protector of the world of four types. O lady of excellent countenance, he causes delight to the entire universe, the three worlds consisting of mobile and immobile beings.

Everything offered as Homa and Dāna becomes stationed in the moon and everyone makes use of it to sustain itself. When Soma is in the state of Vanaspati i.e. New Moon (Amāvāsyā), O lady of excellent countenance, if a wealthy man takes food in another man's house, he is deluded and forfeits the merit of a year.

If men cut or chop off trees and plants on the new moon day, O goddess of Devas, they go to Yama's abode due to that sin. If anyone indulges in sexual intercourse on a new-moon day, he incurs a sin on a par with that of murder of a Brāhmaṇa undoubtedly. If anyone churns curds with a churning rod on a new-moon day, his cows collected before perish. If, on a new-moon day, a person undertakes a journey, his Pitṛs will have only dust particles for food for a period of one month.

101-108. O Mahādevī, if a person performs a Śrāddha on a

1. This is a slip on the part of the author, as the dialogue here is supposed to be between Śiva and Pārvati, not between Mārkaṇḍeya and Yudhiṣṭhira.

new-moon day, certainly his Pitṛs become propitiated for a year, O lady of wide eyes. If he gifts gold, silver or cloth to Brāhmaṇas, O goddess, everything shall undoubtedly increase a hundred thousand times.

Thus the Patriarch in the form of the Moon, became the first son of Anasūyā.

The second one, O great goddess, was named Durvāsas. He is (an incarnation of) Maheśvara himself, the cause of creation and annihilation. O fair lady, in the middle of the sages he performs a severe penance. When the annihilation of all living beings takes place, he attains Rudratva. It was by this Durvāsas that even Indra was cursed, O lady of excellent countenance. Thus the birth of the second son has been recounted by me.

In the form of Dattātreya (manifested there) Lord Madhusūdana himself, Lord Janārdana, the omnipresent Lord of the universe.

Thus, O Maheśvarī, the Devas took incarnations on the earth, by way of granting boons to Anasūyā. They became her three sons.

Mārkaṇḍeya said:

109-120. O son of Kuntī, a Tīrtha was created by Anasūyā on the northern bank of Revā. It causes the acquisition (birth) of a son and destruction of all sins.

Śrī Mārkaṇḍeyā said:

This is an ancient Tīrtha of wonderful efficacy on Narmadā in this world. O king, a Brāhmaṇa's sin of foeticide was dispelled there.

Yudhiṣṭhira said:

May that story be told, the story that dispels all the sins in this world, of any person distressed with misery. O sinless excellent Brāhmaṇa, do narrate that Itihāsa to me.

Śrī Mārkaṇḍeya said:

A farmer named Govinda, born in the family of Gautama, lived in the village of Suvarṇaśilaka along with his wife and son. He was always engaged in protecting his house and field.

One day, he came home in a cart filled with wood. The

wood was unloaded by him single-handedly and he became hungry. On hearing the sound of father's arrival the son came there crawling and was soon covered with the pieces of wood. He was not seen by the father. The cart and the bullock tied with rope were left at the doorway. The thirsty father, O king, entered the house in haste. The obedient wife who was aware of the feelings of her husband became engaged in serving him. On seeing the son fallen down with the head crushed by the pieces of wood, she put him in a hammock compassionately but uttering nothing.

When the husband finished his bath and meal and went to sleep, the lady tried to make the son get up. The son had died and did not get up. The sad lady cried and swooned.

121-130. On hearing the sound of lamentation, Govinda became frightened. He fell down on the ground crying "What is this?"

Both of them fell on the ground, O king, with tresses of hairs left loose. They heaved deep sighs and lamented, O great king:

"Whom else shall we see as the son eagerly playing about? How shall we sustain the heart broken due to you? The line of the family will be perpetuated. I had this faith when you were born. Now whom shall we look up to for the purpose of attaining the highest goal after becoming free from indebtedness? O my son, I have become old and wretched and you ought to have been my support. All the cherished desires of the mind have become futile. Your mother is wretched, bereft of her son and kinsmen. She has fallen down lamenting on the ground; save her.

A son saves the father from the Naraka called *Put*. So he is called *Putra* by the Self-born Lord himself. The house of a man without a son is a void. The quarters are void when there are no kinsmen. The heart of a fool is a void. If there is poverty there is a void in everything.

The world says that sandalpaste is cool. It is wrong. The close embrace of the limbs of a son is cooler than sandalpaste.

Men without merit do not see a son sitting on their laps with dust particles making the face dirty and playing with the whiskers.

131-140. Men without merit do not see a son resembling the Holder of Gaṅgā (Śiva) with the quarters for clothes (naked), bereft of shame, dusty and matted locks of hair (wafted about).

The note of a musical instrument, of a lute, is heard as very charming (to the ears). But the cry of a child is more delightful than that.

Learned men say that even among crows, animals and birds, the young one, the calf is very endearing (to them). Fishes, horses, tortoises, crocodiles etc. are pleased when young ones are born and become distressed when some danger befalls them.

Devas and Gandharvas take delight when sons are born. They bewail at the time of their death. O son, I am very unlucky.

King Rāghava (i.e. Daśaratha) convened an assembly of sages for the sake of (obtaining) a son since the seat of Indra occupied by him was purified by sprinkling water. Residence in Svarga is not (possible) without a son, O son of Pāṇḍu. Hence Daśaratha performed an excellent Yajña for the sake of sons. Rāma, Lakṣmaṇa, Śatrughna and Bharata were born to him.

Even while he was only eight years old Rāmacandra defeated Paraśurāma of unmeasured brilliance, by whom Kārtavīrya had been conquered earlier. Vāli, the monkey who was invincible to enemies, was killed by him single-handed. Rāmacandra killed Rāvaṇa, the son of Brahmā, along with his sons and kinsmen of whom the three worlds were afraid.

141-150. Thus, without a son there is no happiness in the mortal world. He who indulges in sexual intercourse for perpetuating the line, who makes use of learning to attain Svarga, who prepares excellent sweet food for the sake of Brāhmaṇas attains residence in heaven. There is no greater sin than Brahmahatyā and no greater meritorious thing than a horse-sacrifice. There is no greater happiness than birth of a son and no greater calamity than danger to his life. Why should I speak in this vein more, O dear one? Without a son there is no happiness."

After lamenting thus again and again in various ways, the Brāhmaṇa was consoled by the people. He took the body of the boy and went out.

Afterwards they cremated the child in accordance with the injunctions. Extremely distressed, they came back to the abode together.

Thus, when the Brāhmaṇa came home. O Yudhiṣṭhira, night

had already set in. Govinda afflicted with the grief for his son, lay asleep on the ground. When the wife looked at her husband afflicted with misery, she saw him infested with clusters of worms. On seeing him overwhelmed with sins, she became all the more distressed. Even as she was thus immersed in grief, the night came to an end.

The servant who looked after the cattle went to the forest for leaving the buffaloes (to graze) and having kept them there he returned home.

Govinda, the excellent Brāhmaṇa, was informed by the cowherd, "O master, even as I take food, kindly look after the buffaloes."

151-161. Then the Brāhmaṇa hastened towards the buffaloes. He did not see the buffaloes there. Then he rushed towards the field. On his way he came to the confluence of Eraṇḍī and Revā and entered the waters.

Excessively thirsty he drank some water. After washing the eyes well and drinking the water without any desire (for sacred results) he came home towards the close of the day. With great misery Govinda went to bed at night after taking food.

He became overwhelmed with sleep after being afflicted with grief and fatigue. At midnight, O Yudhiṣṭhira, his wife saw his limbs partly infested with worms and party not infested. The wife of excellent qualities was struck with wonder thereby. She said with her mind afflicted with fear that this was his sin.

The wife said:

Five days ago, you were throwing down the fuel. Hence the boy who came to the backyard was killed inadvertently by you. That secret of your terrible sin was not divulged by me. I am being scorched by that concealed sin day and night. I do not see any happiness either in your limbs or in mine. Sleep has been suppressed in my case along with my loving pleasure towards you. It is heard that a verse is recited by the great sages in the Mānava Dharmaśāstra. Distress does not get subdued by recollecting it frequently in the mind. By speaking about it, Dharma perishes and gets increased by concealing it in this world as well as in the other one. The case with sin also is the same.

162-169. Thinking about this like this I spent the night in great terror. What can I say and to whom about you infested with a crowd of worms? Again you were seen today infested with the worms of foeticide (infanticide). In some places they bite into the body and in some places they have disappeared altogether.

I recollect this now and then and ponder over it again and again. But I fail to notice the cause thereof. May I ask you? Will you kindly let me know? This is what I feel. This is the effect of either the adoration of a deity or taking the holy bath in a lake or river or a holy Tīrtha you may have visited and not due to anything else.

Śrī Mārkaṇḍeya continued:

On being told thus, O descendant of Bharata, the Brāhmaṇa told his wife what had happened in the course of the day, O excellent king, because he himself had certain suspicions.

"Today I had gone with the buffaloes. I visited Eraṇḍī confluence and stood in the water coming upto my navel. I drank much water as well. I do not know of any other Tīrtha, lake or river. This is the truth. This is the truth. O beautiful lady, the truth has been averred."

The lady understood everything and began to observe fast. O lady of excellent complexion (?), the Brāhmaṇa went to the confluence along with his wife.

170-180. After taking the holy bath in the charming water and bowing to Lord Bhāskara, he bathed Śaṅkara, the Lord of Devas, along with Umā with Pañcagavya[1], ghee, milk, curds, honey, ghee (*sic*) and water. Then he worshipped the Liṅga identical with the Vedas and the auspicious goddess Kātyāyanī with fragrant flower garlands, incense and splendid Naivedyas. After keeping awake in the whole of the night along with her husband, the chaste lady honoured the Brāhmaṇas assiduously when the day dawned clearly. Govinda honoured the excellent Brāhmaṇas in accordance with his capacity by means of the gifts of cows, gold, cloth and food, O descendant of Bharata. Accompanied by his wife, he came home rid of all sins.

1. Five cow Products, viz. milk, curds, butter and liquid and solid excreta.

If anyone devoutly listens to or reads with great devotion, this excellent story of Govinda, the sin of foeticide perishes. He sports about in the world of Śaṅkara until the annihilation of all living beings.

The person should control his sense-organs and observe fast on the seventh lunar day in the bright half of the month of Aśvayuj or Caitra, O excellent king. He must adopt all Sāttvika feelings and emotions.

In the shrine of Śiva, he must meditate upon the Odd-eyed, Trident-bearing Lord. Then he should meditate upon Lord Viṣṇu who slew Kaṁsa and who holds the conch-shell, discus and club and rides on the Lord of birds and bestows boons on the three worlds.

Then he should meditate on the four-faced Pitāmaha who rides on the swan. He is the creator of everything; he is resplendent on the lotus-seat. The devotee should stay in that excellent spot of Triyāma (of threefold mental control).

181-190. After the day has dawned clearly on the eighth day, O king, the devotee should honour Brāhmaṇas devoid of all faults or disqualifications. They should have all the limbs and organs complete. They should be adepts in all scriptures. They should be regularly practising study of the Vedas and they should be devoted to their own wives. The Brāhmaṇas should be deserving ones for Śrāddha, Dāna and Vrata, O son of Pāṇḍu.

He should begin the adoration of the departed ones after that of the Devas. With the offering of balls of rice and libations in Eraṇḍī one is rid of ghosthood.

Dāna (gifts) with cooked foods as the chief item should always be made (along with) gold, plot of land, a virgin, a pair of bullocks of splendid features with a ploughshare, foodgrains weighing so many Droṇakas. An adorned young cow yielding plenty of milk should be gifted along with her calf. She may be white, red, black, pink or tawny in colour. A milk-pot made of brass should invariably be given. The hoofs of the cow should be adorned with (plates of) gold and the horns covered with gold top. The same should be made over to a Brāhmaṇa uttering the Mantra: "May the Lords of the universe, Hara, Kṛṣṇa and Pitāmaha, be pleased with me. May the divine Surabhī, the saviour of the world, redeem me."

If women desire progeny and take the holy bath at the confluence of Eraṇḍī, the Rudrasūktas of all the four Vedas should be recited by four Brāhmaṇas or at least two in a praiseworthy manner. The couple should be sprinkled with a single well-filled pot.

191-202a. The person showering with the water-pot shall be one well-versed in astrology or one who can sing Sāma verses. The water-pot must contain five jewels. The water should be rendered fragrant with sweet scent. All types of herbs and medicines should be put therein. Leaves or sprouts of mango and Aśvattha or Madhūka should also be put there.

It should be covered with a white cloth and white sandalpaste applied over. White flowers should be strewn and white mustards should be scattered in the middle.

Everything should be put by a seeker of progeny in a vessel of brass to be placed (before) the excellent preceptor.

A cloth that has been worn once should be taken off and placed there along with bangles or other ornaments in the Maṇḍala (mystic diagram) for the sake of one's own fulfilment. He bows down to Bhāskara at the outset and then to the Ācārya who is Rudra personified.

In the excellent shrine of the goddess the dovotee tastes something sweet and makes gifts of fruits, betel leaves, umbrella, shoes or vehicles to a Brāhmaṇa. He shall become free from misery. He sports about in the world of Bhāskara until all the living beings are annihilated.

All *Dānas* whether auspicious or inauspicious shall have a crore times benefit. Just as rivers ultimately fall into the ocean and get merged, so also the sins of men perish at the confluence of Eraṇḍī. Śaṅkara has said that a sin on a par with foeticide perishes at the confluence of Eraṇḍī and within a radius of an arrow's throw all round.

Immolation of one's life should be carried out in fire with devotion. Death due to voluntary starvation or voluntary drowning come thereafter (? in efficacy).

If the death is in fire, the devotee enjoys five thousand years' stay (in the divine world); if it is in water, three thousand years; and if by starvation, sixty thousand years.

202b-210. Even crows, cranes, doves, owls and animals attain the highest goal after coming into contact with the waters of the confluence. Trees go to that region which Yogins will attain after realization.

O goddess(?), Eraṇḍikā is the divine Māyā. If Manmatheśvara is visited, even angry Yama is incapable of doing anything. The gentle one sees all weal.

If the devotees apply the clay taken out of the confluence all over the body everyday, all the sins such as that of foeticide perish. There is no doubt about this.

A man who rolls about at the confluence of Eraṇḍī shall become rid of all sins and attain the region free from ailment.

If staying in hermitages, men glorify the confluence of Eraṇḍī, they become free from sins. Such is the truthful statement of Śaṅkara. One dispels sins by perceiving the tips of Eraṇḍī plants.

Those men who read this meritorious narrative of the Tīrtha and those others who listen to it devoutly, become rid of sins.

Thus the entire details of Eraṇḍīsaṅgama have been recounted to you, O king. I shall further describe another Tīrtha that destroys all sins.

CHAPTER ONE HUNDRED FOUR

The Greatness of Suvarṇaśilā Tīrtha

Śrī Mārkaṇḍeya said:

1-8. Thereafter, one should go to the excellent Sauvarṇaśilā Tīrtha, O king. It is on the northern bank (of Revā) and is reputed as destructive of all sins.

This Tīrtha was formerly created by groups of sages near the confluence within a radius of a hundred steps all round. It is a very rare holy spot on Revā.

Even a spot measuring a cubit in length is considered a holy spot, O king. After taking holy bath in Suvarṇaśilā (Suvarṇaśilaka) and adoring the great Lord Maheśvara, Sun-god should be bowed down to. Then the devotee should perform Homa in holy fire with a Bilva fruit mixed with ghee or with the leaves of Bilva.

The Mantra to be uttered is "May the Lord of the universe be pleased. May my ailment perish positively."

Listen to the benefit when gold is gifted to a Brāhmaṇa (there). He who gifts gold obtains all the excellent benefit that has been mentioned as accruing from a Yajña with much gold as Dakṣiṇā.

By that Dāna a devotee becomes a purified soul and on death he shall attain Svarga. He will become an attendant of Rudra for a period equal to fourteen Indras' reign.

After coming down from Svarga, he is born in a celebrated family richly endowed with wealth and foodgrain. He then remembers that holy Tīrtha once again.

CHAPTER ONE HUNDRED FIVE

The Greatness of Karañja Tīrtha

Śrī Mārkaṇḍeya said:

1-3. Thereafter one goes to the Tīrtha called Karañja. There he takes the holy bath, O great king, and observes fast with the sense-organs completely controlled. He is liberated from all sins.

He should adore Mahādeva and make gifts devoutly of gold, silver, jewels, pearls, coral, sandals, shoes, umbrella, quilt and bed-sheets. Everything becomes crores of times beneficial. There is no doubt about this.

CHAPTER ONE HUNDRED SIX

The Greatness of Kāmada Tīrtha

Śrī Mārkaṇḍeya said:

1-7. Thereafter, O king, one should go to the excessively excellent heavenly Tīrtha that is conducive to conjugal bliss and fascinating to both men and women.

O excellent king, if an unfortunate man or a woman in wretched state takes the holy bath and adores Umā and Rudra, conjugal bliss accrues to him or her.

The person should control his sense-organs and observe fast for a day and a night on the third lunar day. He should devoutly invite a Brāhmaṇa of handsome features along with his wife.

He should be adorned with fragrant garlands and rendered sweet-smelling with incense etc., and clad in good garments.

He should be devoutly fed with milk pudding and Kṛsara (milk, gingelly seeds and rice mixed and cooked well) and then duly circumambulated.

He should recite in his mind this Mantra: "May the bull-emblemed Mahādeva along with his wife, be pleased with me. O Lord of the chiefs of Devas, be kind to me and see that there is no separation at any time (between us), just as there is none in your case."

If this is done, the merit that is said to accrue to him I shall recount entirely to you, as has been stated by the Lord.

8-19. O Yudhiṣṭhira, none of the following (evil things) shall occur to him in the course of seven births: misfortune, wretchedness, penury, grief-incurring bondage and infertility.

He who devoutly goes there (specially) on the third lunar day in the bright half of the month of Jyeṣṭha and practises the penance of the five fires, undoubtedly becomes free from all sins.

The devotee should have full concentration of the mind and burn Guggula (fragrant gum-resin). If in the vicinity of Gaurī, the devotee splits his body and if this ends in the departure of the soul, even as he is engaged in that activity, he shall go to Svarga on death here. So said Śaṅkara.

Regarding the Brāhmaṇa couple (woman and man) as Gaurī and Śiva in physical form, he should honour them with splendid garments of white, red and yellow colours. He should adore them duly with different kinds of flowers and splendid, fragrant incense. A golden necklace should be offered. They should be smeared with saffron. After giving them a fine appearance thus, gifts are offered, such as bangles, earrings, necklaces and rings. Seven kinds of cereals are gifted and they are fed, O excellent king.

The devotee may make other gifts as well at that Tīrtha. There is no doubt about this that he will attain that merit which is incurred by making the gift of everything (all possessions). Everything becomes a thousand-fold in merit.

He enjoys pleasures of great excellence in the company of Śaṅkara. He then derives immense conjugal bliss. There is no doubt there (about this).

He who is sonless gets a son; one without wealth gets wealth. O great king, the Tīrtha that fulfils cherished desires is established on Narmadā.

CHAPTER ONE HUNDRED SEVEN

The Greatness of Bhaṇḍārī Tīrtha

Śrī Mārkaṇḍeya said:

1-3. Thereafter, O great king, one should go to the excellent Bhaṇḍārī Tīrtha. It is the means of averting poverty for a period of nineteen Yugas.

Dhanada (Kubera) performed a penance whereby the Lotus-born Lord was pleased. By making a small gift, he attained the lordship of wealth.

He who goes there and takes holy bath devoutly and then makes the gift of wealth, will regain enormous wealth which will never be lost or become limited in quantity.

CHAPTER ONE HUNDRED EIGHT

The Greatness of Rohīṇī Tīrtha

Śrī Mārkaṇḍeya said:

1-7. Thereafter, O king, one should go to the excellent Rohiṇī Tīrtha well-known in all the three worlds and extremely destructive of all sins.

Yudhiṣṭhira said:

I wish to hear the greatness of Rohiṇī Tīrtha that is destructive of all sins. I wish to hear it succinctly. It behoves you to recount it to me.

Śrī Mārkaṇḍeya said:

At the time of the close of the Kalpa, when all mobile and immobile beings became dissolved in a terrible, single, vast expanse of water, the Discus-bearing Lord of Devas lay down in the ocean. A lotus grew from his navel. It resembled the disc of the sun. It had pericarp and filaments. It was adorned with petals.

Brahmā with four lotus-like faces came into being there. He said, "O Lord of Devas, let me be commanded what I should do."

On being requested thus, the Conch-discus-club-bearing Lord of Devas spoke these sweet words to Lord Pitāmaha:

"O mighty-armed one, at my behest, beget in Sarasvatī the world consisting of all the groups of living beings, the world capable of coming up, abiding and getting dissolved."

8-13. These words of the Lotus-navelled One were listened to by Lord (Brahmā), O descendant of Bharata. He remembered (seven sages and) mentally created the seven sages with a desire for the welfare (of the worlds). These wise ones were remembered in this order: Pulastya, Pulaha, Kratu, Pracetas, Vasiṣṭha, Bhṛgu and Nārada.

Dakṣa, the patriarch of great refulgence, was born of Pracetas. O sinless one, fifty daughters were born to Dakṣa. He gave ten to Dharma, thirteen to Kaśyapa and twenty-seven to Indu (Moon-god).

Among them, O king, the daughter named Rohiṇī was not liked by any of the other women and by the husband also in particular. Thereupon, she developed extreme aversion to Saṁsāra, O excellent king. She came to the banks of Narmadā and performed an elaborate penance.

14-22. She made her body emaciated through fasts for a single night, three nights together, six nights, twelve nights, a fortnight and even for months.

She propitiated the holy goddess, the destroyer of Demon Mahiṣa, the destroyer of all distresses.

She regularly took the holy baths in the waters of Narmadā. (Thus the lady of pure smiles performed the penance.) Thereat the highly illustrious Goddess Nārāyaṇī became pleased, O king.

She said: "O fortunate lady, I am pleased with your Vrata and holy observances." On hearing this, Rohiṇī said: "O bestower of honour, let it be so that I ere long become the beloved of Śaśin (Moon)." After saying, "Let it be so", Bhavānī, the beloved of her devotees, vanished there itself, even while being eulogized by groups of sages.

Ever since then that Tīrtha became well-known. Rohiṇī became the permanent beloved of Śaśin (Moon-god), O excellent king.

A woman who devoutly takes her holy bath in that Tīrtha becomes beloved of her husband like Rohiṇī. A man who regularly bathes in that Tīrtha becomes the lover of the woman (wife).

If a man casts off his life in the Tīrtha, he will never have a broken marriage at any time in the course of seven births.

CHAPTER ONE HUNDRED NINE

The Greatness of Cakra Tīrtha

Śrī Mārkaṇḍeya said:

1-6. Thereafter, O king, one should go to the excellent Cakra Tīrtha well-known as Senāpura. It is conducive to the destruction of all sins.

The Discus-bearing Lord of Devas duly propitiated leading Brāhmaṇas with the gift of lands and brought Mahāsena (Kārttikeya) for ceremonially crowning him as the commander-in-chief (of the army of Devas) for slaying Dānavas in order to bring about victory of the Heaven-dwellers.

Mahāsena was brought there along with the Devas accompanied by Indra as their leader, to the accompaniment of the sounds of conch-shells, Bherī and Paṭaha drums, the notes of flutes, lutes, Mṛdaṅgas and auspicious Jhallarīs (cymbals).

Thereupon the Dānava named Ruru who was proud on account of his strength gave out a terrible roaring shout and came there to create obstacles at the coronation ceremony.

His army consisting of elephants, horses, chariots and foot-soldiers filled all the ten quarters and a great battle ensued.

7-17. The various weapons used by him were Śakti, Ṛṣṭi, Pāśa, Musala, Khaḍga (sword), Tomara (iron rod), Taṅkana (axe), Bhalla (spear), Karṇika, Nārāca etc. Everywhere headless bodies were scattered on the battlefield.

Within a moment Lord Viṣṇu, the destroyer of hosts of enemies, annihilated the army of enemies with arrows discharged from the bow. The elephants, horses and chariots were destroyed and the noble-souled Lord took up his discus.

Discharged from the hand of the Slayer of Madhu, the terrible, blazing, sharp, discus Sudarśana, easily discernible by the Suras and Asuras in the battlefield, cut off the head of the Daitya.

On perceiving this sudden obstacle to his coronation, the Six-faced Lord abandoned the place and performed an elaborate penance.

The discus discharged by Hari, the sustainer of the worlds, for destruction of the Dānava, split him into two and fell down in the pure waters.

Ever since then that Tīrtha is well-known as Cakratīrtha created by the omniformed Lord for the purpose of destroying all the sins.

A man who takes his holy bath in Cakratīrtha and adores Acyuta, the Lord, obtains the merit of a Puṇḍarīka Yajña.

He who takes his holy bath in the Tīrtha there and honours splendid Brāhmaṇas having control over the mind, sense-organs and angry temperament, attains the benefit of a crore of meritorious deeds.

He who devoutly casts off his body into the Tīrtha there, goes to Viṣṇuloka after death, to the accompaniment of auspicious shouts of victory etc.

After sporting about as he pleases and duly honoured by Devas and Gandharvas, he returns here once again and is reborn in a large family.

Thus a meritorious ancedote that is conducive to wealth and destructive of sins and miseries has been recounted to you, O blessed one. Listen further from me.

CHAPTER ONE HUNDRED TEN

The Greatness of Dhautapāpa Tīrtha

Śrī Mārkaṇḍeya said:

1-5. Thereafter, one should go to Dhautapāpa Tīrtha that destroys great sins. It was created by Viṣṇu formerly and is very near to Cakra Tīrtha.

Janārdana, the Lord of Devas, incurred (enormous) sin as a result of the slaughter of the terrible Dānavas. It was to dispel that sin that he made this Tīrtha and performed a severe penance at that Tīrtha after subduing anger.

He observed the vow of silence, too difficult for Devas and Dānavas. He took the holy bath and made different kinds of gifts to Brāhmaṇas. Instantly he was liberated from the sin and he went to his Vaiṣṇava region.

Similarly one who commits grave sin but takes the holy bath there and performs Japa in accordance with the injunctions, becomes free from the sin.

CHAPTER ONE HUNDRED ELEVEN

The Greatness of Skanda Tīrtha

Śrī Mārkaṇḍeya said:

1-6. There is an extremely splendid Tīrtha on the southern bank of Narmadā. It was formerly created by Skanda after performing a very severe penance.

Yudhiṣṭhira said:

O excellent Brāhmaṇa, do recount truthfully the entire story of Skanda[1] beginning with his birth as well as the details of the procedure of the pilgrimage to the Tīrtha.

---

1. VV 3-21 describe the story of the birth of Skanda. If differs from a similar story in Mbh and other Purāṇas on the following points:
   i. Śiva invites Smara (god of Love) to inspire him sexually.

Śrī Mārkaṇḍeya said:

Formerly penance was performed by the Lord of Devas, O Yudhiṣṭhira, but on being requested by all the Suras, Goddess Umā was married by him.

They said, "O excellent one among Suras, Devas have no commander-in-chief. All the Devas including Vāsava are being carried away by the terrible Dānavas.

Just as night without the Moon and day without the Sun, so also army without a leader does not shine even for a short while.

After realizing this, O Mahādeva having great compassion, may a commander of the army bound to be well known in all the three worlds be granted to us."

7-15. On hearing these splendid words of the Devas, Parameśvara who was enamoured of Goddess Umā mentally recollected Smara (god of Love).

With all his limbs intensely excited by him (Smara), the preceptor of the universe assumed a loving form and made love to Rudrāṇī for a period of a hundred divine years.

After coming to know that Hara was engaged in a long-drawn coition, Devarāja Indra had consultation with other Devas and despatched Jātavedas (Fire-god).

He went and saw Mahādeva engrossed in the greatest bliss. On being noticed thus suddenly, the Lord got up exclaiming "Hā-Hā".

Infuriated on that account, the great goddess uttered imprecatory words even as she trembled much, O great king. Listen, I shall tell you what she uttered.

"I was requested earnestly by all the Suras for producing a son, but by sending Jātavedas my experience of sexual bliss has been spoiled and rendered ineffective. Hence all the Suras will undoubtedly be sonless."

Thereupon Vahni (Fire) was told by Hara, "Take up our

---

ii. Śiva when disturbed in his sexual intercourse advises Agni that if he (Agni) finds his(Śiva's) semen unbearable, he should deposit it in Gaṅgā. It is after giving this advice that he gives Agni an oral dose of his semen.

iii. Skanda's penance on the bank of Narmadā to please his parents and creating a Tīrtha after his name on the bank of Narmadā.

seed. It behoves you to do what usually happens in the worlds. O excellent one among Suras, it should be possible for you to take up and bear our fiery refulgence for the purpose of doing the task of the Devas. In all the three worlds, there is no one else competent enough to do so."

Agni said:

O Lord Supreme, what power do I have for carrying your fiery refulgence? It will reduce to ash all the three worlds consisting of mobile and immobile beings.

Īśvara said:

16-26. If there is any pain caused by our seed deposited in your belly, cast off that fiery refulgence in the waters of Gaṅgā, O Hutāśana (Fire).

After saying this Mahādeva deposited into the mouth of Havyavāha (Fire-god) his excellent, never-failing seed. Then he vanished.

When the Lord had vanished, Hutāśana experienced burning sensation. He deposited the seed into the waters of Gaṅgā and went to his own abode.

Unable to bear that fiery refulgence, Gaṅgā, the most excellent one among rivers, deposited it among the Śara reeds and went on her way.

On seeing the child born there, all the Devas including Vāsava sent the Kṛttikās to feed him with breast milk.

On seeing all of them arrived, the highly intelligent god born of the womb of Gaṅgā, became six-faced and drank the milk of the breasts through his six mouths, as he was so eager to drink.

The Lotus-born Lord performed all the consecratory rites beginning with the post-natal rite as enjoined in the Vedas, in accordance with the injunctions.

He was named *Ṣaṇmukha*[1] because he had six faces, *Kārttikeya* because he was nursed by the Kṛttikās, *Kumāra* because he was still a child. He was also called *Gaṅgāgarbha* and *Agnija.*

1. Etymologies of the different names of Skanda.

Thus without formal study he became well-versed in the Vedas and many scriptures. He performed a severe penance.

Then he travelled through divine forests, rivers and all the Tīrthas of the earth as well as oceans, O descendant of Bharata. Ultimately in due course, he reached the banks of Narmadā. On the southern bank of Narmadā, he performed a severe penance.

27-35. Day and night he muttered ritualistically passages from Ṛk, Yujus and Sāman. He meditated upon Mahādeva with great purity. He became so emaciated that all his veins became visible.

When the period of a thousand years was completed Lord Maheśvara came there along with Umā and spoke these words:

Īśvara said:

I am the bestower of boons on you. O dear child, Gaurī is your mother and I am your father. Choose your boon whatever is desired by you, even if it be the rarest thing in all the three worlds.

Ṣaṇmukha said:

O Mahādeva, O Śaṅkara, if you with Umā are pleased with me, O my parents, I choose this boon. In my opinion I don't have any other goal (except you).

On hearing these splendid words that came out of the mouth of his son, the Lord said, "Let it be so" and embraced him with great affection.

Sniffing at his head along with Umā, Śaṅkara said:

Īśvara said:

You will be immutable and everlasting commander-in-chief. A peacock of divine form is being given to you as vehicle. It will hold the Śakti in the battle. Be victorious over Suras and Asuras.

After saying this, the noble soul went to the excellent Kailāsa mountain.

When the Lord vanished, the Peacock-vehicled One installed Mahādeva (Liṅga) and went to the presence of the Suras.

36-44. Ever since then that Tīrtha became well-known as Skandatīrtha. It is the rarest meritorious Tīrtha unto the men of the earth. It is destructive of all sins.

O king, one who devoutly takes his holy bath in the Tīrtha there and adores Śiva with sweet-smelling garlands and Abhiṣeka (ritualistic bathing) shall obtain the benefit of a Yajña.

Listen to the meritorious benefit obtained by one who takes his holy bath in Skanda Tīrtha and worships Pitṛs and Devatās with water mixed with gingelly seeds.

By means of a single ball of rice offered in accordance with the injunctions, O descendant of Bharata, the Pitṛs become pleased with him for twelve years. There is no doubt about this.

O great king, whether it is splendid or otherwise, everything offered at the Tīrtha there becomes everlasting in this as well as the other world.

Whoever casts his life there in the Tīrtha in accordance with the scriptural injunctions goes to the world of Śiva. After staying there for a Kalpa duly honoured by Devas and Gandharvas, he is reborn in Bhāratavarṣa in a pure family. He will be conversant with the principles of the Vedas and Vedāṅgas. He will be devoid of all ailments. Accompanied by sons and grandsons he will live for a hundred years.

Thus, O king, the origin of Skanda Tīrtha has been recounted to you. It is conducive to wealth, fame and longevity. It is excellent. It eradicates all miseries and sins. It is meritorious as told by the Lord himself.

CHAPTER ONE HUNDRED TWELVE

The Greatness of Āṅgirasa Tīrtha

Śrī Mārkaṇḍeya said:

1-11. Thereafter, O great king, a person should go to the Tīrtha of Āṅgirasa. It is situated on the northern bank of Narmadā and is destructive of all sins.

Formerly there was a Brāhmaṇa named Aṅgiras who had mastered the Vedas. At the beginning of the Yuga, he performed a severe penance for obtaining a son.

Everyday he took three holy baths. He performed the Japa of the eternal Lord. He worshipped Mahādeva and observed the vows like Kṛcchra Cāndrāyaṇa etc.

When the period of twelve years was completed Parameśvara became pleased. He asked the Brāhmaṇa Aṅgiras to request for any boon he wanted.

He requested Mahādeva for an excellent son who should be well-versed in the Vedic lore, expert in observing Vratas and a master of all scriptures; who would become advisor to Devas, O king, and honoured in all the worlds; who would be a permanent abode of Brāhmaṇical splendour and immortal too.

Hara told him, "A son so desired and expert in all lores shall be born. There is no doubt (in this matter)." After saying so, Hara went away.

Due to the boon, Bṛhaspati was born to Aṅgiras as the son so desired and an expert in the Vedas and Vedāṅgas. After the birth of the son, Aṅgiras installed Śaṅkara there. With a delighted and contented mind, he went to the northern mountain.

He who takes his holy bath in the Āṅgirasa Tīrtha and worships Śiva, shall be rid of all sins and go to Rudraloka. A man without a son shall obtain a son; a man without wealth shall attain wealth. Whatever the man may desire, he will attain it.

CHAPTER ONE HUNDRED THIRTEEN

The Greatness of Koṭi Tīrtha

Śrī Mārkaṇḍeya said:

1-3. Thereafter, O great king, one should go to the excellent Tīrtha named Koṭitīrtha. A crore of sages attained great Siddhi (spiritual perfection) there.

A person should take his holy bath there in that Tīrtha, remain pure and feed Brāhmaṇas. Even if one Brāhmaṇa is fed, it is as good as feeding a crore of Brāhmaṇas.

A devotee should take his holy bath there in that Tīrtha and adore Pitṛs and Devatās (or Pitṛs as Devatās). When Mahādeva is adored the devotee shall attain the benefit of a Vājapeya (sacrifice).

CHAPTER ONE HUNDRED FOURTEEN

The Greatness of Ayonisaṁbhava Tīrtha

Śrī Mārkaṇḍeya said:

1-3. Thereafter, O great king, a person should go to the extremely splendid Ayonija Tīrtha of great merit, that is destructive of all sins.

The man should take bath in the Ayonija (Tīrtha) and worship Parameśvara. After performing the adoration of Pitṛs and Devas, he is liberated from all sins.

He who casts off his life there in the Tīrtha as per prescribed procedure, O great king, will never thereafter see the opening of vagina (i.e. will not be reborn).

CHAPTER ONE HUNDRED FIFTEEN

The Greatness of Aṅgāraka Tīrtha

Śrī Mārkaṇḍeya said:

1-11. Thereafter, O great king, a person should go to the great Aṅgāraka Tīrtha that accords handsome features to all people. It is situated on the banks of Narmadā and is well-known.

It is said, O great king, that penance was performed by Aṅgāraka (Mars) for millions, billions and trillions of years. Thereupon, Mahādeva was pleased and was filled with great compassion. Appearing before him in person directly, the Lord spoke to the son of Earth (i.e. Mars):

"O blessed one, I am the bestower of boon even if it be very difficult for even Devas. O dear one, tell me. What has been desired by you. I shall grant you that boon."

Aṅgāraka (Mars) said:

O Lord of Devas, O great Lord of all the worlds, with your favour, I shall always move about in the firmament amidst the Planets. Let this boon be of everlasting benefit to me as long as Mountain Meru exists in the world, as long as the Moon and the Sun shine and as long as the rivers and oceans flourish.

After granting the excellent boon saying "Let it be so", the Lord of Devas went away through the sky even as Suras and Asuras made obeisance to him.

The Son of Earth (Mars) installed Śaṅkara there and went to heaven. He was allotted the status of a Planet in the (stellar) world.

He who takes his holy bath there in the Tīrtha, worships Parameśvara, and performs *Homa*, with anger well under control, shall obtain the benefit of a horse-sacrifice.

He who takes his holy bath there on the Aṅgāraka Caturthī day (Tuesday coinciding with the fourth lunar day) and worships Planet Mars duly, shall be in the Aṅgāraka region extending over ten Yojanas and be endowed with a comely form. The creature that dies there itself willingly or unwillingly, shall become an attendant of Rudra and rejoice along with him.

CHAPTER ONE HUNDRED SIXTEEN

The Greatness of Pāṇḍu Tīrtha

Śrī Mārkaṇḍeya said:

1-3. Thereafter, one should go to the Pāṇḍu Tīrtha that is destructive of all sins. By taking his holy bath therein, the man is rid of all sins.

He who takes his holy bath there in that Tīrtha, becomes pure and then gives away gold by way of charity, gets the sin such as that of foeticide destroyed undoubtedly.

By offering balls of rice and libations, one gets the benefit of a Vājapeya. The Pitṛs and Pitāmahas become highly delighted and, therefore, begin to dance.

CHAPTER ONE HUNDRED SEVENTEEN

The Greatness of Trilocana Tīrtha

Śrī Mārkaṇḍeya said:

1-3. Thereafter, O eminent king, a person should go to the meritorious Trilocana Tīrtha. It is there that the Lord of Devas bowed to by all the worlds, is stationed.

He who bathes there in that Tīrtha and devoutly worships Śaṅkara shall undoubtedly go to the abode of Rudra after death.

When the Kalpa ends, he comes back here after sporting there (in Rudra Loka). He shall remain unseparated (from kinsmen) and will be respected (by all) for a hundred years.

CHAPTER ONE HUNDRED EIGHTEEN

The Greatness of Indra Tīrtha

Śrī Mārkaṇḍeya said:

1-9. Thereafter, O great king, a person should go to a highly resplendent Tīrtha on the southern bank of Narmadā. It is well-known as Indra Tīrtha.

Yudhiṣṭhira said:

Why is the Indra Tīrtha on the southern bank of Narmadā? I wish to hear, O eminent Brāhmaṇa, with full details from the beginning, through the middle to the end.

On hearing these words of the intelligent Dharmaputra, he narrated the old legend and the details of the episodes happening there.

Śrī Mārkaṇḍeya said:

Though Vṛtra was an enemy to Dharma (righteousness) that highly powerful one was defeated (killed) treacherously by the Consort of Śacī. As he left the place and was going along the path, the irrepressible Sin of Brāhmaṇa-slaughter followed him tirelessly without resting. He went all over the three worlds.

Wherever the sinner of Brahmaṇa-murder went in his grand vehicle along with the Suras, whichever quarter he passed through, the Sin of slaughter did not leave him alone.

Words of reproach were heard by him such as: "Ways of redemption from grave sins of Brāhmaṇa-slaughter, imbibing of liquor, theft and violation of the chastity of the preceptor's wife etc. are available but not for those guilty of perfidy." "A man or woman engaged in sinful activities gets purified by means of holy bath and *Dāna* but not one guilty of betrayal of trust." The king of Devas heard these and other similar words uttered by different sorts of people and became excessively sad.

10-21a. He abandoned the kingdom along with the Suras and took to the practice of excellent penance. Sons, wives, house, kingdom, different kinds of riches etc., are the fruits of practice of Dharma and they add to the splendour of a king. Even as people watch him, a man must taste the bitter fruits of sin himself, whereas friends, relatives and kinsmen enjoy the good fruits of Dharma.

Indra eschewed all happiness and got his body emaciated through austerities. The king of Devas visited various Tīrthas and shrines. He took holy baths separately in various Tīrthas, in Gaṅgā, Yamunā and Sarasvatī, in all the oceans, rivers, natural lakes and ponds. But the Sin did not leave him despite his association with Devas.

He went on bathing in the Tīrthas on either side of Narmadā and worshipped Mahādeva. Ultimately he reached Skanda Tīrtha.

Halting there he observed fasts and performed the vows of Kṛcchra, Cāndrāyaṇa etc. He made his body lean and emaciated but did not find pleasure anywhere.

During summers he performed penance in the midst of five fires. During rainy season he lay down on bare ground. During winter he performed severe penance wearing wet clothes. Thus Indra spent ten thousand years, O descendant of Bharata, performing penance and trying to know the Ātman.

When the eleventh thousand-year-period arrived, O excellent king, Lord Parameśvara became pleased. Then all the Suras with Brahmā and Viṣṇu as their leaders and also the Brāhmaṇa-sages, Siddhas etc came to the place where Śatakratu (Indra) was present.

21b-28. On seeing that all the Devas and the sages had arrived the highly intelligent preceptor of all the Devas bowed down to them and said: "It is already known to all of you, O Brahmā, Viṣṇu and Maheśvara, that Vṛtra was slain formerly at your behest and concurrence. Still considering him as a Brāhmaṇa-slayer, perpetrator of a crime, though he may have visited all the Tīrthas, the Brahmahatyā Sin does not leave him alone.

All the three worlds including mobile and immobile creatures, are not happy, like the sky bereft of the Moon and the Sun or a kingdom without a leader (i.e. king).

Hence, O ye all excellent Suras, I have something to submit to you now. May all the great sages declare Śakra free from faults."

On hearing those words of auspicious nature that issued forth from the mouth of Bṛhaspati, Lord Brahmā, the grandfather of the worlds, said, "This Sin arising from the slaughter of a Brāhmaṇa is extremely terrible. I am now dividing it into four parts and casting it off to the Devas and the Bhūtas (elements)."[1]

After saying this, that highly intelligent one hurled (the first part of) the Sin over the water.

29-41. Therefore, waters have to be drunk by sensible persons after plunging into them and not otherwise.

The Lotus-born Lord hurled the second part over the earth. Therefore, for all times the earth became unfit to be eaten. The next day, O Yudhiṣṭhira, the Lord deposited the next part within women (on the second day of their menstruation period) and said, "Women in their monthly course are not to be associated with by sensible persons during the four days on account of the enormity of the sin." Then the Lord deposited the fourth part in a Brāhmaṇa who serves Śūdras through cultivation, cattle breeding and business practice.

1. Compare Mbh, *Udyoga*, 13.19

Thereafter, all the Devas and the great sages honoured Devendra who was stationed in the waters of Narmadā. They honoured him through pleasing words (of consolation). Then Maheśvara who was pleased gave him the opportunity of choosing a boon as he pleased: "O Lord of Devas, I shall grant you a boon. Choose whatever you desire."

Indra said:

O Lord of Devas, if you are pleased, if a boon has to be granted to me, then be pleased to be present here always. I shall install you here.

Saying "Let it be so" to him Brahmā, Viṣṇu and Maheśvara went away entering through the sky and they were eulogized by the great sages.

After all the Lords of Devas had gone, Śatakratu, the Lord of Devas, installed Mahādeva and went to heaven.

He who takes his holy bath in the Indratīrtha and propitiates Pitṛs and Devatās will be liberated from all sins even if they are major ones. He who takes his holy ablution in the Indratīrtha and adores Parameśvara, enjoys the full benefit of Aśvamedha Yajña.

Thus the entire excellent greatness of the Tīrtha has been recounted to you. On merely hearing it, men are rid of all sins.

CHAPTER ONE HUNDRED NINETEEN

The Greatness of Kalhoḍī Tīrtha

Śrī Mārkaṇḍeya said:

1-13. Thereafter, O great king, one should go to the excellent Kalhoḍī Tīrtha which is destructive of all sins. It is situated on the northern bank of Revā.

Formerly it was lifted up by sages through the power of their penance and established in the great waters of Narmadā for the sake of the welfare of all living beings.

Listen to the benefit that one attains by making a gift of a

Kapilā (tawny-coloured) cow, after taking the holy ablution in the Kapilā Tīrtha and listening to the divine narrative from a Brāhmaṇa.

Of all the *Dānas*, *Kapilādāna* is the most excellent one. Even Brahmā had recourse to it formerly in the assembly of sages and Devas.

Listen to the meritorious benefit of one who eschews anger, observes fast and makes the gift of a splendid Kapilā cow immediately after it has calved.

There is no doubt about this that it is as good as, O mighty-armed one, the gift of the entire earth along with the caves and oceans, mountains, forests and parks.

O king, sins verbal, mental and physical, committed formerly in the course of seven births, perish by the gift of a Kapilā.

Gifts of plots of land, cash, foodgrains, elephants, horses, gold etc. do not deserve even a sixteenth fraction of Kapilādāna.

A man who takes his holy bath there and makes the gift of a Kapilā cow, goes to Viṣṇu's city on death after being sung about by groups of celestial damsels.

He sports about for a long time in Svarga, for as many thousand years as there are hairs on the body of that cow as well as that of the calf.

After descending down in due course, he is born as a human being in a large family full of wealth and foodgrain.

He will be well-versed in the Vedic lore, an expert in all the scriptures, free from ailments and grief etc. He lives for a hundred years.

Thus the excellent Kalhoḍī Tīrtha has been fully described, by performing (the pilgrimage to) which one is liberated from all sins.

CHAPTER ONE HUNDRED TWENTY

The Greatness of Kaṁbukeśvara Tīrtha

Śrī Mārkaṇḍeya said:

1-9. Henceforth I shall recount the excellent Kaṁbukeśvara Tīrtha.

Daitya Hiraṇyakaśipu who was arrogant due to his might, was well-known in all the three worlds as one who could not be killed by anyone. He had a son of great refulgence named Prahlāda. With the favour of Viṣṇu and due to his own devout nature, he was established in the kingdom of Hiraṇyakaśipu.

Virocana was his son and Bali was Virocana's son. Bāṇa was Bali's son and Bāṇa's son was Śaṁbara. In the family of Śaṁbara was born a great Asura Kaṁbu by name. He was aware of the terror originating from Viṣṇu. He thought that there was none else who could cause the destruction of Dānavas.

Kaṁbu of great intellect, left his wife, sons, friends, relatives and kinsmen and performed penance, observing the vow of silence. He took up a rosary of beads in his hand. He had all the paraphernalia of a sage such as a staff, girdle and tonsured head. He wore barks of trees or antelope-skin and his diet was restricted to greens and barley gruel. Everyday he had his regular bath in the waters of Narmadā. With great fortitude, he worshipped Mahādeva for one hundred million years.

Then Maheśvara, the Lord of Devas, became pleased with him and said to the Dānava in a majestic voice resembling thunder:

10-18. "O Kaṁbu, O blessed one, I am pleased with you. Silence is the greatest of all vows. It is the means of achieving everything. It is difficult for both Devas and Dānavas to observe but you observed it. Welfare unto you. Choose a boon, whatever may appeal to your mind."

Kaṁbu said:

If you are pleased, O Lord of Devas, if a boon has to be granted to me, let me be indestructible and everlasting. May I be free to move about as I please. I shall never have to flee from battles of Dānavas and Devas. There shall be no other source of fear than Lord Gadādhara.

O Śaṅkara, grant this boon unto me, whereby I will not be overwhelmed by him in battle.

Īśvara said:

If you are in my vicinity, O Dānava, there is no fear from Viṣṇu. Stay here free from fever (anxiety). Neither I nor all the Suras and Asuras can be a match in battle unto that over-lord of Devas, the wielder of conch and discus, who holds the Vedas in his womb.

In my opinion there is no doubt that none who cherishes enmity against Hari, the Lord of Lokāloka, can remain happy even for a period of a single wink of the eye. Hence you should be extremely devout and engaged in the welfare of all living beings. Then you will live for a long time.

After saying this the Lord vanished.

19-25. When the Deva vanished, the highly intelligent Dānava installed Śiva, the Lord of Devas, the quiescent one free from ailment, at that Tīrtha.

After installing Mahādeva at that Tīrtha he went to the heavenly world. Ever since then, O son of Kuntī, that became well-known as Kaṁbu Tīrtha. It is reputed in all the worlds as the destroyer of great sins. A man should take his holy bath in Kaṁbu Tīrtha, duly worship Bhāskara and eulogize him with Ṛk, Yajus and Sāma Mantras, O excellent king. His merit has been described by Brāhmaṇas who have mastered the Vedas. Listen to it fully, O king, even as I recount it.

One who knows only the Gāyatrī Mantra attains the benefit obtained when Ṛk, Yajus and Sāma Mantras are recited along with their ancillaries and sub-divisions.

He who takes his holy bath there and propitiates Pitṛs and Devatās and adores Lord Īśāna, attains the benefit of Agniṣṭoma.

One who forsakes the body there in the Tīrtha with or without any desire goes to Rudraloka immediately.

CHAPTER ONE HUNDRED TWENTYONE

The Greatness of Soma Tīrtha

Śrī Mārkaṇḍeya said:

1-5. Thereafter, O king, a person should go to the Candrahāsa Tīrtha where Somarāja (Moon-god), the excellent one among Suras, attained the greatest Siddhi.

Yudhiṣṭhira said:

How did Somanātha, the Lord of the universe, attain the greatest Siddhi? O sinless one, I wish to hear about it entirely. Do tell me.

Śrī Mārkaṇḍeya said:

O descendant of Bharata, formerly he (Moon-god) was cursed by Dakṣa, the leading sage: "You will become a patient of consumptive disease because you did not attend to your (other) wives."

O king, listen to what happens to those men who do not attend to the wives duly wedded.

A son is born by attending to a woman during the monthly period (i.e. after the menstruation on the fifth day). It is mentioned in the Śruti that heavenly pleasures and salvation are attained through the son.

6-16. One not performing what is befitting to those occasions will fall into the Raurava hell. The sinner drinks the blood of that woman for the duration of that period of (unfulfilled) desires.

After coming down (to earth) on completion of the period of stay in the hell, the wicked sinner is born unlucky in every birth he may take.

Ordinarily sexual appetite is very strong in women. Especially during menses, they are afflicted all the more by the arrows of Kāma. Shunned or neglected by their husbands, women naturally think about paramours. A son born of such a woman, makes the excellent family roam about.

The moment such a son is born, Pitṛs, Pitāmahas and other ancestors residing in heaven fall down. Hence the son is called Kulaṭa.

As a result of his own Karma, Moon-god became a patient of consumptive disease. He had to abandon the world of leading Suras and come down to the world of mortals. He wandered over many Tīrthas and holy shrines and ultimately reached Narmadā that is destructive of all sins.

He observed fasts and holy Vratas and restraints. He performed *Dana* rites. Thus his pious activities continued for twelve years. Thereby he became rid of sins.

After bathing Mahādeva, the destroyer of all sins, he regained his full refulgence and went back to the excellent world.

He who installs the Lord and worships him for many years, is himself honoured in Rudraloka for as many thousand years as the number of years he has worshipped.

Hence men install gods as per proper procedure on the earth. Thereby men enjoy for a period which is inexhaustible and unending.

17-26. A man who bathes in Somatīrtha and adores Lord Īśvara, shines in this world and becomes pleasing in looks like Soma.

He who goes to Candrahāsa Tīrtha during solar and lunar eclipses and devoutly takes his holy bath is rid of all sins.

O excellent king, holy ablution taken, Dāna performed, verily all auspicious or inauspicious acts done in Candrahāsa Tīrtha, become everlasting in their effect.

Men who take their holy bath in Candrahāsa Tīrtha and see the eclipse are really blessed. They are noble-souled. Their birth and life are excellent.

Verbal, mental and physical sins committed earlier perish, O great king, merely because a holy bath is performed in that Tīrtha.

Many are entirely deluded ones who do not know it, like the Lord in the form of greatest bliss (Ātman) abiding in the body itself.

Undoubtedly one attains in Candrahāsa that entire benefit which people get after going to Somatīrtha in the western sea (in Saurāṣṭra). By taking the holy bath in Candrahāsa during Saṅkrānti, Vyatīpāta, Ayana and Viṣuva period, one is rid of all sins.

Those who do not know Candrahāsa situated on Revā, are deluded and wicked in action. Their life is purposeless.

A Brāhmaṇa who takes up the life of a recluse at Candrahāsa Tīrtha undoubtedly attains Somaloka from which he never returns.

CHAPTER ONE HUNDRED TWENTYTWO

The Greatness of Kohana Tīrtha

Śrī Mārkaṇḍeya said:

1-2. Thereafter, O king, one should go to the meritorious Tīrtha well-known as Kohanasva. It is destructive of all sins and even of death.

Formerly a certain Brāhmaṇa who had mastered the Vedas and Vedāṅgas lived there along with his wife, sons, friends, and kinsmen. He was always engaged in performing his duties.

Yudhiṣṭhira said:

3-13. Tell me entirely the duties of a Brāhmaṇa, the origin of Kṣatriya, Vaiśya and Śūdra.

I wish to know the excellent procedure regarding Dharma, Artha, Kāma and Mokṣa entirely. It is my opinion that no one else knows it.

Śrī Mārkaṇḍeya said:

Brahmā, the Lord of Devas, is glorified as the primary source of origin of all living beings. He is the preceptor of the universe consisting of mobile and immobile beings.

Brāhmaṇas were born from the face (mouth). Kṣatriyas were born from the arms, Vaiśyas from the region of thighs and Śūdras from the feet.[1]

The Varṇas other than they are separate and they perform their respective duties separately. They are born in the usual order or in the opposite order (*vilomataḥ*).

I shall expound their special duties as enjoined by the Śruti and Smṛti. If they are perfectly performed, all of them attain the greatest goal.

This goal is attained by devout Brāhmaṇas, O king, even without meditation, because they teach one or more Vedas duly.

After the life as a student, a Brāhmaṇa should marry a girl of noble family, marked by all the usual auspicious character-

1. An echo of *Puruṣa Sūkta*, RV X. 90

istics and endowed with beauty, after being duly permitted by the preceptor.

Then he should gradually worship the fire at the time of marriage whether it is Śrauta or Smārta. He should be devoid of hypocrisy and covetousness and earn wealth through *Pratigraha* (gifts).

He should duly perform the five Yajñas. After fulfilling the duties of the second *Āśrama* (i.e. householdership) he should go to the forest.

He should entrust his wife to his sons and severe all connections and associations. He thereby attains all desired worlds. He is not reborn here again.

14-23. A Kṣatriya well-established in the kingdom should protect the kingdom always fixing his mind on *Dharma.* He shall obtain the greatest goal.

There is no doubt about this that the *Dharma* of a Vaiśya is the ardent pursuit of cultivation and breeding of cattle. He too, well-endowed with truthfulness, purity and mental quiescence goes to the excellent Svarga.

A separate duty has not been assigned by Parameṣṭhin to the Śūdra. He need not have any Mantra, consecration or pursuit of lores. He need not have any conventional study of the science of words (i.e. Grammar) and special worship of deities. He has to be, day and night, in the same state as at birth.

Such is the Dharma of all the Varṇas as created by the Self-born Lord formerly. They are richly endowed with the consecratory rites with Mantras. The three Varṇas are called *Dvijāti* (twice-borns).

If anyone lives a wanton life disregarding their opinions and comments, he is reborn as a dog on death. He has no upward progress.

Their missions and errands (should not be ignored by him). Remembering and following their opinions and views, he becomes well-reputed, one abiding by his specific duty, and one deserving Svarga.

Now, the Brāhmaṇa referred to above, possessing all the good qualities lived there, O descendant of Bharata. He heard words like "*Hanasva* (kill), *Hanasva.*"

Thereat he looked up and down and all round. Trembling with fright, he faltered at every step.

He was face to face with a man riding on a buffalo and equipped with fetters, weapons and terrible nooses in hands.

24-31. He had the lustre of a heap of black collyrium. He was clad in black garments. Endowed with all characteristic marks, he had red eyes and long arms.

On noticing him coming along, the Brāhmaṇa turned his attention inwards and repeated words fit to be muttered such as the great *Śatarudriya* hymn.

Thereupon Lord Yama, the great controller of all, said: "O Brāhmaṇa, I am Yama, the controller of all creatures. Withold, O blessed one, the *Rudrajāpya* (Japa of Rudra) which is impregnable, so that I can painlessly bind you with Kālapāśa."

On hearing those ruthless words that issued forth from the mouth of Yama, the Brāhmaṇa became extremely terrified and fled.

All the servants pursued his path along with Yama and said, "Stop, stop" to the Brāhmaṇa. But he continued to run.

By this hurried flight, he became exhausted and cried: "Alas! I have been assailed by evil-minded ones. Save me, save me, O Mahādeva who consider those who seek your refuge as your favourites."

After saying this, he fell down on the ground and closely embraced the Liṅga, O descendant of Bharata. Losing his consciousness, the eminent Brāhmaṇa resorted to the Lord of Suras.

32-38. On seeing him fallen on the ground, Maheśvara, the Lord of Devas, made a *Huṁkāra* ('Hum'sound) and said, "Who dares to kill you? Do not be afraid."

At that Huṁkāra, O descendant of Bharata, all the servants fled away along with Yama like clouds blown away by wind.

Ever since then, that Tīrtha became well-known as *Kohanasva*. It is meritorious and destructive of all sins. It is the most excellent one of all the Tīrthas.

He who takes his holy plunge there in that Tīrtha and worships Parameśvara, attains the excellent benefit of Agniṣṭoma Yajña.

He who sheds his life there in that Tīrtha, O great king, does not see Lord Yama. So said Śaṅkara.

O excellent king, the devotee may immolate himself by entering fire or drowning in water. Thereby he gains a residence in Agniloka for a period of three hundred Kalpas or he may reside in Varuṇaloka for as much time as he pleases and return to this world after which he is destined to become Lord of enormous wealth.

CHAPTER ONE HUNDRED TWENTYTHREE

The Greatness of Karmadeśvara Tīrtha

Śrī Mārkaṇḍeya said:

1-3. Thereafter, O great king, one should go to the excellent Karmadī (*sic*) Tīrtha where Vighneśa, the mighty Lord of Gaṇas, stands.

If a man takes his holy bath there in the Tīrtha on the fourth lunar day and observes fast, he will never have any obstacle in the course of seven births, O descendant of Bharata.

Undoubtedly whatever is offered as gift at that Tīrtha shall have everlasting benefit.

CHAPTER ONE HUNDRED TWENTYFOUR

The Greatness of Narmadeśvara Tīrtha

Śrī Mārkaṇḍeya said:

1-2. Thereafter, one should go to the excellent Narmadeśvara, O king. By taking the holy bath there in that Tīrtha, a man is rid of all sins.

If one meets death by entering fire, or drowning in water or due to ritualistic starvation, his departure (from this world) shall be one from which one has never to return (to Saṁsāra), as Śaṅkara told me.

CHAPTER ONE HUNDRED TWENTYFIVE

The Greatness of Ravi Tīrtha

Śrī Mārkaṇḍeya said:

1-8. Thereafter, O king, a person should go to the excellent Ravitīrtha where the Thousand-rayed Lord performed a penance and went to heaven.

Yudhiṣṭhira said:

How (is it that) Lord Bhāskara, Ravi (Sun-god), the sustainer of the universe, who is bowed to by all the Devas, performed penance? Is the Lord of Devas a sage? He is worthy of being propitiated by all living beings. He is adored by all the Devas. He is seen directly in the world. He is the cause of creation and annihilation (of the world). How did he attain the name Āditya? How is he called Bhāskara? O sinless one, describe all this succinctly.

Śrī Mārkaṇḍeya said:

O great king, what you have asked is a great and relevant question. After making obeisance to the Self-born Lord, I shall describe everything.

Everything in the universe was once enveloped in darkness. It was all unknown and featureless. It was incomprehensible, beyond knowledge; everything was as it were in deep sleep all round.

Thereafter a divine refulgence (appeared) like a highly heated, excellent ball (of iron). Like a meteor from the sky, it came down with face directed downwards for the creation (of the world).

Within that refulgence, a Puruṣa (Person) was born well-adorned with everything. He was without legs and hands. He is Lord Śiva by whom all these visible objects are created and permeated.

9-18. After the appearance of that Being in the form of refulgence Prajāpati who became Kāla (time) appeared in due course. He then became fire for (the sake of) all living beings, mortals, Asuras and Rākṣasas. He is the overlord of all the Devas. Hence he is called *Āditya.*

Obeisance to him should be paid at the outset and to the others only after him. So it is done by all the deities and all the great sages.

In the solar disc three Sandhyās (junctions of time) and three Devas are present. So when the Sun is bowed to, all the Devas are also (automatically) bowed to.

O king, had there been no Sun-god, neither day, nor night, neither the southern transit lasting for six months nor the northern transit would appear.

Without Sūrya (Sun-god) there is neither Snāna (holy bath) nor Dāna, neither Japa nor Homa, neither self-study of the Vedas nor adoration of the deities. Hence Ravi is the most worthy of adoration.

Brahmā, Viṣṇu and Maheśvara are to be known through words of the Śruti (Vedas) chiefly. But Lord Sun is directly visible. He is the sanctifier of all the worlds.

He is the source of origin; the cause of annihilation and dissolution, the storehouse and the immutable seed. The Lord of the universe, the sole cause is none other than Bhāskara. After thus making the universe consisting of mobile and immobile beings issue out of himself, he established the path of piety for the sake of the welfare of the worlds.

He resorted to the banks of Narmadā and installed his own physical form, the thousand-rayed storehouse of refulgence. He then went up to the immutable sky.

19-27. If a devotee takes his holy bath there in that Tīrtha and adores the Thousand-rayed Lord, the great Lord, in accordance with the injunctions regarding the Mantras in the forms of the names (of deities) it is as good as though penance has been performed by him, Homa has been carried out, nay everything has been duly performed. By doing all these things perfectly, the greatest position is attained by him.

Those who take their holy bath in the waters of Narmadā and visit Lord Bhāskara are blessed. They are noble-souled ones. Their life is well lived.

The devotees should constantly repeat the Mantra thrice, O great king and circumambulate the Lord with single-pointed devotion. Thereby they become purified. Their sins are dispelled by that Mantra. Listen with concentration of mind to the merit that shall accrue to them.

There is no doubt about it that the entire earth consisting of mountains, parks and forests along with oceans and caves, has been circumambulated by him.

This entire group of the three worlds consisting of mobile and immobile beings has Mantras at its root. Hence, bereft of Mantras, no undertaking in the world succeeds.

Just as a wooden image of an elephant or a leathern deer cannot be effective in action, so also a pious rite without Mantras (is futile).

Just as an oblation offered on ashes or offering of a gift without use of water is futile, so also (is) Dāna bereft of Mantras.

28-36. In regard to idols made of wood, stone or a lump of clay, particularly in the case of earthen ones, people perform the adoration along with relevant Mantra. They do not make it without uttering Mantra.

By performing Namaskāra (obeisance) once with due utterance of Mantras, one derives the benefit that is usually obtained by ordinary Namaskāras (prostrations) done continuously for twelve years with devotion.

If a devotee takes his holy bath in the waters of Narmadā and worships Ravi during Saṅkrānti, Vyatīpāta, Ayana and Viṣuva, his sins committed knowingly or unknowingly, in course of twelve years, get dissolved immediately like husk burned by fire.

A devotee of controlled sense-organs, observing fast, should take his holy bath during solar and lunar eclipses. By seeing the face of the deity, Āditya, he is liberated from all sins.

On the seventh lunar day in the month of Māgha, O excellent king, one should control anger and stay in the shrine of Sūrya observing fast. In the morning he should take his holy bath in accordance with the injunctions and offer *Arghya* to the Sun duly reciting the Mantras. He shall obtain excellent merit.

After offering the libations to the Pitṛs, Devas and human beings, in the temple of the Lord of Devas, the devotee should perform the worship by means of sweet scents, flowers, incense, lights and auspicious Naivedyas. After worshipping, he should recite the Mantra.

37-44. He shall repeat the twelve names (of the Sun-god) viz. Viṣṇu, Śakra, Yama, Dhātṛ, Mitra, Varuṇa, Vivasvān, Savitṛ, Pūṣan, Caṇḍāṁśu and Bharga (Ravi, the 12th name also) and circumambulate.

Listen attentively to know the benefit that he attains, O son of Kuntī. He will never be poor, sick, dumb, deaf and sluggish for seven births. So said Śaṅkara.

He who wishes for excellent merit should devoutly propitiate Ravi after completely studying and then uttering the Mantra in accordance with the injunctions. The wise devotee then attains the merit.

He who professes to be a devotee without uttering the Mantra, O descendant of Bharata, deceives himself like brutes, worms and insects.

Whoever abandons the excellent physical body there in the Tīrtha, shall go to heaven being adored by the Devas and great sages.

There he lives as he pleases for a long time. Then he shall become a king here in this world richly endowed with sons and grandsons, elephants, horses and chariots etc. He is born in a large family with hundreds of men and maid servants.

CHAPTER ONE HUNDRED TWENTYSIX

The Greatness of Ayoniprabhava Tīrtha

Śrī Mārkaṇḍeya said:

1-7. Thereafter, O great king, one should go to the great Tīrtha called Ayonija. A man, merely by a holy plunge therein, ceases to face the danger of being in a womb.

A man should take his holy bath there in the Tīrtha and worship Lord Īśvara, uttering this Mantra: "O great Lord Parameśvara, just as you are one not born of a womb, so also release me from the inevitable (possible) calamity of being in a womb." He who worships with scented flowers, incense etc. shall be rid of all sins.

He who devoutly covers the Liṅga with rice mixed with curds

shall reside in the world of the Lord of Devas, in proportion to the number of grains of (that) boiled rice (covering the Liṅga).

The devotee should bathe Mahādeva with scented water in the Ayonija Tīrtha. He may bathe with honey, milk or curds also. He shall attain great glory.

On the eighth day in the bright half or fourteenth day in the dark half he should worship Mahādeva and delight him with vocal and instrumental music. He shall reside in the world of Śiva.

Those who celebrate festivals reside in the world of Śiva until the annihilation of all living beings.

8-16. Uttering this Mantra always and submitting his plaint, the devotee should circumambulate the Lord with great devotion: "O great Lord Parameśvara, just as you are one not born from a womb, so also release me, O Śarva, from all possible calamities (befalling one lying) in a womb."

Traditionally men have stated the following good results received from the Lord of Devas. Listen with mental concentration.[1]

Of what avail are the many Mantras that merely make his throat more and more parched? If the Mantra *oṁ namaḥ śivāya* is uttered in the vicinity of the Lord, it is as good as he has studied everything, heard everything and performed everything.

The repetition of the Mantra *oṁ namaḥ śivāya* should be well practised and stabilised. The benefit that is attained by uttering the six-syllabled Mantra cannot be attained by a Brāhmaṇa from any other god or gods.

If the devotee takes his bath there in the Tīrtha and worships a Śivayogin, he will reap the bruit of feeding more than ten thousand Brāhmaṇas.

Or if the devotee consecrates the alms and gives it to one who has controlled his sense-organs, the benefit thereof is more.

Water should be given in the hand (palms) of the ascetic, then the alms and then water again. The alms is on a par with Meru; the water on a par with the ocean.

1. For the sake of continuity in narration verse 10 is taken after 8 and verse 9 follows verse 10.

CHAPTER ONE HUNDRED TWENTYSEVEN

The Greatness of Agni Tīrtha

Śrī Mārkaṇḍeya said:

1-4. Thereafter, O eminent king, a person should go to the excellent Agni Tīrtha. By taking the holy bath there at the beginning of a fortnight, one is rid of all sins.

Listen, O best one among men, to the benefit proclaimed as accruing unto a man who gifts away a virgin well-adorned at that Tīrtha.

By gifting her adorned in accordance with his capacity, the man obtains the benefit of Agniṣṭoma and Atirātra multiplied by hundred times a hundred.

He attains the greatest goal in the world of Śiva for as many years as there are hairs on the bodies of her sons, grandsons and great-grandsons.

CHAPTER ONE HUNDRED TWENTYEIGHT

The Greatness of Bhṛkuṭeśvara Tīrtha

Śrī Mārkaṇḍeya said:

1-8. Thereafter, O eminent king, one should go to the excellent Bhṛkuṭeśvara Tīrtha where the highly honoured Bhṛgu though highly irascible, became a Siddha (enlightened spiritually).

O sinless one, formerly an elaborate penance was performed by him for more than a hundred years for getting a son. The most excellent one among those blessed with sons chose (requested for) a son as the boon.

O highly honoured one, the boon was granted by the Lord who subdued Andhaka. He who takes his holy bath there in that Tīrtha and worships Parameśvara shall obtain eight times the benefit of Agniṣṭoma Yajña.

Whoever seeks a son and devoutly bathes Bhṛkuṭeśa with ghee mixed with honey, does get the desired son.

Listen to the meritorious benefit of the devotee who takes his holy bath there in the Tīrtha and gifts to a Brāhmaṇa, a piece of gold, a cow, or a plot of land.

O excellent king, there is no doubt about this that it is as good as the entire earth along with the oceans and caves, mountains, parks and forests has been gifted by him.

As a result of that gift, he sports about happily in heaven and then comes down to the mortal world as a great king or a highly worshipped Brāhmaṇa.

CHAPTER ONE HUNDRED TWENTYNINE

The Greatness of Brahma Tīrtha

Śrī Mārkaṇḍeya said:

1-6. Thereafter, O king, a person should go to the excellent Brahma Tīrtha which is greater than the greatest of all the other Tīrthas.

There at that Tīrtha, Brahmā, the most excellent one among Suras, the grandfather of all the worlds, resorted to the banks of Narmadā. Merely by seeing him the Lord of Devas washes off the sins of the four Varṇas, committed earlier, including all mental and verbal ones and those arising from activities of the body.

The eminent Brāhmaṇas who take their holy bath and perform the expiatory rites enjoined by Śrutis and Smṛtis have their residence in heaven.

Those who are oppressed by lust and greed and abandon the scriptural texts and then prescribe expiatory rites (as they please) fall into hell.

A sinner should take his holy bath at the outset and bow down to Brahmā. Then he shall confess his sin. His sin perishes quickly like darkness at sunrise.

7-15. He who takes his holy bath there in the Tīrtha and adores Pitṛs and deities, derives the excellent benefit of Agniṣṭoma Yajña.

Whatever is gifted away as *Dāna* there at that Tīrtha with

Brahmā in view, becomes everlasting in its benefits. So said Śaṅkara.

If Japa is carried out merely of the Gāyatrī Mantra there, it shall become as meritorious as one of the Ṛk, Yajus and Sāma Vedas. There is no doubt about it.

If anyone were to cast off his body, usually very difficult to be cast off, in the Tīrtha there, his return from the world of Brahmā is undoubtedly impossible.

He is honoured in Devaloka for as many thousand years as there are bones of embodied beings in the Brahma Tīrtha.

Thereafter, he comes down into the world (here) and is reborn as one knowing Brahman in a noble family. He shall be the most excellent one among all the Varṇas like the great deity among Devas.

He will be well-versed in all the lores and a master of the Vedas and their Aṅgas. He will be undoubtedly honoured in the world by kings.

He will be accompanied by sons and grandsons and will be free from all ailments. By the power of Brahma Tīrtha, he will live more than a hundred years.

The noble souls who visit this meritorious Tīrtha, the most excellent one for those endowed with knowledge, a Tīrtha that destroys all sins, attain immortality.

CHAPTER ONE HUNDRED THIRTY

The Greatness of Devatīrtha

Śrī Mārkaṇḍeya said:

1-2. On the southern bank of Narmadā, there is the excellent Devatīrtha. Parameśvara was propitiated by Devas who came there.

He who is free from lust and anger and takes his holy bath there in the Tīrtha, shall undoubtedly attain the benefit of (the gift of) a thousand cows.

CHAPTER ONE HUNDRED THIRTYONE

The Greatness of Nāgeśvara Tīrtha

Śrī Mārkaṇḍeya said:

1-7. On the southern bank of Narmadā, there is the excellent Nāgatīrtha where the great serpents achieved fulfilment, O king, when a cause of terror occurred.

Yudhiṣṭhira said:

O excellent Brāhmaṇa, usually Nāgas (serpents) cause great terror unto the world (people). How then did a cause of great terror unto them occur whereby they engaged themselves in a severe penance.

O dear one, everything pertaining to the past, present and future in the case of Suras, Asuras and human beings is entirely known to you. Hence my curiosity is great.

The distress that I undergo is due to Duryodhana. When it is flooded with the words issuing forth from your lotus-like mouth, it ceases to oppress.

The more I hear the sin-destroying story narrated through your mouth, O sage of excellent holy vows, the more I recollect this, and the desire for further hearing arises all the more.

Of course, a Brāhmaṇa should not be given further strain but no one else knows the great benefit of the great Vidyādāna (gift of learning) narrated and listened to.

After understanding this duly, may the story with reference to the question put by me be narrated, O Brāhmaṇa, by adopting the compassionate gesture towards me.

Śrī Mārkaṇḍeya said:

8-15. O king, the more you are talking (putting questions), the more fluency comes to my speech. Despite the slackness resulting from my senility, affection for you never perishes, O dear one.

I shall recount the old legend[1] the way it occurred as recounted earlier by elders traditionally, O descendant of Bharata.

1. This is a rehash of the legend of the wager between Kadrū and Vinatā about the colour of the divine horse Uccaiśśravas. The horse was white

Kaśyapa had two wives, the most excellent ones in all the worlds. They were Vinatā, mother of Garuḍa, and Kadrū, mother of serpents. A dispute between them arose at the sight of the horse (Uccaiḥśravas) in the morning, O great king. Vinatā perceived the form of the horse brilliant like the refulgence of the sun.

He was completely white. She said to Kadrū: "See here, O lady of excellent countenance, the wholly white form of the horse Uccaiśśravas that incessantly runs with the speed of wind."

On seeing him proceeding fast, she (Kadrū) was deluded by a fit of internal envy. Considering him black, she prattled thus to her, O excellent king:

"O Vinatā, O cruel one spoiling the whole family! You are a lier. I say, this is black. If you say, this is white, you will fall into the great abysm of Naraka."

Vinatā said:

16-26. A true statement and a false one shall be our stakes, yours and mine. I shall be a maidservant in your house for a period of one thousand years in case my statement proves false.

Thus they pledged each other's plight and went home at night. They had by that time abandoned the paroxysm of anger.

They went to their kinsmen and mentioned the stake, the incident that took place between Kadrū and Vinatā in the pleasure spot.

On hearing it, all the kinsmen as well as the sons of Kadrū thought that a despicable thing was committed by their mother. It was not conducive to their welfare.

They said: "Mother, the excellent horse is not black. How can he become black? On account of this stipulation, O lady of holy rites, you will have to become a slave."

Kadrū said:

Do something immediately lest I should become a slave. This is my suggestion that you should penetrate the hair pores of

---

but Kadrū stated that he was black. To maintain her stand on the colour of the horse, she ordered her sons to assume hair-like forms and cover the body of the horse. Those who refused to do so were cursed with death in fire (Mbh., *Ādi.* 20.8) that horse. If this is done for a very short while, she will become my slave. Thereby, O serpents, you will become happy.

The serpents said:

O fair lady, although you have been considered (and honoured) as the mother of serpents on the earth, still she (Vinatā) cannot be deceived outright.

Kadrū said:

If there are serpents on the earth not caring to carry out my behest, all of them will straightway fall into the jaws of Havyavāha (fire).

On hearing these terrible words that issued from the mouth of their mother, some of them entered the hairs (of the horse). Others stayed on mountains. Some of them entered Gaṅgā and others began to perform penance.

27-36. Then at the end of a thousand years, Parameśvara was pleased. Mahādeva, the creator of the universe, spoke in majestic words:

"O serpents, desist from the austerities. I shall grant you the great benefit thereof which you wish for. You need not worry over it."

The serpents said:

O Maheśvara, O Lord of Devas, we are afraid of the curse of Kadrū. We shall stay near you until the annihilation of all living beings.

Devadeva (Śiva) said:

This mighty Vāsuki, the excellent one among serpents, alone shall stay always near me. He will be the protector of all from fear.

At my bidding the other serpents need not fear at all. Leaping into the waters of Narmadā those serpents can be well protected. They need not be afraid of death. Stay where you desire to. There is no fear of the curse of Kadrū. This is my supreme seat *(vistaraḥ paraḥ?).*

* * *

Thus, after granting them the boon, Maheśvara, the Lord of Devas, went to Kailāsa mountain passing through the sky.

When the Lord vanished, O king, the serpents, the chief of whom was Vāsuki, installed Maheśvara, the Lord of Devas, and went away.

If anyone adores Śiva in that Tīrtha on the fifth lunar day, all the eight families of Nāgas will never injure him.

One who dies in that Tīrtha, O king, shall become Śiva's attendant for a long time and stay there as long as he wishes.

CHAPTER ONE HUNDRED THIRTYTWO

The Greatness of Ādivārāha Tīrtha

Śrī Mārkaṇḍeya said:

1-7. Thereafter, O great king, one should go to the Tīrtha named Vārāha which dispels all sins. It is situated on the northern bank of Narmadā.

It is there that Lord Viṣṇu, the sustainer of the universe and the Lord enabling people to cross the ocean of worldly existence, assumed the form of a Boar and stationed himself for the sake of the welfare of the worlds.

A devotee should take his holy bath there in that Tīrtha and worship Dharaṇīdhara (i.e. Lord Viṣṇu) by means of specially prepared scented garlands. He should indulge in loudly shouting "Victories unto the Lord" and similar auspicious activities.

O excellent king, he should observe fast on the twelfth lunar day. He should shun the very touch of Vṛṣalas of sinful activities as well as *Andhapiśācins* (blind ghostly beings), since sin will be transmitted by them if they talk, touch their body and take food along with them. Even when they breathe out, sin is transmitted.

On the other hand, Brāhmaṇas should be duly and devoutly adored in accordance with one's capacity. During the night, the devotee should keep awake listening to pious stories.

Those who have conquered bad temper and take holy bath in the pure Tīrtha, should visit the Lord, the preceptor of the universe. Thereby they will be rid of all sins.

8-13. On seeing the face of the Lord in the form of a Boar, all sins perish quickly just as on seeing Suparṇa (Garuḍa) serpents perish discharging their poison and terrifying fiery nature.

Just as on seeing the Sun, the most excellent one among Devas, the darkness in the sky perishes, so also the sins very difficult to counteract perish on seeing the face of Dharādhara (Lord Viṣṇu), O son of Kuntī.

Of what avail are numerous Mantras to a person who has devotion to Lord Janārdana! The very Mantra *namo nārāyaṇāya* is the means of achieving every object.[1]

Even a single obeisance offered to Kṛṣṇa is on a par with the valedictory bath after ten Aśvamedhas. A person who performs ten horse-sacrifices takes birth again, but one who makes obeisance to Kṛṣṇa is not reborn.

Those persons who have conquered the sense-organs and the noble souls who meditate upon the Nārāyaṇa form of Hari and cast off their body there in the Tīrtha attain that place devoid of impurities, not available even to Suras. That is the greatest region of Viṣṇu free from Kṣara (perishable) and Akṣara (imperishable).

CHAPTER ONE HUNDRED THIRTYTHREE

The Glory of Kaubera and other Tīrthas

Śrī Mārkaṇḍeya said:

1-7. Thereafter, O king, a person should go to the great group of four Tīrthas, a mere visit to which brings about the destruction of all sins. They are Kaubera, Vāruṇa, Yāmya and Vāyavya. It was here that the highly intelligent and powerful Guardians of Quarters became Siddhas.

Yudhiṣṭhira said:

What for, O sinless one, was penance performed by the Guardians

1. This shows the influence of or leaning to Pāñcarātrism.

of Quarters formerly on the bank of Narmadā? It behoves you to narrate this to me.

Mārkaṇḍeya said:

Inasmuch as the world (worldly existence) is weak, feeble and unstable like a drop of water hanging from a blade of grass, all people crave for a stable base. All the four types of living beings whether mobile or immobile are fickle, free of essence like the core of a plantain tree and unreal like mirage. That being the case, Dharma is mother, Dharma is father, Dharma is kinsman as well as friend. Dharma alone is the support of all living beings in all the three worlds consisting of mobile and immobile beings.

After realizing this all the Guardians of Quarters waited for an opportunity and performed an unparalleled penance taking in wind alone as their food.

8-17. When half of Kṛtayuga passed off, Mahādeva was pleased. O great king, Parameśvara granted them an open choice of a boon saying, "Whoever wishes for anything, whatever he may desire, I shall grant it."

Thus in accordance with the Yuga, the mighty Guardians of Quarters were asked to choose. On hearing these words of Śiva, the Guardians of worlds intending to do what is good for the world requested the Lord for an excellent boon.

Kubera said:

O Mahādeva, if you are pleased, if a boon has to be granted to me, let me be the Lord of Yakṣas and Dhanada, the bestower of wealth.

Then Yama engaged in controlling (all) said to the Lord of Devas: "O Lord, let me be the chief of all living beings."

After bowing down to Maheśvara, Varuṇa said thereafter: "Let me sport about in the Varuṇa world accompanied by the groups of aquatic beings."

After bowing down to Maheśvara, Vāyu asked immediately, O descendant of Bharata. It was the ability to spread all over the three worlds that he requested for.

After granting the cherished desire to all the Guardians of the worlds, Śaṅkara vanished along with Umā. When Lord Mahēśvara had vanished, they remained in their respective places. Installation of the Lord was carried out by them severally after their own names. Kubera installed Kubereśa, Yama Yameśvara, Varuṇa Varuṇeśa and Vāta Vāteśvara, O king.

18-27. With different kinds of auspicious Mantras duly chanted, they offered libations after worshipping the Lord of all in accordance with the injunctions.

All of them like the Lords of all, invited Brāhmaṇas who had fully subdued the sense-organs and mind, who had subdued anger, who granted freedom from fear unto all living beings, who were clever in the Vedic lore and were masters of all scriptural texts, and who were embellished with Ṛk, Yajus, Sāman and Atharva Vedas.

They said, "We shall give four types of *Dānas* unto ye all. Accept." After saying this they did the excellent Bhūmidāna (gift of plots of land) unto all those Brāhmaṇas.

(The Brāhmaṇas said,) "Your *Dāna* will last as long as the Moon and the Sun shine and as long as the Earth exists. There shall be no enemy."

Whether it is a king or someone on a par with a king, if one loses what is given by the Guardians of the worlds, he is deluded. What is in store for him may be listened.

O descendant of Bharata, Dhanada will dry up the assets of that sinner; Varuṇa will make his body dried up. Wind-god will make his lineage dried up (extinct). His life becomes defunct. Yama, the great controller of all, takes away his life quickly. Hutabhuk (Fire-god) reduces him to ashes and goes away, O descendant of Bharata.

Hence, O Yudhiṣṭhira, all kings should have devotion to Brāhmaṇas if they wish their own welfare.

King is a tree. Brāhmaṇas are like the root thereof. Attendants are the leaves and ministers its branches. Hence the root should be protected with effort. If the root is well preserved the tree does not die.

28-38. A person making gifts of land dwells in heaven for sixty thousand years. One who seizes it or slights or denigrates others shall stay in Naraka for as many years.

Land given by one's own people or others should be well-protected. Whoever has the land has the fruit (benefit) thereof.

Those kings who remember the command of the deities and preserve the earth shall always reside in heaven. O Yudhiṣṭhira, land given by one's own people or others should be well-protected by a king. Protection of land is better than the gifting thereof.

If kings are scrupulously engaged in the protection of the subjects, their longevity, fame, strength, wealth and progeny shall be everlasting certainly.

After saying thus to the excellent Brāhmaṇas(?) all the Guardians of the worlds adored them duly and sent them off after bowing down duly.

After the leading Brāhmaṇas had gone the Guardians of the worlds took their holy bath and performed Homa. Being hungry they wandered here and there for alms. Their bodies were reduced to mere bones and skin, with their hands holding the alms bowl. They did not get even a moiety of half of a morsel. They set out from the city and after angrily cursing the Brāhmaṇa(?), O Yudhiṣṭhira: like "You shall be poor always and also fools", they went home.

Ever since then all the Brāhmaṇas were deprived of their wealth. As a result of the curse those in the northern region became miserable.

Śaṅkara said thus: "The wealth of father is not always enjoyed by sons, nor that of sons and gurdians by father for all the period." Kāla alone enjoys (eats up) all.

39-48. A man who takes his holy bath in the Kubereśa Tīrtha and worships Śiva with scents, incense and prostrations shall derive the benefit of a horse-sacrifice.

One who takes his holy bath in Yama Tīrtha and visits Yameśvara shall be liberated from all sins incurred in the course of seven births.

Listen to the meritorious benefit of a person who takes his holy bath on a full-moon and a new-moon day and performs *Pitṛtarpaṇa* (offering libations to Pitṛs). Pitṛs and Pitāmahas become well-pleased. Prapitāmahas (great-grandfathers) remain sporting about in heaven for twelve years.

A man who takes his holy bath in Varuṇeśa Tīrtha and worships Maheśvara obtains the excellent benefit of a Vājapeya

Yajña. On death after a long time he goes to the world where Jaleśvara (Varuṇa) is present by means of a (special) vehicle. He will be sung about by groups of celestial damsels.

A man who takes his holy bath in Vāteśvara Tīrtha and worships Maheśvara becomes blessed and contented by seeing the Guardians of the worlds.

Of what avail to him are many Yajñas with plenty of Dakṣiṇā or Dāna, if he takes his holy bath in all the four Tīrthas and obtains the benefit of the birth.

They are blessed, they are noble souls, their birth and life is well-lived who stay in Kaurilī (?Kauberī) always after inviting the Guardians of the worlds.

This narrative is destructive of sins. It is meritorious, conducive to wealth and capable of augmenting the span of life. The sins of those who read and listen to it shall be dispelled entirely.

CHAPTER ONE HUNDRED THIRTYFOUR

The Greatness of Rāmeśvara Tīrtha

Śrī Mārkaṇḍeya said:

1-2. On the southern bank of Narmadā, there is the excellent Rāmeśvara Tīrtha that is meritorious, destructive of sins and capable of dispelling all miseries.

Those who take their holy bath there in the Tīrtha and worship the great Lord Mahādeva, the great soul, are liberated from all sins.

CHAPTER ONE HUNDRED THIRTYFIVE

The Greatness of Siddheśvara Tīrtha

Śrī Mārkaṇḍeya said:

1-5. Beyond that itself is another excellent Tīrtha named Siddheśvara. It is endowed with all good qualities and is honoured in all the worlds.

One who takes his holy bath there in that Tīrtha and worships Umā and Rudra, shall attain the excellent benefit of a Vājapeya Yajña.

On death he shall attain heaven due to that great merit. There he will be surrounded by groups of celestial damsels of auspicious features proclaiming his victory.

He shall sport about there as he pleases for a thousand years. Then he shall be reborn in a great family rich with wealth and foodgrains.

O best among men, he will be master of the Vedas and Vedāṅgas and honoured by all. He will be free from ailments and grief and live a hundred years.

CHAPTER ONE HUNDRED THIRTYSIX

The Greatness of Ahalyā Tīrtha[1]

Śrī Mārkaṇḍeya said:

1-7. Thereafter, O king, one should go to the excellent Ahalyeśvara Tīrtha where the blessed ascetic lady Ahalyā received redemption and fulfilment formerly.

There was a Brāhmaṇa named Gautama who was like another Brahmā. He was endowed with truthfulness and piety. He was engrossed in the Vānaprastha stage of life.

---

1. Here the Ahalyā episode is the same as in *Vālmīki Rāmāyaṇa* (VR), Sargas 48-49. But Ahalyā's penance and installation of a Liṅga on Narmadā is a new feature.

His blessed wife named Ahalyā was very famous in all the three worlds as a woman endowed with beauty and prime of youth.

Śatakratu, the king of Devas, was infatuated by the exceptional beauty of Ahalyā. The Slayer of Bala, therefore, tempted her.

"O beautiful lady of uncensured features, resort to me, the king of Devas. Sport about with me. You shall be one honoured in all the three worlds. What will you do with this Brāhmaṇa who has become lean and emaciated due to his over-zealousness for purity and conventional rites and austerities and Vedic studies! O lady of beautiful eyes, you must be rather undergoing sufferings now."

On being told thus, the beautiful lady, very fickle by nature as all women are, became confused and defiled by the god of Love. Mentally she became overwhelmed by Śakra.

8-16. Sensing her emotional upheaval the Lord who slew Pāka was so overcome by wicked intentions that he deceived Gautama.

Getting an opportunity, he assumed the excellent guise of the sage and carnally delighted Ahalyā who believed (that he was Gautama) in the inner apartment.

Within a moment thereafter, O descendant of Bharata, the excellent sage hurriedly entered the apartment.

On seeing Gautama come Purandara became terrified and he went out. Seeing him he thought (knew) that it was Śakra. So Gautama became highly enraged and he cursed Devendra: "Since you could not control your senses, be one with a thousand vaginal apertures." On being cursed thus, Devendra was instantly covered with a thousand vaginal apertures. He became bereft of all glory. He left the kingdom and the Suras too. He performed elaborate penance on the earth.

Ahalyā too was cursed by Gautama: "Since you have been caught red-handed in your wicked actions, since you have carnally delighted Śakra within my view, you shall be turned into a rock. At the end of a thousand years you will see Rāma, the renowned one, who would be coming here during his pilgrimage. Thereby you shall be rid of your sins."

17-24. As the stipulated period of time elapsed she was seen by the intelligent Rāma in the company of Viśvāmitra. She absolved herself of her rocky form and adored Rāma duly. Thereby she became free of sins and malignant features. She came to the Tīrtha on the banks of Narmadā and duly took her holy bath.[1]

For a month she performed the Cāndrāyaṇa rites and thereafter the Kṛcchra rites for another month. Mahādeva became pleased and granted her excellent boons. Umāpati vanished and sported about for a long time.

When the Lord went away, Ahalyā installed the preceptor of the universe by the name Ahalyeśvara and went back to her abode.

He who takes his holy bath there in the Tīrtha and adores Parameśvara, shall obtain heaven after death. He will sport about in the place where Lord Maheśvara is present in that Loka.

The performer of great penance, at the end of a thousand years, will be reborn in human form endowed with wealth and foodgrain in plenty and be accompanied by sons and grandsons. He will be born in a pure family and be the receptacle of Vedic lore. Intelligent and handsome; he will be very fortunate. He will live for more than a hundred years afflicted with no ailments as a result of his resorting to Ahalyā Tīrtha.

CHAPTER ONE HUNDRED THIRTYSEVEN

The Greatness of Karkaṭeśvara Tīrtha

Śrī Mārkaṇḍeya said:

1-8. O Dharmaputra, thereafter one should go to the excellent Karkaṭeśvara Tīrtha on the northern bank of Narmadā. It is destructive of all sins.

He who takes his holy bath there in accordance with the injunctions and adores Śiva, shall never return from Rudraloka. Undoubtedly his departure will be one without a return.

It is very difficult to describe in detail the greatness of the Tīrtha as heard by me in the Purāṇa. Hence I shall recount it briefly.

---

1. This portion is not in VR. It is added for the glorification of Narmadā by the Purāṇa writer.

Whatever is done by one at that Tīrtha, whether auspicious or inauspicious, O great king, out of delight or arrogance, shall entirely become everlasting.

After performing penance there at that Tīrtha Vālakhilyas and Marīcis rejoice in the different worlds even today as they please, O scion of the family of Kurus.

Men staying there do not know it as they are excluded from its knowledge in the same manner as one is not aware of the immutable Ātman, the imperishable refulgence stationed in the body.

There at the Tīrtha, Goddess Nārāyaṇī began her penance formerly and even today she continues the severe austerities which she has been doing for the last one hundred million years.

A devotee should take his holy bath in the Tīrtha and propitiate the Pitṛs and deities. His Pitāmahas become satisfied for twelve years thereby.

CHAPTER ONE HUNDRED THIRTYEIGHT

The Greatness of Śakra Tīrtha

Śrī Mārkaṇḍeya said:

1-5. Thereafter, O son of Pāṇḍu, a person should go to the excellent Śakratīrtha where Śatakratu (Indra), the illustrious king of Devas, became a Siddha.

On knowing that the Lord of Suras was cursed by Gautama, the deities beginning with Brahmā and all the sages who regard penance as their wealth pleaded to Gautama through splendid words: "O Lord of sages, Śakra is bereft of his kingdom and glory. O Brāhmaṇa, none will have any interest in the domain without Indra, whether he be a Deva or a human being. O venerable one, this is already known to you. Hence, O excellent Brāhmaṇa, take pity on him on whom innumerable vaginal apertures have been foisted. Defiled by his own sin, Śakra is absconding now."

6-10. On hearing the words of the Devas, Gautama, the greatest of those conversant with the Vedas, consented and began to grant a boon unto Śakra: "O Śatakratu, the thousand vaginal apertures that were earlier produced (on your body) shall now become a thousand eyes with my favour."

On being told thus the Thousand-eyed One bowed down to the excellent sage and the virtuous Brāhmaṇas. Thereafter, he came to Narmadā.

He took his holy bath in the pure waters and installed god Trīpurāntaka. After that he went back to heaven, being adored by groups of celestial damsels.

A man who takes his holy bath there in that Tīrtha and adores Parameśvara, becomes absolved of the sin of violating the chastity of other men's wives..

CHAPTER ONE HUNDRED THIRTYNINE

The Greatness of Somatīrtha

Śrī Mārkaṇḍeya said:

1-5. Thereafter, O great king, one should go to the excellent Somatīrtha where Soma performed penance and attained a permanent place in the stellar path.

Listen, to the meritorious benefit of a person who takes his holy bath there in that Tīrtha after duly and ceremoniously sipping the holy water, and having performed Japa meditates on Ravi.

Merely by reciting the Gāyatrī Mantra here, one gets that benefit which is cited as the benefit of one who recites the Mantras of Ṛk, Yajus and Sāma Vedas, O descendant of Bharata.

If a devotee remains pure and feeds a few Brāhmaṇas there at that Tīrtha, it becomes as meritorious as a crore Brāhmaṇas fed properly in accordance with the injunctions.

If a person makes gifts of sandals and shoes, garments, umbrella, blankets and horses to an eminent Brāhmaṇa, it is on a par with such things gifted to a crore such Brāhmaṇas.

6-13. The feeding of thousands and thousands of Brāhmaṇas utterly ignorant of the Ṛk verses does not merit even a sixteenth part of the feeding of one Brāhmaṇa fully conversant with the Mantras.

A person need feed only one master of the Vedas knowing many Ṛks (by heart), or if he belongs to another Śākhā (branch of Vedic study), he should be an Adhvaryu (i.e. Yajurvedin) or Chandoga (i.e. Sāmavedin) or Samāptiga (i.e. one who has concluded Vedic Studies).

In Somatīrtha if one person well-versed in the Vedas (is fed), one gets the merit said to result from performing a thousand Agnihotras by learned men.

If a man feeds a hundred, he gets the merit of feeding a thousand. (There) learned men know that the merit of (feeding) one well-versed in Yoga (is on a par with it).

Wherever a sage resides after restraining the sense-organs, the holy place should be deemed as Kurukṣetra, Naimiṣa or Puṣkara.

Hence one should assiduously feed a Yogin at the time of solar and lunar eclipses, during Saṅkrānti or Vyatīpāta in particular.

One who enters into Saṁnyāsa stage at that Tīrtha, O Yudhiṣṭhira, becomes glorious and goes to heaven by means of an aerial chariot. He becomes an attendant of Soma. He rejoices along with him.

CHAPTER ONE HUNDRED FORTY

The Greatness of Nandāhrada Tīrtha

Śrī Mārkaṇḍeya said:

1-6. Thereafter, O great king, a devotee should go to the excellent Nandāhrada where the glorious Goddess Nandādevī, bestower of boons, became a Siddha.

Formerly there was a notorious Dānava Mahiṣāsura with a huge body in Kṛta Yuga. He caused terror unto the Devas. He was killed by the Trident-wielding Goddess. His body was pierced with the spear.

It was this powerful Asura who, in Kṛta Yuga, defeated eleven Rudras, (twelve) Ādityas, along with the group of (fortynine)

Maruts, (eight) Vasus along with Moon-god and Sun-god. He defeated Brahmā, Viṣṇu and Maheśvara.

When the terror of the Devas was thus killed in a fierce battle, Goddess Nandā of wide eyes, after the terrible slaughter, took her bath in the Hrada (pool). Hence it is remembered as Nandāhrada.

He who takes his holy bath there in that Tīrtha and offers gifts to Brāhmaṇas with Goddess Nandā in view, shall attain the merit of performing an Aśvamedha.

7-11. Bhairava, Kedāra, Mahālaya Rudra and the fourth one Nandāhrada (are the excellent shrines). A fifth one is very rare to find.

Many who are overwhelmed by Kāma and Rāga do not know that Hrada in Narmadā which is meritorious and destructive of all sins.

If a person takes his holy bath there, in that Tīrtha, and worships Goddess Nandā, of what avail is the departure unto Himālaya to him?

Those who are ignorant of reality, wander here and there as they are enveloped in Tamas. One experiences only tiresomeness in associating with them.

O son of Kuntī, by taking the holy bath in Nandāhrada, O king, one attains that merit which is mentioned as the merit of taking holy bath and offering Dāna everywhere on the earth encircled by the oceans.

CHAPTER ONE HUNDRED FORTYONE

The Greatness of Tāpeśvara Tīrtha

Śrī Mārkaṇḍeya said:

1-5. Thereafter, O king, one should go to the excellent Tāpeśvara Tīrtha where a doe frightened by a hunter became a Siddha.

After casting off her limbs (body) into the water, she rose up unto the outer space. The hunter was dismayed at the sight of the doe. He set aside his bow and arrows and started performing excellent austerities. Penance was performed by the hunter for a period of a thousand divine years.

When the time elapsed thus, Maheśvara became pleased. He said, "O great hunter, speak up what appeals to your mind. What boon shall be granted?"

Vyādha said:

O Lord of Devas, if you are pleased, if a boon is to be granted to me, let my stay beside you be granted to me, O Mahādeva.

Īśvara said:

6-11. Let it be so, O hunter. You are granted the boon desired by you.

After saying this, Mahādeva, the Lord of Devas, vanished. When the Lord disappeared the Vyādha installed Maheśvara, worshipped him in accordance with the injunctions and went to heaven.

Ever since then that Tīrtha became well-known in all the three worlds. It is heard that Tāpeśvara Tīrtha originated from the repentance of the Vyādha.

He who takes his holy bath there in the Tīrtha and worships Śaṅkara attains Śivaloka. So said Maheśvara to me.

Men who bathe in the Tāpeśvara Tīrtha in the waters of Narmadā, are liberated from the three types of distress. No hesitation need be felt in this respect.

For the sake of the suppression of sins, a devotee should take the holy plunge on the eighth and fourteenth lunar days and particularly on the third lunar day.

CHAPTER ONE HUNDRED FORTYTWO

The Greatness of Rukmiṇī Tīrtha

Śrī Mārkaṇḍeya said:

1-7. Thereafter, O great king, a person should go to the excellent Rukmiṇī Tīrtha. By taking the holy bath only therein, one shall become handsome and fortunate.

If a devotee takes his holy bath on the eighth, fourteenth or the third lunar day in particular, he will never be born here again.

He who takes his holy bath and makes the gift of gold, will never incur sorrow due to the power of that Tīrtha.

Yudhiṣṭhira said:

O great sage, how did this Tīrtha come to possess such a great efficacy? Kindly tell me how this Tīrtha became capable of according beauty and good fortune.

Śrī Mārkaṇḍeya said:

O descendant of Bharata, I shall recount the old legend in the manner it occurred and also as traditionally narrated by elders from early days. That I shall recount to you. Listen with concentration of mind.

Bhīṣmaka was a ruler of the city named Kuṇḍina.[1] He was richly endowed with horses, elephants and chariots. He was wealthy and very powerful. Shining in the midst of a thousand women, he administered the splendid kingdom.

8-15. Mahādevī ('great queen') was his wife dear to him more than his own very vital breaths. He begot of her a son named Rukmaka.

The second child born was a daughter named Rukmiṇī. At that time an unembodied etherial voice told him, "O Bhīsmaka, this girl should be given to a Four-armed One (born) on this earth."

On hearing these words, he and his beloved became delighted. Along with learned Brāhmaṇas, he entered the lying-

1. Kundiṅapura near Amaravati in Vidarbha (Maharashtra).

in-chamber and made them recite the Svastika prayers and the girl was duly named Rukmiṇī.

O descendant of Bharata, she was proclaimed Rukmiṇī by the Brāhmaṇas then because she had a freckle golden in colour congenitally.

As time passed on she became a girl of eight years. The king recollected the words of the unembodied being and became worried. 'To whom shall I give this daughter? Who will be the four-armed one?'

In the meantime Damaghoṣa, the chieftain of Cedi came there from the excellent mountain Raivata[1].

16-27. He entered the royal palace where King Bhīṣmaka was present. On seeing him arrived in the abode, the king duly adored him.

He was taken to the Royal Court and given a proper seat. 'This day has dawned meritoriously. I was eager to see you. O great king, my daughter has come to the age of eight years. The ethereal voice of an unembodied being has told that she should be given to a Four-armed One".

On hearing the words of Bhīṣmaka, Damaghoṣa said thus: "My son is well known in all the three worlds as Four-armed One (*Caturbhuja*). O Bhīṣmaka, let this girl be given to Śiśupāla."

On hearing the words of Damaghoṣa, O king, Rukmiṇī was betrothed to Śiśupāla by Bhīṣmaka.

The auspicious ceremonial beginning was made by Bhīṣmaka, O Yudhiṣṭhira. All the kinsmen and members of the family who were staying in far-off countries in every direction, were invited and they duly arrived.

Then Bala and Kesava, the distinguished members of the Yādava clan, were also invited. They came to the city of Kuṇḍina of Bhīṣmaka. The most excellent scions of the family of Yadu were duly received and honoured by Bhīṣmaka.

At the time of dusk, Rukmiṇī, the bride of seductive charms, went out of the city accompanied by her female companions for the worship of Aṁbikā.

There she saw Hari, the Lord of Devas, in the guise of a cowherd. On seeing him, she was excited by the god of Love and became completely fascinated.

1. *Cedi* is Bundelkhanda and Raivata or Girnar is in Gujarat. The author has faint ideas about Indian Geography.

On seeing her, Keśava said to Saṅkarṣaṇa, "O dear brother, in my view the excellent jewel of a girl should be taken away."

28-40. On hearing the words of Keśava, Saṅkarṣaṇa said: "Go ahead, O Kṛṣṇa, O mighty one. Let the jewel of a girl be seized quickly. I shall follow you closely behind causing much havoc unto all these demons."

On getting the consent of Saṅkarṣaṇa, Keśava, the slayer of Keśin, seized the girl, immediately put her on the chariot and went off.

Setting off in quick speed like wind, O king, he went ahead. There arose a great hue and cry in the city of Bhīsṃaka.

The enraged demons came out like billows (of flowtide) in the great ocean. All of them were perfectly armed and they roared as they ran after the chariot along the highway.

They overtook Baladeva who was following the chariot along the highway. A battle that threatened annihilation of all the worlds ensued between them and Bala, as in the case of an earlier well-known battle for Tārā (Bṛhaspati's wife).

Wielding the club in his hand, Bala, the mighty one, had no match in all the three worlds. He forcefully dragged them by means of his ploughshare and struck them down with blows of the club.

The powerful Balabhadra could not be struck by the Dānavas. He smashed all the demons and stood there unshakeable like a mountain.

On seeing Bala much infuriated and unassailable even by gods, the highly refulgent son of Bhīṣmaka, the well-renowned warrior named Rukmin, took an Akṣauhiṇī (large divisions of chariots, horses etc.) of men of great heroism, attacked and tried to repulse Balabhadra.

Accompanied by Rukmiṇī Lord Keśava hurried along the path in the chariot dodging the arena of the battle.

Crossing Vindhya, the immutable preceptor of the three worlds came to the banks of Narmadā where he had earlier achieved perfection and invincibility by the power of this Tīrtha.

41-48. It is for this reason, O dear one, that it is called Yodhanīpura. Rukma (Rukmin) the leading Dānava too came to that excellent spot.

He furiously spoke (challengingly): "Stop! Stop! Do not go away. I shall despatch you unto the abode of Yama by means of sharp arrows."

Both of those heroes roared like this against each other. Their fight became terrible like that between Tāraka and Skanda (who was born of Agni). The demon discharged volleys of arrows against Keśava. Ignoring them, Keśava, the slayer of Keśin, too discharged arrows against him.

The infuriated Rukma took up an excellent bow and pierced his chest with a sharp arrow. Thereupon Viṣṇu himself became furious, seized his discus Sudarśana and was about to hurl it at Rukma when he was restrained by Rukmiṇī.

"The fellow does not know you as the four-armed Janārdana, the Lord of Devas. Reveal your own real form taking pity on me."

On being requested thus by Rukmiṇī, the Lord revealed his form, O descendant of Bharata. On seeing that form the Devas stationed in the sky began to eulogize. At that time, O descendant of Bharata, the Lord granted to Rukma the divine vision.

Rukma said:

49-57. O Lord Keśava, unlucky and sinful that I am, I had hit your chest with arrows. It behoves you to forgive me.

Formerly Jānakī was given over to you by Janaka himself. Now, O Lord of Devas, Rukmiṇī is offered unto you by me. Marry her duly in accordance with the injunctions.

On hearing the words of Rukma, the Preceptor of the universe became pleased. The Lord of the chiefs of Devas spoke thus to Rukmin, the son of Bhīṣmaka: "Go back to your own city. Do not be afraid. Rule the kingdom free from thorns (hindrances from enemies)."

On hearing the words of Keśava, Rukma, the leading Dānava[1], bowed down to the Lord of the universe and went back to the abode of his father.

When Rukma went back Kṛṣṇa invited excellent Brāhmaṇas. They were the seven mental sons of Brahmā, namely Marīci, Atri, Aṅgiras, Pulastya, Pulaha, Kratu and Vasiṣṭha, the highly honoured one. These seven have been mentioned decisively in the Purāṇa.

O highly intelligent one, these sons of Brahmā are truthful,

---

1. Rukma (Rukmi in *Harivaṁśa*) was not a Danava but a bonafide Kṣatriya. But to this Purāṇa all opponents of Kṛṣṇa are Dānavas or Rākṣasas.

men of fortitude, great ones endowed with progeny. They were embellished by the great ones. They have come down to the banks of Narmadā to stay. They have conquered the sense-organs. They are engaged in penance and self-study of the Vedas. They are devoted to Japa and Homa.

58-67. They were invited, O great king, by the noble-souled Keśava. After duly performing the Śrāddha in accordance with the injunctions of Brahmā, Hari honoured those seven great Brāhmaṇa-sages.

Janārdana granted them twelve villages there. "The gift offered by me shall be yours as long as the moon and the sun shine and the earth remains. There shall never be any enemy. I shall bestow welfare on those kings of no sins, who will keep up what has been offered by me. I will grant them the greatest goal.

Those who preserve what has been given by me rejoice in heaven as long as the five great elements move about in the worlds.

A fool who deprives you of what has been given on the earth, will have to live invariably in Naraka until the annihilation of all living beings.

The earth has to be protected whether bequeathed by one's own men or others. The benefit belongs to the person to whom the earth belongs for the nonce.

He who takes away the earth bequeathed by one's own men or others, becomes a worm in faeces and sinks along with his Pitṛs (ancestors).

If the land is illegally confiscated or illegally caused to be confiscated, the primary confiscator and the other who caused it to be confiscated, are born as worms in faeces.

He who gifts a plot of land stays in heaven for sixty thousand years. The confiscator (usurper) and he who abets it, shall stay in Naraka for as many years.

68-79. Which gentle (good) man will take back the gifts made over earlier by leading men, causing religious merit, wealth and renown? They are on a par with the remnants of the offerings made unto a deity."

In this manner the Slayer of Madhu honoured them duly and perfectly and then grasped the hand of Rukmiṇī in marriage.

After finishing his task splendidly i.e. after conquering the leading Dānavas, Musalin (i.e. Balarāma) came back to his abode.

Both of them, Kṛṣṇa and Saṅkarṣaṇa, set off to Dvārakā.

On seeing Keśava, the destroyer of sufferings, going away, the truthful Brāhmaṇas of esteemed holy vows also started.

On seeing those Brāhmaṇas closely following the chariot along its path, Keśava stopped for a short while and spoke these words:

"O excellent Brāhmaṇas, speak out everything, what makes you come along? Your duty towards me yet remains. Do carry out your own tasks."

On hearing the words of the Lord, the sages spoke thus: "You have been venerated by us with truthful mental fervour for thousands and crores of Kalpas. You are very difficult to be attained by men but attained (now) by us; why do you abandon us (summarily)?"

On hearing the words of the Brāhmaṇas, the Lord spoke thus: "This is the truth, the sole truth. Again and again I repeat this that I shall come on three occasions (everyday) to Mathurā, Dvārakā and Yodhanīpura."

On hearing this, the Brāhmaṇas returned to Yodhanīpura. After manifesting himself in Mathurā, the Lord incarnate, manifested himself in three ways.

Thus everything past, present and future connected with the origin of the Tīrtha has been recounted to you. On hearing this, one is sure to be rid of all sins undoubtedly.

80-89. He who takes his holy bath there in that Tīrtha[1] and worships Bala and Keśava has actually venerated the sustainer of the universe, the soul of three Guṇas.

A man who observes fast and then circumambulates it shall be liberated from all sins. No worry or hesitation be entertained in this respect.

Those men who see even the trees growing there in that Tīrtha are rid of sins though they may be as heinous as the sin of foeticide.

Those who see Bala and Keśava after getting up in the morning shall become equal to the Lord of Devas, the wielder of the discus. They are worthy of being adored, worthy of being bowed to. Their life is an excellent life.

1. Though *Skanda* follows *Harivaṁśa* in the story of the abduction of Rukmiṇī by Kṛṣṇa, the creation of Rukmiṇī Tīrtha on Narmadā is a Skanda contribution.

O king, the Dāna, the holy bath and the adoration of the Lord there in that Tīrtha shall entirely be everlasting. So said Śaṅkara.

O excellent king, listen to the merit cited as accruing to those who die there entering fire. It shall be recounted completely.

They shall go to the palace of Agni-god by means of an aerial chariot shining with tinkling bells and solar splendour. He shall rejoice there for as much time as he pleases.

Those who die getting drowned in water within the precincts of Yodhanīpura shall stay in Varuṇa-Loka until the annihilation of all living beings.

If people die in that Tīrtha by ritualistic fast and starvation, O king, their departure shall be one without return. There is no hesitation or worry in this respect.

90-102. Listen to the benefit of this also, namely the excellent gift of a Kapilā (tawny-coloured) cow there at that Tīrtha in accordance with the injunctions.

They shall be honoured with the fulfilment of all their desires. They will rejoice in heaven for as many years as there are hairs on that cow and her calf.

He is honoured (in heaven) for as many years as there are hairs on the cow. After slipping down from heaven on the *Trilokī* (one of the three worlds) he shall be born in the family of those with plenty of cows.

He who gifts silver or gold there in that Tīrtha is transported to Viṣṇuloka in a golden aerial chariot and he is honoured there.

He who gifts a pair of sandals or garments there at that Tīrtha obtains the desired Svarga by the power of the gift.

There at that Tīrtha, one obtains by means of Gāyatrī, that benefit which is usually obtained by the study of the passages of Ṛk, Yajus and Sāmaveda.

Undoubtedly one obtains by merely bathing in that Tīrtha all the benefits of the following: the merit accruing from Prayāga, Gayā, Tripuṣkara, Kurukṣetra when the sun is swallowed by Rāhu, O great king, and the merit accruing from Someśvara at the time of a lunar eclipse.

If a man takes his holy bath on the twelfth lunar day and bows down to Janārdana, the Pitṛs are redeemed by him. The fruit of his birth has been obtained by him.

If someone feeds a single Brāhmaṇa there at the time of Saṅkrānti (Transit of the Sun), Vyatīpāta and particularly on the twelfth lunar day, it shall then become one on a par with the feeding of a crore of Brāhmaṇas.

All the Tīrthas and the holy oceans on the earth are present there on Dvādaśī day, O son of Pāṇḍu.

Ordinary Dāna, Yajña, Bali (oblation) and other rites may get lost but, O great king, what is performed there in that Tīrtha never gets lost.

Everything connected with the greatness of the Tīrtha, past and future, has been recounted to you in detail, O descendant of Bharata.

CHAPTER ONE HUNDRED FORTYTHREE

The Greatness of Yojaneśvara Tīrtha

Śrī Mārkaṇḍeya said:

1-8. Thereafter, O great king, one should go to the excellent Yojaneśvara Tīrtha where, in a former Kalpa, the sages Nara and Nārāyaṇa became Siddhas.

It was after performing a penance there at that Tīrtha that both of them, Nara and Nārāyaṇa, of noble souls, gained victory in the battle between Devas and Dānavas.

Again, when Tretā Yuga arrived, Lords Rāma and Lakṣmaṇa took their bath in that Tīrtha. Thereby the invincible demon Rāvaṇa could be killed.

Again after the advent of Kali[1] age (*sic*) Lords Balarāma and Keśava were born in the family of Vasudeva. They performed formidable deeds. Balarāma and Keśava killed Naraka, Kālanemi, Kaṁsa, Cāṇūra, Muṣṭika, Śiśupāla and Jarāsandha[2](*sic*).

1. Kali Age began after Kṛṣṇa's death. Hence he belongs to Dvāpara Age.
2. Bhīma killed Jarāsandha (Mbh, *Sabhā* 24.7).

That Lord will kill in the battle Karṇa, Duryodhana and others with Bhīṣma and Droṇa as their leaders.

They will engage themselves in fighting in Kurukṣetra, the sacred battlefield, making Bhīma and Arjuna, the disciples of each, as instruments.

They will go to that Tīrtha again and perform a severe penance. After devoutly honouring Brāhmaṇas, they will return to Dvārakā once again.

9-17. If a person takes his holy bath there in the Tīrtha and worships Balarāma and Keśava, it is as though the Supreme Lord, the sustainer of the universe, endowed with the three Guṇas (Sattva, Rajas and Tamas) is honoured by him.

A man who observes fast, keeps awake at night and sings his splendid story, becomes absolved of all sins.

As many trees men see there in that Tīrtha so many sins such as those of Brāhmaṇa-slaughter etc. become dissolved (at once).

Those who get up in the morning and see Balarāma and Keśava, become by that very act of seeing, similar to the Discus-bearing Lord of Devas.

Those who bow down to Hari, Lord Nārāyaṇa, worthy of being adored by the whole universe become themselves worthy of adoration and obeisance. Their life is well-lived.

Whatever is performed in that Tīrtha by way of Dāna, Snāna and adoration of the deity, the fruit thereof becomes everlasting.

It is (traditionally stated) that gold is the first progeny of Agni. The earth (plot of land) belongs to Viṣṇu and cows are the children of Sun-god. If a person makes a gift of a cow, a piece of gold or plot of land, it is as though all the three worlds have been gifted by him.

Thus the entire excellence and greatness of the Tīrtha, its great efficacy past, present and future has been recounted to you.

By listening to this and by narrating this to righteous persons, one is rid of all sins. No hesitation or worry in this regard (is needed).

CHAPTER ONE HUNDRED FORTYFOUR

The Greatness of Dvādaśī Tīrtha

Śrī Mārkaṇḍeya said:

1-3. Thereafter, O great king, one should go to the excellent Dvādaśī Tīrtha. All the Dāna as well as Japa, Homa, Bali and other rites performed (elsewhere) perish. But what is performed in Cakratīrtha (?) never perishes.

Whatever is there in regard to the excellent greatness of the Tīrtha, past, present as well as future has been entirely recounted by me separately, O descendant of Bharata.

CHAPTER ONE HUNDRED FORTYFIVE

The Greatness of Śiva Tīrtha

Śrī Mārkaṇḍeya said:

1-3. Thereafter, O Lord of the Earth, a person should go to the excellent Śiva Tīrtha; by seeing the Lord there one is liberated from all sins.

One who has subdued (his) anger and the sense-organs and takes his holy bath in Śiva Tīrtha and worships Mahādeva shall attain the merit of performing Agniṣṭoma.

One who devoutly observes fast there in that Tīrtha and worships Śiva, reaches Rudraloka from which he never comes back. There is no doubt about it.

CHAPTER ONE HUNDRED FORTYSIX

The Greatness of Asmāhaka Tīrtha

Śrī Mārkaṇḍeya said:

1-7. Thereafter, a devotee should go to the excellent Pitṛtīrtha named Asmāhaka where by (offering) a single ball of rice ancestors are liberated from the state of ghost.

Yudhiṣṭhira said:

O sinless one, recount to me the greatness of Asmāhaka as well as the merit that accrues to one through performing Snāna, Dāna, offering libation and balls of rice.

Śrī Mārkaṇḍeya said:

In a former Kalpa, O excellent king, in the assembly of sages and Devas, this same question was put by me which you ask me now, O dear one.

(If there be) on one side the seven seas (Sāgaras) along with Prayāga and Puṣkara, they do not attain equality with this. No doubt need be felt in this respect.

A man obtains that merit which one gets (by Snāna) at the time of a lunar eclipse in the well-known Somanātha Tīrtha that was established by Soma.

At the end of a month (i.e. on Amāvāsyā day) Pitṛs look up to their human progeny to ascertain whether someone will offer them Piṇḍa here in this Tīrtha. So also do Prapitāmaha (great-grandfather) and Ādityas. This is (mentioned in) the eternal Śruti. So say Devas and sages and ascetics.

8-14. Listen, O king, to the merit that accrues to one by offering libation and Piṇḍas but once. O eminent king, they enjoy the splendid Yoga for twelve years.

In every Yuga, O great king, Pitāmahas wait eagerly for the arrival of a scion of their family in the Asmāhaka Tīrtha wishing, "Will our Amāvāsyā occur in Amāhaka (Asmāhaka)?"

Those who perform the rites of *Snāna, Dāna* and *Tilatarpaṇa* (libation with gingelly seeds and water) unto the Pitṛs become free from all sins. They attain all their desired objects.

In the midst of water, O king, there is Agnitīrtha as well. By visiting that Tīrtha a heap of sins gets dissolved. Through a holy bath alone, O leading king, one dispels the sin of the slaughter of a Brāhmaṇa.

A person should always wear white clothes with self-restraint and subduing of the sense-organs. He should stay in the vicinity of the Tīrtha for a month taking food only once a day. Thereby he obtains in full, the merit arising from the gift of a hundred virgins adorned with gold. He is honoured in Pitṛloka.

15-20. He shall be a lordly enjoyer of all pleasures on the earth encircled by oceans. He shall be endowed with wealth and foodgrains and become righteous and munificent.

One who remains pure and observes fast shall obtain the world of Brahmā. One who casts off his life after coming to Asmāhaka is honoured in Rudraloka for crores of thousand years. Thereafter, slipping down from heaven when the meritorious Karmas dwindle, he shall be born in a family rich in gold, jewels and pearls and will be endowed with handsome features.

After performing the ceremonious bathing in accordance with the injunctions, he shall attain the merit of performing a horse-sacrifice. He shall be wealthy, handsome, alert, clever, munificent and righteous.

By taking the holy bath there in that Tīrtha, a devotee attains that merit which is acquired by the study of the four Vedas and by speaking only the truth. This Tīrtha that is greater than all the other Tīrthas, was created by Śaṁbhu formerly.

21-32. Viṣṇu himself, the Lord of the heart, performs the Japa of Maheśvara. So also do Gandharvas, celestial damsels, Maruts, Mārutas, Viśvedevas, Pitṛs, Moon, Sun, Marīci, Atri, Aṅgiras, Pulastya, Pulaha, Kratu, Pracetas, Vasiṣṭha, Bhṛgu, Nārada, Cyavana, Gālava, the great sage Vāmadeva, Vālakhilyas, Gandhāras, Tṛṇabindu, Jājali, Uddālaka, Ṛṣyaśṛṅga, Vasiṣṭha, Sanandana, Śukra, Bharadvāja, Vātsya, Vātsyāyana, Agasti, Mitra, Varuṇa, Viśvāmitra, Munīśvara, Gautama, Pulastya, Paulastya, Pulaha, Kratu[1], Sanātana, Kapila, Vahni, Pañcaśikha and many other sages of esteemed holy rites. All the Devas, sages, ascetics, human

1. VV 22-26 contain repetition of names, probably inadvertently done by the redactor of SkP.

beings, Yogīndras, Pitṛs, along with Pitāmahas etc. stay in Asmāhaka. There is no doubt about it.

Everything offered to them whether good or bad is permanent. Whatever is done in Yodhanīpura is everlasting.

One forsakes his mother, father, all kinsmen, friendly folks, wealth, foodgrains, dear sons and even very body, O excellent king, and goes in the form of air accompanied solely by *Śubha* (merit) and *Aśubha* (demerit). He is invisible to all living beings like the greater supreme Ātman. By means of his own Karmas, O king, he attains good and evil states.

Yudhiṣṭhira said:

33-45. What is the reason for this? Neither Śubha nor Aśubha befalls kinsmen. A creature at birth is alone. It is alone when it gets dissolved (dies). He solely enjoys the meritorious benefits and alone he experiences the evil effects (of his actions).

Śrī Mārkaṇḍeya said:

This great question put by you is remembered by me. What is uttered by the very mouth of Pitāmaha, I shall recount to you. It was known from Pitāmaha formerly in the Assembly of Sages.

(Really) no one is mother, father, kinsman or friend unto anyone at any time. As the embodied being becomes aerial in form, his form is not known to anyone.

If such were not the case in the world, O dear king, everything would have gone beyond proper limits. The mobile and immobile beings would have perished.

This was realized even very early by the creators of the worlds, O king; Norms have been established lest Dharma (piety, righteousness) should perish in the world.

If Dharma perishes the unrighteousness of men will prevail. As a result thereof people will go astray from their path and it inevitably leads to downfall into hell.

All people are uncontrolled by nature. All are intent on (i.e. love) transgressing the norms of decency. Hence the bounds of decorum were established by the great sages in the light of the scriptural texts.

The various righteous acts are: *Snāna, Dāna, Japa, Homa,* self-study of the Vedas, worship of the deities, offerings of libation and balls of rice (to Pitrs) and hospitality unto guests. The Pitṛs, Pitāmahas (grandfathers) and Prapitāmahas (great-grandfathers) are to be remembered as well as the three deities Brahmā, Viṣṇu and Maheśvara.

All of them were adored by men of esteemed worth. So also the three (generations beginning with) maternal grandfather. Hence by means of all endeavour a devotee should follow the acts of righteousness urged by the Śruti and Smṛti texts. By practising piety for ever, one is not defiled by the particles of sin. One should not even think of transgressing the pious rites laid down in the Śruti and Smṛti (Texts).

46-56. If one desires for one's own welfare in this world as well as in the other, one should scrupulously practise pious rites. Father and son are always identical, the original and its replica, whether (living) together or separately. This is the implication of the Śruti and Smṛti passages.

One should lift oneself up by one's own effort. One should not allow oneself to sink in dejection and suffering, O son of Kuntī, by not offering libations and balls of rice. There is no doubt about it. After realizing this one should be a person regularly offering libations and balls of rice. Thereby longevity, piety, fame, refulgence and progeny flourish.

I shall mention unto you all the Pitṛkṣetras (holy spots specific for the Manes) all over the earth encircled by the oceans, where things offered yield great benefits. They are Gayā, Puṣkara, Jyeṣṭha (?) Prayāga, Naimiṣa, Sannihati, Kurukṣetra and Prabhāsa, O scion of the family of Kuru.

Undoubtedly, by means of the offering of libations and balls of rice in Asmāhaka on Narmadā one obtains the benefit proclaimed by learned men in the case of all those holy spots of the Manes.

There all these are present: Brahmā, the Slayer of Mura (i.e. Viṣṇu), Rudra along with Umā, Devas beginning with Indra, all the Pitṛs, sages, oceans, rivers, mountains, clouds and the Manes too. Hence it is the Supreme Tīrtha of all the Tīrthas.

Brahmaśilā (stone-slab of Brahmā) is also there, O king, and it resembles the forehead of an elephant. It is not visible in Kali age. It is the most important part, the Gayāśiras. On the new-moon day in the month of Vaiśākha, the holy rock resembling the forehead of an elephant, pervades the Tīrtha to an extent of a Gavyūti (six Kilometers). That is cited as the Tīrtha.

57-66. If a person goes there on that day and performs Śrāddha, the Pitṛs will become perfectly satisfied for a hundred years.

One may take his holy bath there on any other new-moon day as well. With sense-organs under control, one should perform Śrāddha duly reciting the prescribed Mantras.

Listen to the meritorious benefit he derives, O king. He obtains that benefit which is ordinarily obtained by performing Agniṣṭoma, Aśvamedha and Vājapeya. So Śaṅkara has told me.

The fathers, grandfathers on the paternal and maternal sides detained in all hells beginning with Raurava, if offered a ball of rice or libations of water at least once, sport about in the Pitṛloka until all the living beings are annihilated. There is no doubt about this.

Those who regularly performed their pious rites or those who performed the opposite thereof and those who have become ghosts and spirits due to sins—all these are liberated undoubtedly through a single Piṇḍa (ball of rice).

A divine rock resembling an elephant stands in the Asmāhaka Tīrtha. It was created by Brahmā formerly and it is destructive of all sins. Upon this rock, O descendant of Bharata, a wise person should offer balls of rice placed on Darbha grass with the tips pointing to the south. They shall offer these with the Pitṛs in view.

The cooking of the food intended for the Śrāddha shall be done on the ground below duly (not on the rock). With the Pitṛs in view, O descendant of Bharata, various kinds of monetary and other gifts should be made to Brāhmaṇas invited for the Śrāddha, such as a pair of clothes, umbrellas, shoes, waterpot etc.

67-78. Listen to the meritorious benefit of the person who offers these to an excellent Brāhmaṇa. The Pitṛs undoubtedly become contented for a period of twelve years.

O great king, Pitṛs and Pitāmahas assuming aerial forms (at Asmāhaka) eagerly wait for a member of their family to arrive there. "The son shall arrive here at the Tīrtha, take his holy bath and offer the libation. He may perform Śrāddha or offer balls of rice. Thereby we shall attain *sadgati* (good position) (i.e. *Mokṣa*)."

The drops that fall from the garments after taking the holy plunge shall delight the Pitṛs staying in Naraka. There is no doubt about it.

If any member of the family was not properly cremated in funeral fire after death, the drops of water falling from the hairs (of the performer of Śrāddha) and other things wet therewith will propitiate them.

A person should perform the Śrāddha in accordance with the injunctions in the Tīrtha there and perform the Japa of *Pitṛ-Saṁhītā.* They immediately redeem the ancestors.

When Amāvāsyā coincides with a Monday, the man need offer only a single ball of rice. The Pitṛs attain everlasting worlds. There is no doubt about this that everything becomes everlasting if performed or offered there.

Persons performing the Japa of *Pitṛsaṁhitā* redeem immediately the Pitṛs from Naraka.

Vṛṣotsarga

Even Vācaspati is not competent to recount the meritorious benefit of a person who ritualistically discharges a Nīla Bull[1] perfect in every limb, after duly bathing it in the Tīrtha on an Amāvāsyā day with the Pitṛs in view, O descendant of Bharata. Because you have been listening attentively, O descendant of Bharata, I shall recount the merit that accrues by ceremoniously discharging a bull in Asmāhaka. He shall redeem twenty-one generations of the members of his family who have been baked in Narakas beginning with Raurava.

A bull that has a pink-coloured face, grey tail and tawny-coloured hoofs and horns, is called *Nīla Bull.*

79-89. A bull that is tawny-coloured in all the limbs and white in tail and hoofs is called *Piṅga Bull.* It increases the delight of Pitṛs.

A bull resembling a pigeon in colour, that has a Tilaka (freckle mark) on the forehead is called *Babhru.* It should be perfect and splendid. A bull that has the same colour all over the body but has a tawny-coloured tail and hoofs is called *Khura-piṅga.* It gives a good position to Pitṛs.

Some say that a bull that is blue in colour throughout the body is a *Nīla Bull.* His eyes are bright red in colour.

Nīla Bull is of five types: A Nīla Bull bred in the house of a Vaiśya is the best of the lot.

1. The term is explained in verse 78 below.

A calf bred in the house should never be yoked to a plough. The rite of Vṛṣotsarga should be performed only through it in order to become free from indebtedness to Pitṛs.

If a twice-born yokes to a plough, a calf bred in his house, the Pitṛs slip down even if they have attained the world of Brahmā.

After drinking (water) the bull should shake its head. By drinking the bull delights Pitṛs. By shaking its head it redeems the Pitṛs from Naraka. When it shakes the tail and the drops of water reach the shoulder the Pitṛs of the family of the person fallen into Naraka are redeemed.

In rainy season, it may bellow and scratch the ground with the horns. It pleases the sages through the mud kicked up by the hoofs.

By drinking, the bull delights Pitṛs. Through eating (grass etc.) and scratching (the ground) it delights Suras and by roaring and bellowing, sages and human beings. O son of Dharma, the bull is Dharma personified.

90-97. One possessed by spirits or vampires or affected by quartan fever should go to Asmāhaka Tīrtha, the destroyer of the anguish of all.

After taking the holy bath in the pure waters, a piece of Darbha grass should be tied on the head, armpit, navel or round the neck.

He should then approach the deity Keśava and circumambulate him. After uttering the Gāyatrī or any Vaiṣṇava Mantra, he should eulogize Nārāyaṇa, the Lord of persons worthy of being sought in refuge, the Lord saluted and venerated by all the Devas.

(Prayer) "Obeisance to you, O Lord born of a part of Yajña. Obeisance to you, O omnipresent one. Obeisance, Obeisance to you, O Lord of Devas, O eternal Lord with the lotus as the womb. O Dāmodara, be victorious. O infinite one, protect me who have sought refuge in you.

You are the maker. You are the annihilator in this world consisting of mobile and immobile beings. You protect living beings. You support the universe. Be pleased, O Lord of the chiefs of Devas. Waken the sleeping (paralysed) limb. I am always engaged in meditative absorption in you. I consider devotion to you as the greatest. O Lord Acyuta, you have been eulogized thus. Be pleased with me. Protect, protect me who have sought refuge in you. Save me from sins."

98-107. After eulogizing Hari, the Lord of Devas, and the destroyer of Dānavas, the devotee should take the holy bath once again uttering the Mantra mentioned before.

He should then feed Brāhmaṇas. After taking the holy plunge in accordance with the injunctions laid down in the Vedas and after duly offering the balls of rice, the person should recite Svastika prayer.

This rite is repeated thrice. After making them repeat the blessings, the Brāhmaṇas should be sent off.

What is uttered there should be mentioned to the Brāhmaṇas. After taking the holy bath in the Tīrtha the devout man or woman should give monetary gifts after Śrāddha is performed duly.

When the devout person duly bathes the deity with milk, honey, curds, or cold water, the Pitṛs drink water in *Puṣkarapātras* (ethereal vessels).

A devotee who worships the Lord of Devas with flowers and offers Naivedya at the time of Ayana (transit of the Sun), Viṣuva (equinox), Yugādi (beginning of the Yugas) and Sūryasaṅkrama (passage of the Sun to various Zodiacs) derives the full benefit of an Aśvamedha sacrifice.

A man who performs rites connected with solar eclipse there in the Tīrtha, O king, goes to Viṣṇuloka by means of vehicles resembling solar splendour and is honoured there.

A dutiful son who performs the Śrāddha unto the Pitṛs there at the Tīrtha has attained the benefit of his very birth (as a son).

108-117. On hearing this, all the Devas with Śakra as their leader, Brahmā, Viṣṇu and Maheśvara installed the Lord who subdues all ailments and destroys all sins.

If a person remains pure and offers balls of rice on Amāvāsyā days throughout the year in the Asmāhaka Tīrtha, O king, he obtains here itself that benefit (merit) which performers of Śrāddha attain in Tripuṣkara, Gayā, Prabhāsa and Naimiṣa.

A person, facing the south, should offer water mixed with gingelly seeds and Darbha grass on holy days such as Manvādi, Yugādi, Vyatīpāta and Dinakṣaya (evening). He who offers thus to the fathers and mothers shall obtain the benefit of an Aśvamedha.

A man who takes his holy plunge in Asmāhaka and adores Hari, Brahmā and Śaṅkara with devotion and keeps awake at night, shall be liberated from all sins and get the hospitality of Śakra in heaven.

If a man takes his holy plunge there in the Tīrtha and visits Janārdana and adores with special procedures and bows down again and again, he is considered a good son. The salvation of the Pitṛs has been effected by him.

There is only one Mūrti (image) for the three deities Brahmā, Viṣṇu and Maheśvara. They are associated with good results and causes. They are subtle and yield great benefits.

Thus, O king, the greatness of Asmāhaka has been recounted to you. It is destructive of great sins. What else do you ask?

CHAPTER ONE HUNDRED FORTYSEVEN

The Greatness of Siddheśvara Tīrtha

Śrī Mārkaṇḍeya said:

1-5. Thereafter, O king, a person should go to the excellent Siddheśvara Tīrtha. It is an extremely fine spot situated on the southern bank of Narmadā.

One who takes his holy bath there in that Tīrtha and adores the Bull-emblemed Lord, shall be rid of all sins and attain the status of those who perform a horse-sacrifice.

If a person takes his holy bath there in that Tīrtha and assiduously performs Śrāddha in order to propitiate the Pitṛs, it is as if he has done everything for that purpose.

No inclination for further stay in womb will be evinced, O excellent king, by creatures that die there in that Tīrtha.

A stay in the womb brings one to misery and never to happiness. There is no possibility of rebirth in the case of one who bathes in the waters of that Tīrtha.

CHAPTER ONE HUNDRED FORTYEIGHT

The Greatness of Maṅgaleśvara Tīrtha

Śrī Mārkaṇḍeya said:

1-8. Thereafter, O king, a person should go to the auspicious Aṅgāraka (Maṅgaleśvara) Tīrtha on the northern bank of Narmadā. It is destructive of all sins.

On the fourth lunar day coinciding with a Tuesday the devotee should perform the Saṅkalpa-rite (ritualistic announcement of the decision) resolutely and take his bath after sunset. He then proceeds to perform the Sandhyā rites of dusk.

He should adore Lohita (Mars) devoutly with sweet scents, garlands and ornaments. The idol should be installed on the ground and smeared with red sandalpaste.

Uttering "Obeisance to Aṅgāraka" he should adore on the pericarp of the lotus figure (drawn). Then on the petals beginning with the one in the east, he should perform the worship uttering respectively. "Obeisance to Kuja", "Obeisance to Bhūmi-Putra", "Obeisance to Raktāṅga", "Obeisance to Suvāsas", "Obeisance to Harakopodbhava" ('born of the anger of Hara'), "Obeisance to Svedaja" ('born of sweat'), "Obeisance to Atibāhu", ('of extremely powerful arms') and "Obeisance to Sarvakāmaprada" ('bestower of all desires').

After duly worshipping thus, he (the devotee) should offer the *Arghya* in accordance with the injunction. Then he utters the Mantra: "Obeisance to you, O son of Earth, O highly powerful one, O deity born of the sweat of the Pināka-bearing Lord, O Lohitāṅga (red-bodied one). O Aṅgāraka, I make, obeisance to you."

He then makes the gift of a water-pot filled with paddy rice to a Brāhmaṇa along with gold and clothes and placed on sweetmeat. At that time he repeats the Mantra, "May *Kuja* be pleased with me."

9-19. He should then offer *Arghya* with water mixed with red sandalpaste. On an auspicious circular Maṇḍala (mystic design drawn on the ground) a copper vessel is placed, filled with gingelly seeds mixed with rice and strewn with red flowers. He then places the vessel on his head and kneels on the ground. The clever devotee then offers the *Arghya* sanctified through

Mantras. Thereafter the devotee who wishes for his welfare takes in silently his food, soft, smooth and sweet. He should avoid saline, bitter and sour foodstuff.

The devotee celebrates this festival on three Caturthī-Aṅgāraka combinations and when the fourth occasion arrives he should make an idol of Aṅgāraka in gold within his capacity. It should be beautiful. It is to be placed on an altar made of jaggery.

The devotee should worship the deity placed on jaggery with sweet-smelling flowers. The idol is to be placed in the north-east along with jaggery and water. A vessel made of white copper (?*Kāsāreṇa*) shall be placed in the south-east and a pot filled with red rice in the south-west. The wise man should place a fourth *Karaka* (pot) filled with sweetmeat in the north-west. This *Karaka* should be tied with a thread round its neck and it shall be adorned with scented garlands.

A conch should also be blown and musical instruments played. There shall be auspicious shouts of victory etc. A Brāhmaṇa well-versed in the Vedic texts should be made to sit on a high seat or in the middle of the platform. He should wear red clothes, red garlands and unguents. He should be quiescent, handsome and lucky-featured. He should be one engaged in what is conducive to the welfare of all living beings. He should be a master of all scriptural texts. After duly adoring him, O son of Pāṇḍu, he should be asked to recite Vedic passages.

20-26. A red cow along with a red bull should be gifted to him while uttering the Mantra, "May the deity, the son of Earth, who is venerated by all Devas, be pleased."

The devotee then circumambulates the Brāhmaṇa along with his wife and sons, father, mother and friends too. After asking for his forgiveness he should be sent off.

I shall tell you fully the meritorious benefit that accrues to one when this rite is performed, especially at that Tīrtha.

Due to the power of this Tīrtha, O great king, he shall be a handsome man with lucky features for seven births. No hesitation or doubt need be entertained in this respect.

If the man dies in the Tīrtha willingly or otherwise, he shall go to the City of Aṅgāraka and will be adored by Devas and Gandharvas.

After duly and befittingly enjoying the divine pleasures of excellent nature, he is reborn here in the human world as a pious king.

He will be handsome and lucky. He will be free from all ailments. He will live for more than a hundred years and all the world will pay respects to him.

CHAPTER ONE HUNDRED FORTYNINE

The Greatness of Liṅga Vārāha Tīrtha

Śrī Mārkaṇḍeya said:

1-6. Next to it is the holy spot well-known as Liṅgeśvara where by visiting the Lord of Devas, sins perish.

O Yudhiṣṭhira, after working terrible havoc among Dānavas, the Lord assumed the form of a boar and stationed himself on Narmadā.

One who takes his holy bath there in the Tīrtha and venerates the Lord, O excellent king, is rid of great sins committed earlier.

On the twelfth day of the dark half as well as the bright one, one should observe fast and then worship the Lord of the universe with fragrant garlands, O son of Pāṇḍu.

O blessed one, he should honour Brāhmaṇas through Dāna, special devotion and gift of foodstuff. Listen to the meritorious benefit thereof.

By feeding Brāhmaṇas there, the devotee gets the same benefit as a person attains through the performance of a Sattra extending to twelve years.

7-15. After due offering of libations to the Pitṛs and Devas and taking a holy dip, the person should concentrate his mind therein and repeat the twelve names of the Lord while sitting before him. This should be done every month on the twelfth day, O scion of the family of Kuru.

A wise devotee should always worship Keśava in the Mārgaśīrṣa month. He worships Lord Nārāyaṇa in the month of Pauṣa and Mādhava in the month of Māgha. He should adore Govinda in the month of Phālguna and Viṣṇu in Caitra. In the month of Vaiśākha he worships Madhuhantṛ (Madhusūdana, the slayer of Madhu) and Lord Trivikrama in the month of Jyeṣṭha. In the month of Āṣaḍha, he should worship Vāmana and remember Śrīdhara in the month of Śrāvaṇa. He should worship Hṛṣīkeśa in the month of Bhādrapada and Padmanābha in that of Āśvina. One who glorifies Dāmodara in the month of Kārttika never gets feeble and tired. (The above are the first twelve names of Viṣṇu.)

By glorifying the names in different months a sin committed earlier perishes, whether it be verbal, mental or due to physical activities. There is no doubt about it.

He should be alert always, whether winking or opening the eyes. He shall take food looking over it quickly. Then he should utter the name without (any other) Mantra.

This is the natural reaction of a creature caught in a great disaster, that he utters the name of Lord Viṣṇu, the ruling deity of different months, which is appropriate to that particular month.

Those nights, those days, those months and those years of men are fruitful wherein Lord Hari is remembered.

16-22. If from the lotus-like heart of the devotee, though he is in the midst of great disaster, Lord Janārdana does not move away, he is undoubtedly a Yogin.

Those who are devoid of devotion to Lord Ananta are unwise. They are on a par with brutes. Those unfortunate people are really worthy of being pitied. They have come to the earth only to add to the burden of the earth.

Those who are equipped with devotion to Lord Ananta, are persons who have fulfilled tasks on the earth; they sanctify the universe when their limbs come into contact with it. They are clever, they are the veritable ornaments unto the universe.

If Lord Janārdana is present in one's mind, words and body, he alone is meritorious. He has secured the fruit of the tree of his life.

This excellent Tīrtha is meritorious, for it has Janārdana as the Liṅga. After deceiving the enemies in the battle in the guise of Boar, the eternal Lord (is installed here).

A pure man should offer here water mixed with gingelly seeds to the Pitṛs on the following occasions: during the eclipses of the Sun and the Moon, on the Aṣṭaka days and during the two Ayanas.

May Lord Hari in the form of Boar make you quiescent (by

blessing you). With his curved fangs he made a series of holes in Meru. He is like a raft unto those who sink down in the ocean of misery. His hoofs were partially immersed in the vast expanse of mud that came out from the bowels of Rasātala (nether worlds). When he produced a hissing snort, it nudged the wind in the atmosphere which split the trumpeting sound of the Elephants of Quarters. The reputation of his stiffened physical form has been dealt with in the Śrutis. May that Lord Hari give you peace and quiescence.

CHAPTER ONE HUNDRED FIFTY

The Greatness of Kusumeśvara Tīrtha

Śrī Mārkaṇḍeya said:

1-6. Thereafter, O great king, one should go to the excellent Kusumeśvara. It is destructive of Upapātakas (minor sins).

The deity named Kusumeśvara was installed by Kāma. The eternal Lord of Devas is well known all over the world.

Kāma is mind-born one. He is a universal being having flowers for his weapons and bow. On being worshipped the Fish-emblemed Lord bestows all desires.

After his body was burnt, Anaṅga (Body-less) regained Aṅgitva (the state of being an embodied one) on the banks of Narmadā.

Yudhiṣṭhira said:

Do tell me the (story of) destruction of Anaṅga when he was one possessing all the limbs. It has neither been heard nor seen by me as having ever taken place. O excellent Brāhmaṇa, do recount everything in the manner it happened. O eminent Brāhmaṇa, I along with Bhīma, Arjuna and the twins (Nakula and Sahadeva) wish to hear it.

Śrī Mārkaṇḍeya said:

7-17. At the outset, in Kṛtayuga, O dear one, Maheśvara, the Lord of Devas, performed an elaborate penance when he was staying at Gaṅgā Sāgara.

The worlds along with Suras and Asuras became scorched by that penance. All of them sought refuge in the Lord of Devas, the Consort of Śacī.

"O Gopati (Lord of heaven), Maheśvara, the Lord of Devas, who pervades all living beings scorches the three worlds. Do stop him."

On hearing the words of those Devas, the Slayer of Bala and Vṛtra thought mentally and commanded (his subordinates) to bring about an obstacle in his penance. They were: the Apsarās, Menakā, Rambhā, Ghṛtācī and Tilottamā and also Vasanta (Spring Season), Cuckoo, Kāma and the excellent Southern Wind.

On being told thus by the king of Devas, O descendant of Bharata, the Devas accompanied by the Apsarās went near Hara.

The time was Vasanta (Spring) with abundance of flowers. Peacocks, Cātaka birds and cuckoos became excessively excited. The Devas danced and the Apsarās sang making all love-stricken and agitated. The (Southern) Wind blew on making even Yama and Nairṛta confounded. Thereat everyone went into a swoon. Excellent birds engaged in mutual contacts, along with Kinnaras and the great serpents were agitated by the fragrance of the Spring Season.

Even as he glanced round, the whole forest was in a great upheaval. The people were seen experiencing the state of (intoxication following) a poisonous sting (of an insect or reptile).

Even the Lord of Devas passed through the three states of Devas viz. Sāttvika, Rājasa and Tāmasa. O king, listen to it.

18-27. (Out of the three eyes of Śaṅkara) one eye became closed like a bud due to Yogic mental absorption. As for the second eye, it had a lethargic repose (due to the intensity of the sentiment of love) on the loins, hips and breasts of Pārvatī and another eye of Śambhu became kindled with the fire of anger at Madana who far away from him, had (held) his bow to shoot off (an arrow). May the triad of Śambhu's eyes depicting different sentiments at the time of his meditation, protect you all.

Thus was Kāma seen by the Lord. He was reduced to ash along with his bow and arrows. It amounted to the destruction of all embodied beings.

On seeing Kāma annihilated there, the Devas and the groups of celestial damsels became frightened. All of them fled away in the ten different directions.

All the worlds including Suras, Asuras and human beings, bereft of Kāma, sought refuge in Brahmā. The Devas with Indra as their leader sought refuge in Brahmā.

On seeing the universe dejected and despondent, they spoke to Parameṣṭhin: "O Lord, you know that the world remains (alive and active) when copulation becomes possible. But, O Lord, now without Kāma, all the subjects have become dried up."

On hearing the words of those Devas, Prapitāmaha accompanied them and went to the place where Lord Maheśvara was present.

He propitiated the Lord of all living beings, the Lord of the universe, by means of the eulogy of his Tāṇḍava dance and passages of prayer taken from the Vedas and Vedāṅgas.

Then the delighted great Lord Parameśvara became pleased with the Devas. He spoke these sweet words to the Devas with Brahmā at their head:

"What is to be done? What is the distress? What is the cause of this arrival of the Devas and sages? May this be told me without delay."

The Devas said:

28-39. O Śambhu, the destruction of the universe will occur as a result of the destruction of Kāma in mobile and immobile beings. It behoves you to create all the three worlds once again.

On hearing these words, Parameśvara pondered over them and thought of the physical form of Kāma, rare on the earth.

Thereupon Anaṅga came there quickly as an embodied one even as all the living beings were watching. O excellent king, he bestowed the vital breath on them.

Thereupon the Suras, Asuras and the great Serpents honoured and greeted the Lord with the sounds of conchs blown and Bherī-drums played on: "Obeisance to you, O Lord of the chiefs of Devas; we are blessed and contented." O destroyer of enemies, on being sent off, the excellent Suras went back the way they had come there.

When all the Devas dispersed, O descendant of Bharata, Kāmadeva resorted to the banks of Narmadā and performed an elaborate penance lasting for a hundred divine years. He became lean and emaciated through penance and Japa. Then he was pestered by great horrible beings causing obstacles from all around.

In order to annihilate all the obstacles he remembered Kuṇḍaleśvara. Showering arrows everywhere he accorded him protection.

Mahādeva became pleased with his steadfast devotion. The Destroyer of Kāma was inclined to bestow boons. He accorded Kāma the freedom of choice of a boon he wanted.

On coming to know that Mahādeva was pleased the Fish-emblemed One bowed down to the Three-eyed Lord of Devas and spoke with palms joined in reverence: "O Lord of Devas, if you are pleased, if a boon has to be granted to me, O Lord of the universe, be present here in this Tīrtha always."

Saying "So be it", Maheśvara, the Lord of Devas, went away piercing through the sky. He was then eulogized by the groups of celestial damsels.

40-51. When the Lord had vanished, Kāmadeva, O great king, installed the preceptor of the universe named Kusumeśvara.

On the fourteenth day of the month of Caitra or on the day of Madana, a person should take his holy bath there in the Tīrtha and observe fast.

Early in the morning itself, he should bathe and adore Divākara. Then he should offer libations to the Pitṛs and Devas with water mixed with gingelly seeds.

After taking the holy bath in accordance with the injunctions and after adoring him, one should offer balls of rice. Listen to the benefit thereof.

Undoubtedly, by offering the balls of rice the devotee derives that benefit which one gets by performing a Sattra for a period of twelve years.

If, with the Pitṛs in view, the devotee offers a ball of rice at the root of Aṅkula(?) his grandfathers become contented for twelve years.

O Yudhiṣṭhira, even worms, insects and locusts that die there in that Tīrtha attain heaven. All the more so in the case of men who die there!

He who conquers his anger and the sense-organs and devoutly takes to Sannyāsa (renunciation) shall go to Śiva's Palace.

There he sports about with the divine Apsarās and musicians of Devas and Gandharvas serving him for a hundred crores of Kalpas, O king.

When that period is complete, he will be born as a man here. He becomes a great king adored by great emperors.

He will be handsome, lucky in features, eloquent, valorous, intelligent and pure (sinless). He will live for more than a hundred years. He will be free from all ailments.

This Tīrtha well-known as Kusumeśvara is meritorious and destructive of sins. It is superior to hundreds of other Tīrthas. It is venerated by all the Devas.

CHAPTER ONE HUNDRED FIFTYONE

The Greatness of Śvetavārāha Tīrtha

Śrī Mārkaṇḍeya said:

1-7. On the northern bank of Narmadā there is an excessively splendid Tīrtha. The greatness of Jayavārāha (or Śvetavārāha) is destructive of all sins.

The Earth bowed to by all the Devas was lifted up by that Lord with the intention to bless all the worlds. He stationed himself on the banks of Narmadā with the same idea.

One who takes his holy bath in that Tīrtha and visits Madhusūdana, is liberated from all sins by repeating the names of the ten births (i.e. ten incarnations of the Lord). Those ten are: the Fish, the Tortoise, the Boar, the Man-lion, the Dwarf, Paraśurāma, Rāmacandra, Kṛṣṇa, Buddha and Kalki.

Yudhiṣṭhira said:

O dear one, what was done by Matsya (the Divine Fish)? O excellent sage, what was done by Kūrma, the Divine Tortoise? What was the act of Varāha, the Divine Boar? What was done by Narasiṁha (the Man-lion)? By Vāmana (the Dwarf), by Paraśurāma, by Rāghava? What was done by the Lord in the form of Buddha? What was done by Kalki? Tell me:

On being asked thus by the intelligent son of Dharma, the leading Brāhmaṇa spoke these sweet words to him:

Śrī Mārkaṇḍeya said:

8-17. In order to please Brahmā in a former Kalpa, the Lord became a Fish, recovered the Vedas that were immersed in the great sea and handed them over to Brahmā.

At the time of the production of Amṛta, O king, the Preceptor of the universe became a Tortoise and supported Mandara as well as the Earth.

Janārdana, the Lord of Devas, assumed the form of a Boar and lifted up Goddess Earth who was submerged in Pātāla.

He assumed a body partially human and partially leonine and tore up the chest of Hiraṇyakaśipu with the goad-like claws.

In the form of Vāmana with matted hair the Lord was eulogized by excellent Brāhmaṇas. Taking up that divine form, he covered the earth (etc.) by means of his steps and later made Bali a resident of Pātāla. After establishing all the Suras, Viṣṇu went back to his own city.

He became son of Jamadagni, Paraśurāma, the most excellent one among warriors wielding weapons, and killed Kṣatriya kings beginning with Haihaya. After giving the earth along with mountains, forests and mines, to Kaśyapa, the Lord of Devas is performing penance even today on Mahendra Mountain, O descendant of Bharata.

Then the Lord became Rāma, son of Daśaratha, and killed Rāvaṇa, the thorn unto Devas, in battle along with his hosts. He gave the kingdom to Vibhīṣaṇa. He ruled the kingdom with justice. By means of Yajñas, he propitiated Devas. Then the lotus-eyed Rāma went back to heaven.

18-28. The Lord of the earth, Vāsudeva, took his birth in the abode of Vasudeva, with Saṅkarṣaṇa as his help-mate (brother) for the purpose of slaying the wicked kings like Kaṁsa, Keśin, Jarāsandha and Cāṇūra, O Yudhiṣṭhira. With your (moral) support he killed them. With him as your excellent ally, O king, you will kill the enemies and enjoy the earth consolidated by your brothers.

Similarly, Acyuta will take up the next birth as Buddha. The Slayer of Madhu, the Lord of the chiefs of Devas, who is fond of the spring season, will be very quiescent. With Lord Parameṣṭhin in the form of Buddha the entire universe consisting of mobile and immobile beings will become enchanted. Ever since then, O descendant of Bharata, sons do not pay heed to the words of fathers, relatives do not pay heed to the words of elders, nor students to the words of preceptors. Everything will become topsy turvy. Dharma is defeated by Adharma, truthfulness by falsehood, kings by thieves, and men by women.

With the advent of Kali, O Yudhiṣṭhira, Agnihotras get defunct, adoration of preceptor comes into disuse and all the pious precepts of Manu get lost. Girls of ten and twelve become pregnant, only girls are born and Brāhmaṇa becomes Haripiṅgala (tawny like monkeys). Thereupon, the Lord will take up his tenth incarnation as Kalki.

Thus, O king, I have told you the reason for the ten incarnations of Lord Parameṣṭhin. It is destructive of all sins.

CHAPTER ONE HUNDRED FIFTYTWO

The Greatness of Bhārgaleśvara Tīrtha

Śrī Mārkaṇḍeya said:

1-3. Thereafter, O protector of the earth, one should go to the excellent Bhārgaleśvara Śaṅkara, who is the very life-breath of the world. It (this Tīrtha) destroys sins by merely remembering it. One who takes his holy bath there in that Tīrtha and adores Parameśvara attains the merit of performing a horse-sacrifice. Undoubtedly his departure to Rudraloka is one without a return therefrom.

If someone gives up his life in the Tīrtha, he gets the goal of Rudraloka from which there is no return.

CHAPTER ONE HUNDRED FIFTYTHREE

The Greatness of Ādityeśvara Tīrtha

Śrī Mārkaṇḍeya said:

1-11. Next to it, there is another excellent Ravi Tīrtha. Merely by seeing it, men are liberated from all sins.

The fruit of a man who takes his holy bath in Ravi Tīrtha and visits Bhāskara has been laid down by the Lord himself. Listen to it.

In the course of sixteen lives hereafter, of that devotee, there shall never be anyone blind, dumb, deaf, ugly or having deformed nails in his family. White patches, herpes, scabs, cutaneous eruptions etc., perish within six months in the case of a devotee of the Lord.

The story of that Lord heard by me in the Purāṇa cannot be briefly recounted, O excellent king.

If with Ravi in view, a gift is made to a deserving Brāhmaṇa in accordance with the injunctions, there is no end to its merit at all.

Excellent indeed is the fruit of *Dāna* made at Ravitīrtha at the time of *Ayana* (transit of the Sun), *Viṣuva* (equinox) and of solar and lunar eclipses.

Like that of the waters of the ocean, there is no end unto the merit of *Dāna, Havya* and *Kavya* offered at the time of Saṅkrānti (when the Sun passes from one Zodiac to another), O descendant of Bharata.

Savitṛ (the Sun-god) recompenses at the proper time, the persons who make gift or perform *Homa* (there).

The Sun-god grants boons for the next seven births again and again. The gift made during the waning of the Moon has a hundred times return and that when there is Dinakṣaya, a thousand times return. If it is during Saṅkrānti, the return is a hundred thousand times and if at Vyatīpāta, it is infinite.

Yudhiṣṭhira said:

12-24. How did Ravi Tīrtha come to be remembered as more meritorious than other meritorious ones? Kindly recount to me in detail. My ears are covetously eager.

Śrī Mārkaṇḍeya said:

Listen attentively to the excellent Ādityeśvara on the northern bank of Narmadā. It is destructive of all ailments.

Formerly in the beginning of Kṛtayuga, there was a Brāhmaṇa named Jābāli born of the family of Vasiṣṭha. He was a master of the topics dealt with in the Vedas and scriptural texts.

His chaste and well-behaved wife was a woman of excellent mind. During the days after the menstrual cycle, she approached her husband and said thus: "This is the period of my menstrual cycle. I have approached you, my husband. I am actuated by love and I wish for a son. Hence enjoy me with love."

On being told thus, the Brāhmaṇa said: "O my beloved, today I am observing a holy vow. Do go away now, O beautiful lady. I shall grant you the boon in the next menstrual cycle."

The next month, when the menstrual cycle recurred, she approached him again. On the plea that he was observing a holy vow, she was dissuaded by him.

Thus many times, she was again and again kept away. She became disappointed with her husband and the beautiful lady was overwhelmed by an excess of grief. She undertook fast unto death and gave up her life.

Owing to this sin of foeticide, the Brāhmaṇa was suddenly assailed by leprosy when his nose and feet became infested with sores. All his penance was lost. Realizing that he had contracted the fell disease of leprosy, the excellent Brāhmaṇa became grief-stricken. He came to the banks of Narmadā and asked the other Brāhmaṇas about Bhāskara Tīrtha, thinking in his mind, 'One should seek health and freedom from ailments from the Sun.' He asked the other Brāhmaṇas: "O Brāhmaṇas, where is that Bhāskara Tīrtha? May it be pointed out to me. I shall go to that Tīrtha with mental purity and perform penance."

The Brāhmaṇas said:

25-34. On the northern bank of Revā, there is a Bhāskara Tīrtha known by the name Ādityeśvara Tīrtha. It is destructive of all ailments. Do go there unhesitatingly, if you can.

On being told thus by the Brāhmaṇas, the Brāhmaṇa (Jābāli) prepared himself to go. But afflicted with the foul and fatal disease, he was unable to move.

Thereupon he thought: 'Indeed the power of Brāhmaṇas is famous all over the three worlds. The Liṅga (penis) of the Trident-bearing Lord of Devas was made to fall down by Brāhmaṇas. The ocean was dried up by Brāhmaṇas. Vindhya was restrained. I too, stationed here itself, shall bring Bhāskara here by means of the power of penance. I shall bring the deity named Ādityeśvara.'

After determining thus, he engaged himself in a severe penance without taking food and with the sole intake of air for food. In summer he stationed himself within five fires. During winter he stood in water. During rainy season he remained without any covering for the body.

When more than a hundred years passed, Ravi became pleased and said thus:

Sūrya said:

Welfare unto you. Choose your boon, whatever be in your mind as you desire. Even if it is one not to be granted, I shall give it to you. Do not delay. O Brāhmaṇa, since you are engaged in a penance (for such a long time), what is it that cannot be achieved, for you now?

Jābāli said:

35-43. If you are pleased, O Lord of Devas, if a boon has to be granted to me, (I would like to tell you that) I had taken a vow of visiting Ādityeśvara, O Lord of Devas. But being afflicted with disease, I have not been able to fulfil it. Hence you station yourself here at Śukla Tīrtha assuming the form of Ādityeśvara.

On being told thus, the multiformed Divākara appeared instantly on the northern bank of Narmadā.

Ever since then, they consider and speak of that Tīrtha as one destructive of all sins and all miseries.

If a devotee takes his holy bath everyday, particularly on every Sunday, makes seven circumambulations, continuing this for a full year, and visits Bhāskara, listen to the benefit that is to be obtained by him.

Prasupta (latent leprosy), patches, herpes, white leprosy and scabs perish immediately, O king, like a heap of cotton in blazing fire. Within three years, his house will be filled with wife, sons and wealth.

If a devotee performs Śrāddha there with the Pitṛs in view on the day of the transit of the Sun, his Pitṛs become contented. Indeed Bhāskara is the Lord of Pitṛs.

Thus the excellent Ādityeśvara Tīrtha has been entirely recounted to you. It is divine and destructive of all sins and ailments.

CHAPTER ONE HUNDRED FIFTYFOUR

The Greatness of Kalakaleśvara Tīrtha

Śrī Mārkaṇḍeya said:

1-9. On the southern bank of Narmadā is the famous Kalakaleśvara Tīrtha well-known in all the worlds. It was created by the Lord himself.

After killing Andhaka in the battle, Maheśvara, the Lord of Devas, created it in the company of the Devas, Gandharvas, Kinnaras and great Serpents. They sang and played on the musical instruments like trumpet, drums like Mṛdaṅga, Paṇava etc., lutes and flutes. They sang a number of eulogies. They sang Sāman verses, Yajus and other Vedic passages. Others recited Ṛks. Other dignified persons eulogized Maheśvara with many prayers.

There was heard the *Kalakala* (indistinct but sweet to the ears) sound of Pramathas and bards. Since the Liṅga was installed in the midst of Kalakala sound, it came to be known after it.

A man who takes his holy bath there in that Tīrtha and visits the deity, Kalakaleśvara, obtains a greater merit than that of Vājapeya here on the earth itself.

By that merit, he will become a sanctified soul and on death he will go to heaven seated on an excellent vehicle. He will be sung about by groups of celestial damsels. After enjoying great pleasures, he will be reborn as a noble soul in a pure family after lapse of much time. He will be a Brāhmaṇa of excellent luck and handsome in features. He will be a master of the Vedas and Vedāṅgas. Devoid of ailments and grief, he will live for a hundred years.

CHAPTER ONE HUNDRED FIFTYFIVE

Attainment of Siddhi by Cāṇakya

Śrī Mārkaṇḍeya said:

1-7. Henceforth I shall extol Śukla Tīrtha, the most excellent one of all Tīrthas. It is on the northern bank of Narmadā, O Yudhiṣṭhira.

From the point of view of meritoriousness and auspiciousness in appearance, all the other Tīrthas on the earth do not merit even a sixteenth part of that Tīrtha.

Yudhiṣṭhira said:

I along with my brothers and all the excellent Brāhmaṇas wish to hear the real greatness of that Tīrtha.

Śrī Mārkaṇḍeya said:

O king, listen to the origin of Śuklatīrtha. Merely by visiting it, a sin of Brāhmaṇa-slaughter gets dissolved.

Narmadā is the most excellent one among all the rivers and is destructive of all sins. A sin committed in childhood perishes merely at its sight.

Except Śuklatīrtha, O king, no Tīrthas are bestowers of salvation anywhere.

The greatness of Śuklatīrtha was listened to by me formerely in the company of Devas and sages. O descendant of Bharata, it was narrated by Śitikaṇṭha (the blue-throated god Śiva), the Lord of Devas, on Kailāsa, the most excellent one among mountains. That I shall now recount to you.

8-21. Formerly, in the beginning of Kṛtayuga, Viṣṇu performed an elaborate penance for a thousand years in order to propitiate the Consort of the Daughter of the Mountain. He remained without taking any food except the intake of air. He had stationed himself in Śuklatīrtha.

Thereafter, Maheśvara, the god of Devas, became directly visible. He manifested himself all of a sudden in that Tīrtha, O king.

The area extending to two Krośas (i.e. 2 x 3=6 Kms) was made capable of yielding worldly pleasures as well as salvation. A man who takes his holy bath in the Tīrtha is rid of all sins.

Gaṅgā is meritorious in Kanakhala; Sarasvatī in Kurukṣetra. Whether it be a village or a forest, Narmadā is meritorious everywhere.

Intake of food is the most important of all medicines; of all beverages, water is the most important. Sleep is the most important of all happy and pleasing things, a young woman among the yielders of pleasures, and head is the most important of all the limbs.

Just as the forehead of one who has taken the holy bath is the most meritorious, O excellent king, O Yudhiṣṭhira, so also is Śuklatīrtha the most meritorious on Narmadā.

Just as Gaṅgā is the most meritorious among all rivers, just as Janārdana is the greatest of all deities, so also Śuklatīrtha is declared as the most meritorious on Narmadā.

Just as Surabhi (celestial cow) is the most important one among all quadrupeds, just as Brāhmaṇa is the most important of all Varṇas, so also, O king, Śukla Tīrtha is the most important of all Tīrthas.

Just as the Sun is the most important one among the Planets, just as the Moon is the most important one among the stars, just as head is the most important of all the limbs, just as truthfulness is the most important of all righteous acts, so also, O son of Kuntī, is Śuklatīrtha the most excellent one of all Tīrthas.

Just as the eternal Supreme Soul is difficult to be comprehended and cannot be pointed out because it is very subtle, so also, O king, is the Śuklatīrtha.

One who is full of great delusion and suffers from slow-wittedness, does not understand clearly Śuklatīrtha established on the banks of Narmadā.

O son of Dharma, of what avail is too much of talk repeated frequently in this context? Śuklatīrtha is highly meritorious and can be approached only through the destruction of sins.

If a devotee offers here a handful of the waters of Revā, it is as though the Pitṛs have been propitiated for thousands and crores of Kalpas.

22-29. The only one that destroys the distress of Pitṛs on the earth is a son.

There was a king named Cāṇakya[1]. Only he knew Śukla Tīrtha.

Yudhiṣṭhira said:

O excellent Brāhmaṇa, who was this person named Cāṇakya? Who was the only person who knew Śuklatīrtha which no one else knew? By what means was it (the Tīrtha) known by him on the surface of the earth? I wish to hear about it. I am very eager.

Śrī Mārkaṇḍeya said:

He was a king born of the family of Ikṣvāku. He was the great- grandson of Śuddhodana. The saintly king named Cāṇakya enjoyed the entire earth. He was not deceived by any man but all of a sudden the excellent king was deceived by two roguish crows.

Yudhiṣṭhira said:

How was that king deceived by the two crows? Formerly the intelligent noble soul had vowed, "I shall not continue to live if any being be deceived by another. I will certainly cast off my life. There need not be any doubt about it." O leading Brāhmaṇa, explain this to me. My eagerness is intense.

Śrī Mārkaṇḍeya said:

Realizing that he had been deceived, the king caught hold of the crows and sent them to the abode of Yama inflicting severe punishment.

The crows said:

30-39. We are the sons of Sunda and Upasunda. We have attained the state of crows for some reason. O blessed one, do

1. As vv 25ff show, this Cāṇakya is a king. He is different from Cāṇakya of *Mudrārākṣasa*.

not kill us. We have come to a decision in this respect. O bestower of honour, whether we are hurled away through anger or not, we shall attain the greatest goal. Hence command us, O leading king. After carrying out something that pleases you much we shall be freed from the curse in accordance with the utterance of Brahmā.

On hearing the words of the crows Cāṇakya, the excellent king, said: "After knowing that I have been deceived by anyone anywhere, I will not continue to live. Hence (try) to find out the Tīrtha, O birds, at the abode of Yama. I shall send you there duly. After hearing about it, you will tell me."

Then he adorned the crows with garlands and sandalpaste. He sent them asking them to go to Yama's abode quickly and told them:

The king said:

After going to the city of Dharma, you may move about here and there. If the pious-souled Yama, the great controller, were to ask you, "From where are you coming? Tell me by whom you have been adorned", my words should be repeated to him without any fear or hesitation: "There was a righteous king named Cāṇakya born of the family of Ikṣvāku. On the twelfth day after his death we were propitiated with food and the like."

On hearing those words of the king, they went to the abode of Yama. With the full embellishment of garlands and sandalpaste, they began to sport about in the courtyard of Yama. The bold crows were seen by Dharmarāja. He asked them:

Yama said:

40-49. From which place have you come? By whom were you two adorned? O crows, what has happened may be mentioned unhesitatingly.

The crows replied:

There was a righteous king named Cāṇakya born of the family of Ikṣvāku. On his death, on the twelfth day, we were propitiated through food etc.

* * *

On hearing their words, Yama, the son of Vivasvān, looked at Citragupta, Kali and Kāla and said to them thus: "It has been enjoined by Brahmā that living beings, such as the oviparous, sweat-born etc., among mobile and immobile beings should come to my presence. Where has that man of evil action named Cāṇakya gone? Let this be searched and found out from the Purāṇas and Itihāsas as to what the fate (of such ones) is." Thereupon those Dharmapālas (officers of god Dharma) urged by Dharmarāja looked into the opinion of the Purāṇas regarding the coming and going effected by Karmas.

Thereafter Dharma, the most excellent one among those who uphold righteousness, said in a voice as majestic as the thunder of a rumbling cloud, even as the Dharmapālas were listening: "The oviparous, sweat-born and other living beings that die in the pure waters of Narmadā in Śuklatīrtha do not come to my presence. That Tīrtha is highly righteous in the world. It was created by Brahmā, Viṣṇu and Maheśvara with great devotion and a desire for the welfare of the worlds. Men defiled by major and minor sins who die in the waters of Narmadā in Śuklatīrtha become pure. They are not at all under my jurisdiction."

50-59. On hearing these words uttered by Yama, the two crows quickly surveyed the great city of Yama, O son of Kuntī, and returned.

They bowed down to the king who asked them about what happened and what was heard by them. The two crows who were Dānavas turned into crows, said: "From this place we two went to the excellent city of Yama on the southern side of the earth, after crossing many Yojanas.

That city had divine features with golden ramparts and ornamental gateways. It could bestow everything desired. There were many groups of houses. The city was embellished with jewels and gold, crossing roads, quadrangles and royal highways. The whole region was covered with gardens and parks with clusters of lotuses adorning the ponds. Swans and ducks cackled loudly while the cooings of cuckoos added to the confused noise. The forests were infested with lions, tigers, elephants and monkeys and bears resorted to them.

It was teeming with men and women. It was beautified by continuous festivals. It was resonant with the sound of blowing of conchs, of lutes and flutes. Yama-mārga also is made like the region called Svarga. Having reached the place we were found out by the messengers of Yama. At the behest of Yama, we were sent to the place where the Lord of the universe was present. The Lord was seated on a throne and we were afraid for our very life when we saw him. He had huge thighs, calves, shoulders, belly, chest, arms, face, eyes, nay the whole body was very huge.

60-62a. Another Kāla was also present there seated on a great buffalo and adorned with a great crown. Kali and the highly intelligent Citragupta were seen arriving with fires blazing in between.

They were experts in the interpretation of the Vedic passages. They were discussing the merits and sins of the creatures. They stayed there day and night forever.

62b-70a. At the end of the customary obeisance, Yama with a well controlled form, asked us the reason for our visit. Do listen to what we told him, 'In Ujjayinī there was a valorous king named Cāṇakya. On the twelfth day after his death we had our food and then came to this abode of Yama.'

On hearing our words Yama shook his head and smilingly spoke these truthful words in the midst of the assembled courtiers, 'There is a reason why this sinful person Cāṇakya has not come to my world that terrifies all sinners. All the creatures that die in Śuklatīrtha on Narmadā attain the greatest position. There is no need to doubt anything in this matter. Whether a creature is forced or does it voluntarily, if it dies in the area around the holy spot, it shall undoubtedly become an attendant of Rudra.'

On hearing these words of Dharma, we set out and came out of the city. We saw the terrible tortures of various kinds of people in Naraka. O excellent king, there are thirty crores of these horrible hells. Seeing these on the great highway we became terrified and extremely distressed.

70b-79a. The Narakas there are: Raurava and Mahāraurava. Then there are the other hells: Peṣaṇa, Śoṣaṇa, Kālasūtra, Asthibhañjana, Tāmisra, Andhatāmisra, Kṛmipūtivāha. Another hell Mahājvāla was seen. There itself is Viṣabhojana. There are the pairs of hells, Daṁśa and Maśaka and the Yamalaparvatas (twin mountains).

River Vaitaraṇī, the destroyer of all sins was seen. Meritorious persons drink the cool nectar-like water thereof. The same water gets transformed into blood in the case of sinners.

Asipatravana is another hell. Another great rock was seen having the form of a mass of fire. Another large Śālmalī was seen. There are hundreds and thousands of similar hells.

All types of acutely horrible hells were seen where men suffered much. They had committed sins verbally, mentally and physically.

Different types of sins due to arrogance and deceptive words (were seen). Fathers, mothers, elders, brothers—all were in helpless states with imperfect sense-organs. Those who had not redeemed them wandered there in Raurava. These base people spend twelve years in Raurava. Coming back to the mortal world, they become wretched and blind.

79b-89a. Men of sinful deeds who misappropriate the property of temples or of Brāhmaṇas fall into Mahāraurava in the abode of Yama and stay there certainly.

Like insects in chrysalis stage in cocoon, they are subjected to piercing with thorns.

Killers of animals, birds etc., and meat-eaters go to the hell named Peṣaṇa. Those who keep living beings in bondage fall into Śoṣaṇa hell. After enduring the tortures as laid down in the scriptural texts, they come back to the human world as lame, blind and deaf men.

Those who utter falsehood jeopardising cows and Brāhmaṇas fall into the Kālasūtraka hell. The torture therein as per the authors of the scriptural texts is indeed terrible. After experiencing those sufferings those who come back to the human world are born as men of low caste.

Those who forsake the progeny of their own family and keep living beings in bondage fall into the Asthibhañjana hell undoubtedly. After spending a hundred years there they are born as human beings. Those sinners undergo misery as dwarfs and hunchbacked ones.

Those deluded fools who profess to be learned but forsake their own wives go to the terrible Tāmisra hell. There is no doubt in this respect. At the end of a hundred years there they come back to the human world. Those men are congenitally unlucky with skins morbidly affected.

89b-99a. The base men who speak deceptive words and who use fraudulent measures and weights are cooked in the Andhatāmisra hell. After staying there a hundred thousand years they come back to the mortal world and wander in the abodes of enemies as blind and ill-formed wretches.

Those who nourish themselves alone by eating without giving food to Pitṛs, Devas and Brāhmaṇas fall into the Kṛmibhakṣya hell. Even at the time of birth they will have wounds eaten by worms.

One who lives upon the fortune of others emits a foul odour. Those who swerve from their duties, the sinners bereft of the discipline of *Varṇa* and *Āśrama* endure sufferings in the Pūyasaṁpūrṇa hell (filled with putrid things) for ten thousand years. When the period is complete they take human birth but afflicted with ailments they become repulsive to all other living beings.

A man of greed and delusion, a wicked man who administers poison and an arsonist alike sink into the Viṣasaṁpūrṇa hell. After a period of a hundred years he comes up from it. He is reborn as a miserly, unlucky human being.

Those who fail to make gifts of sandals, shoes, umbrella, quilt and covering sheets are eaten by Daṁśas (flies) and Maśakas (mosquitoes) for seventy births.

Those who take away the wealth of their fathers, those who are engaged in abusing and beating them are afflicted in the place where the *Yugmaparvatas* (twin mountains) are present.

99b-110a. Those who approach a woman in her menses will drink blood in the terrible Vaitaraṇī river with blood in the stream. The perpetrators of sins are subjected to torture in the terrible Asipatravana.

Those who always inflict pain on others, men who cohabit with low-class women are also tortured there.

Great sinners engaged in intimacy with the wives of preceptors are compelled to embrace (heated) Śilās (rocks) for a period of seventy births.

Those who sport about with the wives of others are made to embrace terrible (heated) images of iron full of many spikes in the hell Śālmalī.

One who abducts other men's womenfolk or misappropriates the assets of a Brāhmaṇa shall become a cruel Rākṣasa in a waterless forest region.

A sinful soul who takes away the properties of deities in temple or Brāhmaṇas out of avariciousness has to sustain himself with the leavings of the food of vultures.

These are the sins for which punishments are meted out at the bidding of Yama. Merely the sight of these and the listening to their descriptions generate fear.

There are others who enjoy in the abode of Yama the benefits of the gifts they had made. They were seen even as the messengers of Yama who were narrating to them at the bidding of Yama.

They were surrounded by (and carried by) chariots, elephants and horses. O blessed one, those who had performed series of penances and derived their benefits were seen there.

That world accords the desires of the men who gift cows, gold, plots of land, jewels, quilts, food, houses etc. Men who offer food here along with beverages sport about in the abode of Yama fully satisfied and contented.

110b-115a. O excellent king, whatever is given as gift here in Śuklatīrtha, even if it be as little as the tip of a hair, has everlasting benefit. Thus everything seen and heard has been recounted to you. Carry out whatever you desire if you are capable and if possible release (us)."

On hearing their words Cāṇakya was delighted in his mind. He congratulated the two birds again and again and sent them off.

When both of the crows departed, O descendant of Bharata, he gave everything he possessed to Brāhmaṇas, discarded lust and anger and went to Amara mountain (*Amarakaṇṭaka*).

There he fastened firmly a raft with black strings. Meditating on Lord Janārdana he floated on quickly. One shall wish for health from the Sun and wealth from the sacred fire. One attains knowledge from Īśāna and salvation from Keśava. The string that was dark blue in colour became red and shone like pure crystal. On seeing the rope shining so the highly intelligent (king) immersed himself in the pure water and attained the Vaiṣṇava region.

115b-116a. One should desire (pray for) health (absence of ailments) from the Sun, wealth from Fire-god. From Īśāna one obtains (spiritual knowledge). One attains Mokṣa (final beatitude) from Keśava.

116b-119. The black-coloured ropes (of the raft) became blue, red (and finally) resembling pure crystal (which was the effect of the waters of Śuklatīrtha) and the highly intelligent king immersed his body in the auspicious Śuklatīrtha. The noble-souled prince attained the region of Nārāyaṇa, the eternal one called Acyuta (Unswerving or Eternal), which the knowers of the Vedas sing about.

Thus the Siddhi (attainment of perfection) of king Cāṇakya has been described to you. I shall describe another thing also. Listen with concentration.

CHAPTER ONE HUNDRED FIFTYSIX

The Greatness of Śuklatīrtha

Śrī Mārkaṇḍeya said:

1-8. There is no other Tīrtha, O king, in all the worlds, which is on a par with Śuklatīrtha which is on the earth. No other Tīrtha is sung about in comparison with it.

The great Śuklatīrtha is stationed on Narmadā in the north-eastern region. It is resorted to by groups of sages.

On the fourteenth lunar day in the dark half of the month of Vaiśākha, Śaṅkara himself comes here from Kailāsa along with Umā.

He takes his holy bath in Śuklatīrtha with great mental concentration at midday and sees himself through his self. He is accompanied by Brahmā, Viṣṇu and Indra.

Especially on the full-moon day in Kārttika and Vaiśākha, O best of men, (Indra) after taking bath sees Brahmā, Viṣṇu and Mahādeva.

After taking bath, Indra, the king of Devas, along with Suras stays (and waits) on the way of the wind (i.e. the firmament) and sees Śaṅkara on the fourteenth day of the dark half.

On that day, Gandharvas, Apsarās, Yakṣas, Siddhas, Vidyādharas and Uragas (Serpents) see the Lord of Devas and shed off their sins.

Extending to half of a Yojana and half thereof wide, Śuklatīrtha is highly meritorious and destructive of great sins.

9-21a. Excellent men stand in a place from where they can see the tops of the trees thereof. Such people stationed there are rid of great sins accumulated earlier.

A man defiled by major and minor sins, is liberated by the holy bath therein. Even the sin of infanticide which is very difficult to be removed, perishes when acquired.

Especially on the full-moon day in Vaiśākha Śaṅkara comes here from Kailāsa. Since the Lord of Devas stays there along with Umā, the Tīrtha is highly meritorious and destructive of all sins. It was earlier said to me by Brahmā and it has been mentioned to you, O king.

Just as a cloth washed by a washerman becomes free from impurities, so also the body of a man becomes pure through the holy bath therein.

A man who has committed sins earlier in his life can dispel them by staying at Śuklatīrtha for a day and night.

O great king, if on a full-moon day a handful of the waters of Revā is offered to Pitṛs, they will enjoy welfare for thousands of crores of Kalpas.

Neither one's mother nor father nor kinsmen will redeem one's fall into the ocean of hell, O king, but the merit acquired from Śuklatīrtha will do that.

One does not attain through penance or continuous celibacy that good state which a creature that dies by casting off its body in Śuklatīrtha attains.

One should observe fast, remain pure and bathe the deity with ghee on the fourteenth day in the dark half of the month of Kārttika. At dawn he should take his holy bath in Revā. Keeping Lord Śaṅkara in view one should offer Ghṛtakaṁbala along with gold according as his resources permit.

Concluding the offering to the Lord with Ghṛta (ghee) is called Ghṛtakaṁbala. That man becomes highly refulgent on death and shall go to the world of Śiva accompanied by twenty-one generations of his family and remain there till the destruction of all living beings (i.e. *Pralaya*).

21b-33a. A man who takes his holy bath in Śuklatīrtha and worships Umā and Rudra with sweet scents, incense, flowers etc., shall obtain the merit of a horse-sacrifice.

O king, he who observes fast for a month there at that Tīrtha is liberated from great sins incurred in the course of seven births. The following sins undoubtedly perish by observing Cāndrāyaṇa at Śuklatīrtha: Taking in milk of a camel; taking milk of sheep and taking food in Navaśrāddha; co-habitation with a Vṛṣalī; eating prohibited foodstuff, buying a sheep or buffalo under false pretext, performing Yajña on behalf of undeserving fellows; usury; administering poison to a number of persons; and reviling deities and Brāhmaṇas: these and others of this sort.

If a person takes his holy bath in Śuklatirtha and offers libation to Pitṛs and deities they become highly propitiated and contented for twelve years.

Persons who offer sandals and shoes, umbrella, quilt, seat, gold, money, foodgrain, Śrāddha, fully yoked plough, meal, drinking water etc., in that Tīrtha, will undoubtedly go to Śivaloka on death delighted and well nourished.

Men who devoutly keep Śiva in view, O descendant of Bharata, and offer an alms-bowl and cooked food, go to heaven.

Even something as little as the tip of a hair, gifted to the residents of the Tīrtha, those who perform Yajñas and observe vows, becomes everlasting in its merit.

He who has rid himself of too much attachment and hatred, meditates in his heart on Janārdana and enters fire with concentration shall go to the City of Varuṇa with all his desires fulfilled. There is no ailment and old age where the Lord of waters is present.

33b-44. He who observes ritualistic fasting (unto death), O Yudhiṣṭhira, there in that Tīrtha shall certainly depart to Rudraloka never to return therefrom.

Whether of his own accord or under duress, if a creature, dies in the region of that holy spot, he shall undoubtedly become an attendant of Rudra.

He who gives a virgin well adorned according as his resources permit at Śuklatīrtha (derives great merit thereby). What has been declared by Rudra by way of indicating the merit of ritualistic dedication of a bull in accordance with the injunctions, O excellent king, I shall recount it: O king; listen to it with an attentive mind. He is honoured in Rudraloka for as many thousand years as the number of pores in the separate limbs of the bull. What is gifted in Śuklatīrtha at the time of solar and lunar eclipses gets increased fifteen times.

If a person remains pure and circumambulates Śuklatīrtha, he attains merit of circumambulating the entire earth.

If a devotee honours an excellent couple with Rudra in view, he will never meet with separation (from his beloved) for seven births.

Thus, O king, the great merit has been succinctly recounted to you, i.e. the merit of (visiting) Śuklatīrtha in the manner heard by me from the Lord.

He who devoutly listens to this, shall undoubtedly obtain the merit laid down in the Purāṇa.

This is true. This is true. Again and again it is asserted (to be true). He who seeks salvation shall obtain salvation as the great fruit of the holy bath and the gift made.

CHAPTER ONE HUNDRED FIFTYSEVEN

The Greatness of Huṁkārasvāmī

Śrī Mārkaṇḍeya said:

1-9. Next to it, O king, and in the vicinity of Śuklatīrtha is the Tīrtha of Vāsudeva honoured in all the worlds.

Indeed that is an ancient, well-known, meritorious Tīrtha on Narmadā where Revā flows to a distance of a Krośa (3 Kms.) merely making the hissing sound of *Hum.*

O leading king, ever since the river began to flow with a hissing sound, the deity is named *Huṁkāra* by learned men.

A man who takes his holy bath in Huṁkāra Tīrtha and visits the immutable Acyuta, is rid of all sins incurred in the course of seven births.

Excepting Nārāyaṇa, the Lord of the universe, there is no other deity capable of redeeming a man immersed in the ocean of worldly existence, perpetrating more and more sinful activities.

That tongue is the real tongue which eulogizes Hari; that mind is genuine which is dedicated unto Him. Only those hands are worthy of praise that worship Him.

Nothing inauspicious happens at any time in any of the activities of those persons in whose hearts is present Lord Hari, the abode of all auspiciousness.

Merely by prostrating before Hari, a man obtains the same merit as (is derived) from the adoration of other deities.

He is honoured in Viṣṇuloka for as many thousands of years as there are dust particles sticking to his dusty limbs.

10-15. By sweeping, sprinkling with water and plastering the temple premises, all sins of men and women perish. By visiting with devotion, the sins of excellent persons get dissolved.

If Lord Vāsudeva is adored by anyone, the sin incurred by him in the course of life perishes. With the sins shaken off, he goes to the world of the Garuḍa-emblemed Lord and becomes worthy of being worshipped by groups of Suras.

Even if one makes obeisance to the Discus-bearing Lord hypocritically, the sins incurred by him in the course of seven births vanish immediately.

There is no doubt about it. Rudra is pleased by adoration; Divākara (Sun) by means of Japa and Homa. The Lord with the conch, discus and club in his hands, becomes pleased with prostration.

A raft in the form of Viṣṇu can be the sole refuge unto men without a raft, getting immersed in the chaotic waters of sensual objects, entangled in the ocean of worldly existence, assailed by the typhoons of *Dvandvas* (mutually opposed pairs e.g. pleasure-pain) and afflicted with the burden of protecting sons, daughters and wives.

O leading king, O tiger among men, whatever is performed in Huṁkāra Tīrtha, whether auspicious or otherwise, does not get lost.

CHAPTER ONE HUNDRED FIFTYEIGHT

The Greatness of Saṅgameśvara Tīrtha

Śrī Mārkaṇḍeya said:

1-9. Thereafter, a devotee should go to another excellent Tīrtha named Saṅgameśvara Tīrtha on the southern bank of Narmadā. It eradicates the fear of all sins.

Proceeding towards the Kailāsa mountain after his arrival from Pitṛloka, O excellent king, Dhanada had rested there for a short while.

As for the proof, O excellent king, on the earth indeed black stones appear as bright as crystals.

An excellent river Puṇyatoyā (a river of meritorious waters) originating from a spring in the Vindhya mountain enters the waters of Narmadā, destructive of all sins.

One who takes his holy bath at the confluence there and worships Saṅgameśvara, undoubtedly attains the merit of an Aśvamedha sacrifice.

One who offers bells, banners and awning unto the deity, Saṅgameśvara, attains Rudra's region riding in an aerial chariot fitted with swans and surrounded by hundreds of celestial ladies. He shall become an attendant of Rudra.

One who fills (covers) the Liṅga of the Lord with rice mixed with curds shall stay in Śivaloka for a desired period of as many years as there are grains of cooked rice.

One who covers the Liṅga of Lord Śiva with Śrīphalas in spite of being very poor, goes to Svarga (heaven), O king, and attains the same benefit (as the previous one). For seven births the line of his progeny will not be broken.

10-16. Listen to the meritorious benefit of that person who bathes the Lord of Devas with curds, honey or ghee. When Maheśvara is extremely pleased, those men go to that place where rivers of ghee and milk flow and where trees exude honey.

If a devotee offers even water, a leaf, a flower or fruit unto Maheśvara, he enjoys everlasting benefit for seven births.

Maheśvara is the greatest of all deities worthy of being worshipped. Hence Maheśvara should be worshipped with all effort.

One who steadfastly; observes (the vow of) celibacy forever and worships Lord Śiva, lives here in this world as a great Lord and on death attains the region free from ailments.

O son of Kuntī, by worshipping one eminent Yogin one attains the same benefit as is obtained by learned men when Śiva is worshipped.

Their life is an excellent life and blessed are those noble-souled ones in whose houses men engrossed in devotion to Śiva take food.

17-21. The holy spots of Kurukṣetra, Naimiṣa and Puṣkara are there wherever an ascetic with all the sense-organs perfectly restrained stays. By feeding a single Śivayogin, O son of Kuntī, one attains that benefit which is obtained when Vedic scholars hundreds in number are fed.

The Bull-emblemed Lord of Devas takes food along with his consort there where a person with all his limbs smeared in ash takes food irrespective of his being ignorant or learned.

By offering alms alone to Śivayogins one attains that merit which is obtained by feeding a crore of Brāhmaṇas learned in the Vedas.

If anyone casts off his life after reaching Saṅgameśvara Tīrtha, he never returns from Śivaloka.

CHAPTER ONE HUNDRED FIFTYNINE

The Greatness of Anarakeśvara Tīrtha

Śrī Mārkaṇḍeya said:

1-6. Thereafter, O great king, one should go to an extremely sacred Tīrtha on Narmadā named Anarakeśvara. It is of Siddha (spiritually perfect) nature and very rarely obtained. A man who takes his holy bath there in that Tīrtha, O descendant of Bharata, does not see the extremely terrible gate of what is termed as Naraka, even though he may be a sinner.

Yudhiṣṭhira said:

O dear one, men here in this world experience pleasures (and sorrows) as the results (of deeds) auspicious and inauspicious. O excellent one, what are the characteristic features based on which they are born so?

The individual soul coming out after leaving the body is not seen. In the same way, it is not seen while reentering a body constituted of the five elements.

What is the Saṁjñā (?name, consciousness) that comes to men in the conglomeration of faeces, urine and semen, along with skin, bone, flesh, suet, blood and hundreds of hair and nerves and tissues?

On being asked thus, Mārkaṇḍeya, conversant with Yoga meditated upon the eternal Maheśvara, Śarva, the Lord of Devas, and began to say:

Śrī Mārkaṇḍeya said:

7-19. O son of Kuntī, listen to the great problem. I shall recount it in the manner heard earlier by me from Brahmā in the assembly of sages and Devas.

Preceptor is the chastiser of self-controlled ones; king is the chastiser of the wicked ones. The chastiser of those with sins concealed here (in the world) is Yama, the son of Vivasvān.

Those who did not perform expiatory rites are tortured in various ways in the world of Yama. They are then born as various kinds of living beings. After passing through those stages, they take up human birth when they will have distinct marks of their sins. I shall mention them, O king. Listen attentively.

After going to the abode of Yama they endured all sorts of tortures. After undergoing such large-scale tortures, those who rtetrn to the mortal world are marked duly.

A habitual liar becomes a stammerer. One who had uttered a lie jeopardizing cows becomes a dumb man. A person with the sin of slaying a Brāhmaṇa becomes a leper. A drunkard has blackened teeth.

By stealing gold, one gets deformed nails. A man who defiles the bed of the preceptor gets skin diseases. One who is in contact with sinners becomes deficient in generative organs. One who has never made any gifts becomes impoverished.

A person who performs Yajña on behalf of the undeserving becomes a Grāma Śūkara (village pig), O king. One who performs Yajña on behalf of many becomes an ass. One who takes food uninvited becomes a dog.

One who takes food indiscriminately without examination shall be born as a monkey in a desolate forest. One who threatens others becomes a cat. By burning down a forest of dry wood, one becomes a glowworm.

By imparting false knowledge, one becomes a bullock. One who gives stale, cooked rice to a Brāhmaṇa, may become impotent.

On account of rivalry one is born as congenitally blind. One who steals a book is born blind. The child of one who steals fruits dies. There is no doubt about this. On death he becomes a monkey. Getting released therefrom, he becomes Galāḍavān (? with a pendulous fleshy purse hanging from the throat?). A man who eats those fruits without giving (to others) becomes one without children.

One who steals cloth shall become an alligator. A person who administers poison becomes a serpent. By cohabiting with an ascetic woman one becomes a vampire in desert.

20-34a. A person taking away water becomes gouty. A person stealing grain becomes a mouse. The Śruti says that one who ravishes an immature girl becomes a serpent.

One coveting the wife of the preceptor shall become a chameleon and remain so for a long time. A man who breaks water-current shall become a fish. A man who sells an article the sale of which is prohibited, shall become one with deformed eyes. An *Ayoniga* (one who introduces the penis elsewhere than into a vagina) shall become a wolf. One who practises deception in buying shall become an owl.

One who takes food on the eleventh day of the death of a person, becomes a dog. After promising some payment of money to a Brāhmaṇa, if one does not give it, he shall become a Madhūka tree.

One who ravishes a queen becomes a wicked man. A thief becomes a filthy pig. One who spreads scandal about the people of high caste, takes up the form of a tortoise.

A *Devalaka* (one who supports himself by the offerings to an idol) takes the birth of a Cāṇḍāla. A seller of fruits becomes unlucky. A consort of a Śūdra woman becomes a scorpion.

One who treads on fire becomes a cat. One who eats meat

belonging to others, becomes diseased (chronically). One cohabiting with his own sister becomes an impotent fellow. One who steals sweet scents becomes a stinking person.

A Grāmabhaṭṭa (a priest of the rustic multitude) becomes a barber. A Daivajña (street astrologer) shall become a donkey. A person professing to be a learned man, shall become a cat. A person expounding scriptural texts (professionally) shall become a dog. O king, one who reveals secrets of others is seen to be so (a dog). One who does enimical act, whether small or big, takes the birth of a brutish creature. There is no doubt about this.

These and other signs are brought about by one's own actions, wherefrom men are clearly seen what they really are. Birth follows death and death follows birth. This is the case in all creatures, O descendant of Bharata.

When auspicious and inauspicious acts become equal in magnitude and when semen and blood become mixed due to the intercourse of a man and a woman, a creature is born undoubtedly. Equipped with the five elements the creature, the Ātman, the Lord himself becomes the sixth of the series. The Ātman is beginningless and when it wishes to take a birth, all these things come to it: sense-organs, mind, vital airs, knowledge, longevity (life expectation), happiness, fortitude, sustaining (retention), inducement, misery, wish, Ahaṁkāra (ego, I-ness), effort, shape, colour, voice, hatred, birth and non-birth.

Purāṇic Embryology

34b-39. In the first month it is a phlegmatic mass with the full complement of the bodily ingredients. In the second month it is a lump of flesh; in the third it gets equipped with sense-organs. From the element of ether it derives lightness, subtlety, sound, power of hearing, strength etc. From air the Ātman obtains sense of touch, movement, digestive power and roughness. From fiery element the sense of vision, warmth, digestive capacity, colour and illumination are obtained. It takes from watery element chillness, fluidity, dampness and softness. From earth element it takes odour, sense of smell, weight and physical form. These the unborn Ātman takes up in the third month and begins to throb. If the longing of a pregnant woman is not fulfilled, the foetus becomes defective. It may get ugliness or even death. Hence the woman should be kept pleased. In the fourth month the limbs get firmness. Blood begins to flow in the fifth month. Physical strength is obtained in the sixth month. Complexion is fixed and the nails and hairs grow at that time.

40-53. In the seventh month, the foetus becomes endowed with consciousness and mind and the body has all the nails and hundreds of hairs. In the eighth month, the outer skin is fixed and the foetus becomes endowed with the power of memory. It is at this time that his sin pursues the foetus and the mother as well. Hence if the birth is premature and the child is born in the eighth month it dies invariably. Either in the ninth or the tenth month the child comes out naturally forced by the powerful winds at the time of delivery. With feverish haste it comes out like an arrow from the hole in a mechanical device. Now it has its full complement of the limbs of the body. There are one hundred vulnerable joints with three hundred Āsthās (bones?). There are seven skull-pieces in the head created by the Self-born Lord himself. O descendant of Bharata, there are three and half crores of hairs on the limbs. There are seventy-two thousand Nāḍis (nerve vessels) fanning out. They are named Hitā and Śaśiprabhā is one of them. Thus the cycle goes on functioning in all the four types of living beings and the birth and death of all embodied beings are brought about.

The upward progress is due to righteousness and downfall is due to unrighteousness. Everything in regard to all classes of people, O king, is due to the acts of righteousness of the respective Varṇas.

The acts of giving and enjoying give Deva-hood or human birth. O great king, all that is the fruit of action (Karma).

A creature may sink into the inauspicious and terrible hell brought about by its own action and urged by lust and anger. There is no redemption therefrom.

The only means for the redemption of creatures is this single excellent Narakeśvara[1] Tīrtha situated on the banks of Narmadā. It dispels Naraka torture. It is highly meritorious. It is destructive of great sins. It is the rarest on the earth.

1. The name of the Tīrtha is *Anarakeśvara* but due to metrical exigency A is dropped from the verse.

One who takes his holy bath there in that Tīrtha and adores Maheśvara, will never see Naraka though he might have incurred great sins.

One who makes a gift of an auspicious cow which is the redeemer, becomes easily liberated from the Vaitaraṇī river undoubtedly.

Yudhiṣṭhira said:

54-66. What is the form and what is the extent of river Vaitaraṇī which flows near the gateway of Yama's terrible world? O Brāhmaṇa, how does it flow?

How do people escape from it? Who are the people who have to remain in it always? To whom is it favourable? Do expatiate upon all these points.

Śrī Mārkaṇḍeya said:

O mighty-armed Dharmaputra, listen to everything uttered by me. The great river at the threshold of Yama's world, named Vaitaraṇī, is very deep. It is vast and shoreless, Even at the very sight it strikes terror. Putrid blood constitutes its water and flesh is its mud. That water whirls swiftly like ghee in a melting pot. It is full of worms and putrid matter (like pus).

Alligators and sharks of adamantine snouts and iron-like bills resembling big scissors fill it. There are other aquatic beings of violent features capable of tearing vulnerable joints.

Twelve suns burn there fiercely as though at the time of the ultimate annihilation. Men fall therein and shriek awfully. "O my brother! O my son! O my mother!" Thus they cry out frequently. Who can save one falling into the terrible Asipatravana?

Some creatures keep floating, some sink and some get fatigued. That great river must necessarily be seen by all the four types of living beings.

Through the means of good gifts they remain floating, otherwise they go down. The stay there is perpetual in the case of those who do not honour their mothers and slight their preceptors or other elders.

Those sinners who forsake a chaste, wedded wife of decent habits, steadfast in pious habits, remain there (in Vaitaraṇī) permanently.

Those horrible sinners who particularly seek weak points in women, children, old people and wretched ones are cooked (subjected to torture) within it. They continue to shriek and howl.

67-80. An evil-minded one who puts in obstacles in the case of a Brāhmaṇa tired and hungry, is eaten by worms for a period of three hundred Kalpas.

One who promises a gift unto a Brāhmaṇa, invites him and says "No" has to stay there permanently.

The following sinners have to stay there permanently: an arsonist, a person administering poison, a person assailing king, a slanderer, one who causes interruption in the narration of a (holy) story, a perjuror, a drunkard, one who destroys diamonds, one who takes away what is offered by himself, one who breaks the embankments of excellent fields, a ravisher of other men's wives, a Brāhmaṇa who sells spirituous beverages, a paramour of a Śūdra woman, one who disturbs herds of thirsty cows (while drinking), a violator of the chastity of a virgin, one who torments the recipient after making a gift, a Śūdra who drinks the milk of a tawny-coloured cow, a Brāhmaṇa who habitually eats meat etc.

O king, you need not entertain doubts in regard to this.

Do listen to O king, as to how this Vaitaraṇī can be turned into a favourable one. An excellent *Dāna* that is given in the holy periods of the transit of the Sun, the equinox, Vyatīpāta, the close of the day (a day touching three Tithis) etc. and a black or pink-coloured cow make Vaitaraṇī auspicious.

The horns (of the cow) shall be fitted with (caps of) gold and the hoofs with silver. The milking pot shall be made of brass. A pair of black cloths should cover it. Seven varieties of grain should accompany the gift. It must be made to sit above a copper vessel filled with a *Droṇa* (of grain).

The image of Yama should be made of gold. He must have an iron staff. A raft of sugarcane stumps should be tied with silk cords.

On the raft the cow should be placed conceiving it as originating from the body of the Sun. A wise person should make gift of umbrella, pair of shoes, ring and clothes to a Brāhmaṇa. He shall catch hold of its tail and utter this Mantra: "Om, I am desirous of crossing River Vaitaraṇī at the excessively terrible threshold of Yama's abode. O Vaitaraṇī, obeisance to you! I make this over to you." This is the consecratory Mantra.

81-90. "May cows be in front of me. May cows be behind me. May cows be in my heart. I live in the midst of cows.

Oṁ, O excellent Brāhmaṇa in the form of Viṣṇu! O Sir, sanctifying the line of Brāhmaṇas! This has been given to you along with monetary gift, O Vaitaraṇi, obeisance to you."

This is the *Dāna Mantra*. The devotee circumambulates the Brāhmaṇa, (the image of) Dharmarāja, the cow, the auspicious Vaitaraṇī and then makes over the gift of these to Brāhmaṇas.

He then makes the Brāhmaṇa go ahead, holds the tail of the cow and utters, "O dear cow, do wait for me at the extremely fearful threshold of Yama's abode. O cow, I am desirous of crossing Vaitaraṇī. Obeisance to Vaitaraṇi!"

This is the Mantra for following the cow.

The entire household should follow him as he goes after the cow. He leads the entire household. If this is done, O king, the river shall be flowing favourably.

That river flowing with the water redeems the donor of the *Dāna* through that cow. He attains all the cherished desires, both divine and human.

The sick shall be rid of all ailments. All great calamities become quelled. In regard to the healthy, the benefit is thousand times more and in regard to the sick a hundred times. Only in the case of a dead man, the gift is made indirectly. The benefit then is remembered as on a par. Hence the gift should be made by one's own hand. After death who will give to whom? O great king, after thinking along this line, what is offered by one's own hand shall be of great benefit.

Thus, O son of Dharma, the procedure regarding *Dāna* on Vaitaraṇī has been recounted to you. One who listens and recites with devotion goes to the immeasurable region of Viṣṇu.

Śrī Mārkaṇḍeya said:

91-102. At the advent of the month of Aśvayuja on the fourteenth lunar day in the dark half, one should take one's holy bath, perform the Śrāddha rite and worship Maheśvara. The gift on behalf of the Pitṛs is to be given by people with devotion and faith.

Thereafter the person should keep awake listening to the stories about saintly persons and the like. Early at dawn he should take his holy bath in the waters of Narmadā and duly perform the rites of libation unto the Pitṛs and Devas. A lamp of gold should be gifted to a Brāhmaṇa with ghee in the basin of the lamp. Thereafter he should feed Brāhmaṇas and take food himself without feelings of jealousy.

If this is done, O leader of men, a creature never goes to Naraka. It is compulsory that men should survey the situation in Naraka. But if this procedure is followed, a man never sees Naraka.

If people die in the Tīrtha after these procedures are duly followed, O king, they will stay in the rare Śivaloka for a period of one Manvantara.

By means of an aerial chariot dazzling with the colour of the Sun and resplendent with hundreds of tinkling bells, he goes there, O blessed one, being attended upon by groups of celestial damsels. He enjoys different kinds of pleasures undoubtedly for the period of time as mentioned before.

When the period is complete he comes over here in human form when he will be bereft of all ailments. He shall live for a hundred years.

At the advent of the month of Aśvayuja, on the fourteenth day in the dark half, a devotee should observe fast for a night and a day and worship Maheśvara. Even if he has incurred great sins he shall undoubtedly get rid of them.

O Yudhiṣṭhira, there are twenty-eight crore Narakas. Devotees shall be unaffected by the miseries of Naraka. They go to Śivaloka. After enjoying great pleasures with divine Aiśvarya (richness) they will come again as human beings which (manhood) is difficult to obtain.

CHAPTER ONE HUNDRED SIXTY

The Greatness of Mokṣa Tīrtha

Śrī Mārkaṇḍeya said:

1-9. Thereafter, O son of Pāṇḍu, one should go to the excellent Mokṣa Tīrtha which is resorted to by Devas, Gandharvas, sages and ascetics.

Many who have been deluded by Viṣṇu's Māyā do not know that Tīrtha. Here blessed sages and ascetics have become Siddhas. Pulastya, the learned Pulaha, the highly intelligent Kratu, Prācetasa, Vasiṣṭha, Dakṣa, Nārada and many other fortunate ones, more than seven thousand in number, have attained salvation along with their sons. Hence that Tīrtha is the bestower of salvation.

River Tamahā flows into the stream of that Tīrtha. The confluence there is a Tīrtha that quells all sins.

By a perfect Japa of Gāyatrī in accordance with the injunctions at that Tīrtha, one will obtain that benefit which is obtained when the Vedic passages of Ṛk, Yajus and Sāman are repeatedly recited.

What is given as a religious gift, whatever is consigned to the holy fire in Homa, the Mantras and holy names uttered as Japa-the benefit obtained from all these shall be everlasting and shall be the excellent means of attaining salvation.

If Brāhmaṇas who have renounced the world as Sannyāsins die there in the Tīrtha, their departure shall be one without any return, due to the power of Mokṣatīrtha. Thus the procedure has been succinctly recounted to you by me, O sinless one. The benefit from this Tīrtha is very great and it has been mentioned in the Purāṇa.

CHAPTER ONE HUNDRED SIXTYONE

The Greatness of Sarpa Tīrtha

Śrī Mārkaṇḍeya said:

1-7. Thereafter, O great king, a person should go to the excellent Sarpa Tīrtha where, O Yudhiṣṭhira, great serpents performed penance and became Siddhas.

They are the serpents Vāsuki, Takṣaka the terrible serpent, Airāvata, the highly fortunate Kāliya, Karkoṭaka, Dhanañjaya, the highly refulgent Śaṅkhacūḍa, Dhṛtarāṣṭra, Vṛkodara, Kulika, Vāmana and the sons and grandsons of all these who performed a very difficult penance there at that highly meritorious Tīrtha. (Thereby) now they enjoy different kinds of pleasures. They now sport about as they please.

Śaṅkara has formerly declared that one who takes his holy bath there in that Tīrtha and offers libations to Pitṛs and Devas, obtains the benefit of a Vājapeya sacrifice. O descendant of Bharata, men who have taken their holy baths in the Sarpatīrtha have seldom fear from serpents, scorpions and the like anywhere on the earth.

One who dies there goes to the city of Bhogavatī and is honoured by great serpents surrounded by Nāga maidens. He shall be the Lord of great enjoyments.

8-11. On the eighth lunar day in the dark half of the month of Mārgaśīrṣa, a person should be pure and observe fast. He should cover the Liṅga with gingelly seeds. In accordance with his capacity, he should adore with sweet-smelling flowers. After doing thus duly, he should prostrate and crave for forgiveness.

O leader of men, listen to the benefit that has been enjoyed in his case. O king, he rejoices for as much time in Svarga (Amarāvatī) as he desires, nay as many years as there are gingelly seeds, leaves, flowers and fruits (in the adoration).

Having slipped down from Svarga, he is reborn in a pure family. He will be handsome, fortunate and highly rich. He will become a Lord of crores.

CHAPTER ONE HUNDRED SIXTYTWO

The Greatness of Gopeśvara Tīrtha

Śrī Mārkaṇḍeya said:

1-5. Thereafter, next to Sarpakṣetra, one should go to Gopeśvara where men are liberated from sins merely by a single bath.

One who takes his holy bath there in that Tīrtha and casts off his life, shall go to the palace of Śiva even though he is defiled by sins.

One who takes his holy bath there in the Tīrtha and adores Lord Īśvara is liberated from all sins. He goes to Rudraloka.

After sporting about in Rudraloka as he pleases, the devotee of great austerities attains human birth and becomes a righteous king.

He will be richly equipped with elephants, horses and chariots and will be accompanied (served) by male and female slaves. He will be honoured by other kings and shall live happily for a hundred years.

CHAPTER ONE HUNDRED SIXTYTHREE

The Greatness of Nāga Tīrtha

Śrī Mārkaṇḍeya said:

1-4. Thereafter, O great king, a person should go to the excellent Nāga Tīrtha.

On the fifth lunar day in the bright half of the month of Āśvina one should remain pure and observe regulations. Then he has to keep awake for the whole of the night while offering sweet scents, incense and food.

Early next morning, he should take his holy bath and duly perform Śrāddha. He will be liberated from all sins. No hesitation need be felt in this respect.

O king, one who casts his life off there in the Tīrtha, shall have a departure from which there is no return. So said Śiva himself.

CHAPTER ONE HUNDRED SIXTYFOUR

The Greatness of Sāṁvaureśvara Tīrtha

Śrī Mārkaṇḍeya said:

1-7. Thereafter, a person should go to the excellent Sāṁvaura Tīrtha where Bhānu (Sun-god) is present and is adored by Suras and Asuras.

Those who have become lame, those whose noses and nails are defective, those whose limbs are split due to itches, scabies etc., those whose wounds are infested with flies and worms, those bereaved of mothers and fathers, abandoned by brothers and wives, those helpless creatures defective in limbs who suffer a great deal of misery, do find this deity, the Lord of Sāṁvaura, the source of origin of the universe, very helpful. This deity stationed on the banks of Narmadā is destroyer of miseries of the worlds and quells pains.

Listen to the meritorious benefit of a person who regularly bathes in the Tīrtha there for a month and continuously worships Lord Bhāskara.

O son of Kuntī, the benefit that one derives by taking the holy dip in the four seas, viz. northern, eastern, western and southern seas, is derived by taking holy bath there in this Tīrtha.

Merely by taking the bath in Sāṁvaura all the sins acquired during childhood, youth and old age get destroyed.

8-13. Undoubtedly one obtains that benefit which is usually obtained by fasting on the seventh lunar day and keeping awake at night. O excellent king, by bathing in that Tīrtha one obtains the benefit of offering Arghya with red sandalpaste.

The waters of Narmadā are beautiful and destructive of all sins, especially of the section looked at by the noble-souled Sāṁvaura deity.

Those who take bath and visit the excellent Lord of Devas, Sāṁvaura, are blessed ones. They are great souls. Their life is an ideal one. By resorting to Sāṁvaura for seven births, one can permanently avoid ailments, poverty and separation from beloved ones. A devotee shall stay in Suryaloka until the destruction of all living beings.

CHAPTER ONE HUNDRED SIXTYFIVE

The Greatness of Siddheśvara Tīrtha

Śrī Mārkaṇḍeya said:

1-7. It is heard, O Lord, that the great Tīrtha well known as Siddheśvara on the southern bank of Narmadā was created by Siddhas.

The Tīrtha there is highly meritorious, the most sacred of all the Tīrthas. O great king, it is situated on the southern bank of Narmadā.

Men should take holy bath there in the Tīrtha and offer libation to Pitṛs and Devatās. If a Person should offer Śrāddha there with the Pitṛs in view, O descendant of Bharata, undoubtedly his Pitṛs are propitiated for twelve years.

A devotee should take his holy bath there in the Tīrtha and devoutly worship Śiva.

Keeping awake at night, he should read the Purāṇa. Early in the morning he should perform ablutions duly. Thereafter he should visit the Consort of the Daughter of the Mountain.

He shall attain the greatest goal. Formerly great sages beginning with Kapila, Siddhas of great fortune, performed the Japa of the great Brahman. There of great Vratas achieving perfection in Yoga attained the greatest Siddhi by the power of Narmadā.

CHAPTER ONE HUNDRED SIXTYSIX

The Greatness of Siddheśvarī Tīrtha

Śrī Mārkaṇḍeya said:

1-8. Then there is the Vaiṣṇavī goddess named Siddheśvarī. She is destroyer of sins. By seeing the excellent spot people have attained great bliss.

One should take his bath there in that Tīrtha and adore the Pitṛs and Devatās. He who devoutly visits the goddess is rid of all sins.

A woman whose dear child has died, a barren woman and one who invariably gives birth to girls, (after worshipping the deity) begets a son endowed with good qualities and good conduct.

A devotee should take his bath there in the Tīrtha and visit the goddess with great devotion on the eighth or fourteenth day, or, O king, it may be on any day.

A woman or man should take the holy bath at the confluence. The goddess (if pleased) gives them sons and wealth.

When visited and perfectly adored, the goddess accords good protection to the family. There is no doubt about this that on being adored she protects the progeny always.

A person should take his holy bath on the ninth lunar day, O great king. He should observe fast. With his mind purified with faith, he should worship the goddess with deep devotion. He goes to the greatest world inaccessible even to Suras.

CHAPTER ONE HUNDRED SIXTYSEVEN

The Greatness of Mărkaṇḍeśvara Tīrtha

Yudhiṣṭhira said:

1-8. O great sage, there is a Tīrtha on the southern bank of Narmadā distinguished with characteristic features. Do recount (glory of) this Tīrtha to me along with its origin.

Śrī Mārkaṇḍeya said:

Formerly at the beginning of Kṛtayuga, I lived for a long time in Daṇḍaka (forest) on the excellent mountain Vindhya endowed with all qualities. I was regular in my diet and other habits and the groups of sages extended to me the greatest hospitality.

I lived there very happily for ten thousand years. Then I took leave of those sages, O blessed one. I came to the banks of Narmadā followed by my disciples.

Accompaied by multitudes of Brāhmaṇas, I made a beautiful, meritorious spot as my abode. It was destructive of all sins. It abounded in people of various sorts, such as celibate religious students, those well established in the life of a householder, ascetics, recluses who had controlled their diet as well as their minds fully, saints of esteemed honour and devoid of lust and anger.

I performed very severe penace for ten thousand years and propitiated Lord Vāsudeva, the creator and master of all. Resorting to the banks of Narmadā, I carried on my Japa, Tapas and observance of vows.

9-14. Thereupon, O Yudhiṣṭhira, the two gods (Śiva and Viṣṇu), granters of boons, resplendent like (two) Suns incarnate, embellished as it were (accompanied) by Umā and Śrī arrived there.

I bowed down to the Lords devoutly and spoke these words: I requested the Lords, the auspicious bestowers of boons: "I pray for adherence to righteousness, O highly esteemed Lords, and excellent devotion unto you both. Let me stay here in this spot like a young man of twenty-five years, without getting old and devoid of ailments, undoubtedly along with the Devas."

On being prayed to thus by me, O son of Kuntī, those two Lords, Kṛṣṇa and Śaṅkara, became pleased, O Yudhiṣṭhira, to stay here and told me:

The Lords said:

Know that we are stationed here in this spot along with Devas including Vāsava.

After saying thus, the Lords vanished there itself.

I installed there both Śaṅkara and immutable Kṛṣṇa (Viṣṇu). I adored them with mental concentration. I felt contented (with my achievement).

15-25. A man who takes his bath there in the Tīrtha of Mārkaṇḍeśvara, whether it be Lord Parameśvara or Viṣṇu the Lord of the three worlds, shall go to the greatest region of Viṣṇu or Śiva.

A devotee should offer curd, milk, ghee, honey as well as Narmadā water, sweet scents, incense, splendid offerings of flowers and Naivedyas (food offerings) with full self-control.

With great devotion he should thus keep awake at night propitiating Viṣṇu. Remaining pure mentally and physically, O king, he should perform the holy ablution etc. The devotee should observe fast on the twelfth or fourteenth lunar day in the bright half of the month of Jyeṣṭha. The man devoted to Viṣṇu should carry out the adoration of the Lord. By doing thus he attains Viṣṇuloka and becomes one on a par with Viṣṇu.

A devotee of Maheśvara rejoices like a Gaṇa in the city of Maheśvara.

If a devotee performs with steady mind Śrāddha there with the Pitṛs in view, they undoubtedly attain everlasting satisfaction.

A Brāhmaṇa devotee should take his holy bath in Narmadā silently, with the mind fully controlled. He should perform Sandhyā prayers staying there itself. After performing the auspicious Japa, he should offer libations to the Pitṛs and Devas and human beings too duly.

Staying in front of Kṛṣṇa or of Mārkaṇḍeśvara, he should assiduously recite the Mantras of Ṛk, Yajus and Sāman.

If only a single Ṛk of Ṛgveda is recited he will derive the benefit of reciting the entire Ṛgveda; by reciting a single Yajus verse he will derive the benefit of the recitation of the entire Yajurveda; and by reciting a single Sāman the benefit of the entire Sāmaveda.

26-31. If only a single Brāhmaṇa is fed, it will be as though a crore of Brāhmaṇas have been fed.

A woman whose child is dead, a barren woman and one who successively begets only girls, should make the following arrangement. A Brāhmaṇa fully conversant with the principles of the Vedas, should repeat the Rudra Mantras duly. An auspicious Kalaśa (sacred waterpot) should be placed on the southern side of the Liṅga. Repeating eleven, times the Rudra Mantra (*Rudrādhyāya*) the devotee then pours water from the pot and bathes the deity. A woman who sponsors this, O leading king, obtains a sinless son destined to live long.

One who sees the groves of trees growing at the Mārkaṇḍeśvara Tīrtha, even from very far, is rid of such sins as arise from Brāhmaṇa-slaughter etc. So said Śaṅkara.

He who listens to this or reads it with devotion, O excellent king, becomes undoubtedly one purified of all sins.

In the case of those who read or listen, this brings about destruction of all sins. It is conducive to fame, long life and plenty of wealth. It is destructive of evil dreams.

CHAPTER ONE HUNDRED SIXTYEIGHT

The Greatness of Aṅkūreśvara Tīrtha

Śrī Mārkaṇḍeya said:

1-5. The excellent Aṅkureśvara Tīrtha is on the southern bank of Narmadā. It is endowed with all good qualities and is well-known in all the three worlds.

There a great Rākṣasa propitiated Maheśvara and became a Siddha. He propitiated Śaṅkara, the very life of the universe, the deity that transports a devotee merely when remembered.

Yudhiṣṭhira said:

Who was that Rakṣas (i.e. Rākṣasa)? O excellent Brāhmaṇa, what was his name? In whose family was he born? O sinless one, mention this to me in detail.

Those men who commit sins and who are turned blind due to ignorance, do see the world consisting of mobile and immobile beings, thanks to the people like you who guide them like lamps.

On hearing the words of Dharmaputra, Mārkaṇḍeya, the eminent sage, smiled and began to narrate that tale destructive of sins.

Śrī Mārkaṇḍeya said:

6-15. There was a mental son of Brahmā named Pulastya, O king. He was an expounder of the Vedas and scriptures. He was as if another Vedhas (Brahmā) in person.

The daughter of Tṛṇabindu became the wife of that learned Parameṣṭhin. Thanks to his holy communion, a noble-minded son was born.

Since the Vedas and Itihāsas along with the six Aṅgas, Pada and Krama (Pāṭhas of Vedas) rested in him, the name Viśravas was given to him.

On a certain occasion the great sage Bharadvāja gave his daughter with pleasure to Viśravas, O king.

He sported along with her like Indra with Paulomī (Śacī).

The Brāhmaṇa, the foremost among those conversant with the Vedas, sported with her with great joy (like Indra with Indrāṇī).

After some time a son endowed with all the qualities of a son was born to Viśravas. He became well known as Vaiśravaṇa.

With the guilelessness of a child, O Yudhiṣṭhira, he observed the vow of silence while granting freedom from fear to all living beings.

Mahādeva was pleased with him and granted him his own friendship and the status of Dhanada (giver tof wealth). Along with Brāhmaṇa-sages, Brahmā came to him and told him: "You will become the fourth of the group of Yama, Indra and Varuṇa, and attain Lokapālatva (guardianship of the worlds). After granting this desired Lokapālatva, Brahmā went away quickly.

On another occasion a demoness named Kaikasī left Pātāla, came to the earth and desired Viśravas as her husband.

16-25. O excellent descendant of Bharata, Rāvaṇa was born as her son. So also were Kuṁbhakarṇa, a great Rākṣasa, and the noble-souled Vibhīṣaṇa.

Kuṁbhakarṇa had two sons named Kuṁbha and Vikuṁbha. They were very great, O most excellent one among men. They possessed great strength and virility.

Aṅkūra, the most excellent Rākṣasa, was a great son of Kuṁbha. Emulating Vibhīṣaṇa in good qualities, he became the most excellent one among Rākṣasas.

On attaining mature youth, he came to know that his grandfather was a Rākṣasa. He became very much disgusted and performed a very great penance.

He performed pilgrimage to the four oceans, southern, western, northern and eastern, and came incidentally to Narmadā.

Aṅkūra, the Lord of Rākṣasas, performed a very great penance for a hundred divine years. Thereat Mahādeva, the conqueror of the cities of the enemies, became pleased. The Bull-emblemed Lord granted him freedom of choosing any boon. "O fair one, choose your boon. O devotee of good Vratas, I shall grant it."

On seeing Maheśvara, the god of Devas, standing before him as the granter of boons, he bowed to him again and again and spoke (the following words):

"O Mahādeva, if you are pleased, O Lord of Suras, if you are ready to grant a boon, grant unto me immortality which is very rare in the case of all living beings. O Slayer of Tripuras, stay here after my name by this boon. It behoves you to be always present here."

Īśvara said

26-33. As long as you adhere to piety, as long as you follow the advice of Vibhīṣaṇa with steadiness of the mind, this will be true.

After saying this, the Lord honoured by all deities went away to the Kailāsa mountain by means of an aerial chariot of lustrous hue of the Sun.

When the Lord vanished, the demon took his bath and sipped water ritualistically in accordance with the injunctions, O great king, and installed the excellent Aṅkūreśvara.

He then adored the Lord of Suras with scents, flowers, incense, garments and ornaments, banners, chowries, umbrellas and (saying the) auspicious words like *'Jaya'* ('Be victorious') etc. He eulogized the Lord with plenty of prayers pleasing to the heart. The Rākṣasa then went to the abode where King Vibhīṣaṇa was present.

He was suitably honoured with gifts and other honours. Treated like own brother, he stayed there with great joy.

He who takes his holy bath there in the Tīrtha and worships Parameśvara named Aṅkūreśvara shall obtain the merit of a horse-sacrifice.

The sacred region of Maheśvara begins from the pond known as Māṇḍavya and extends to the auspicious confluence of Revā and Āmalakī.

34-43. The Aṅkūreśvara Tīrtha is to the west of Māṇḍavyakhāta. A devout man should take his bath there in the Tīrtha and remain physically and mentally pure.

He should assiduously say Sandhyā prayers and perform the Japa, O descendant of Bharata. O excellent one among the descendants of Bharata, he should offer libations to the Pitṛs and Devas and human beings. Continuing to wear the wet clothes and observing silence, he should adore the Lord.

Listen to the meritorious benefits of the worshipper who duly observes fast on the eighth and fourteenth lunar days and performs worship (of Aṅkūreśvara).

There are Tīrthas and shrines over an area of a hundred Yojanas. It will be as though all these shrines have been visited by him. Thereafter he is liberated from sins.

After duly bathing there in the Tīrtha, Dāna should be offered to a deserving person with the Lord in view. It shall be everlasting in benefit.

It is said to be ten times more than that of Homa. The benefit in Japa is more than that. By observing fast, the benefit is three times more and by holy ablution it is four times.

One who renounces the world or casts off his life (therein) attains the region of Rudraloka from which there is no return for him.

Even worms, insects and birds that die there in the Tīrtha named Aṅkūreśvara attain liberation.

Thus, O king, the origin of Aṅkūreśvara has been recounted to you. The Tīrtha is endowed with all good qualities. It is destructive of sins.

Those who devoutly listen to this being glorified as yielding great benefit, attain the abode of Śiva. There is no doubt about it.

CHAPTER ONE HUNDRED SIXTYNINE

The Abduction of Kāmamohinī

Śrī Mārkaṇḍeya said:

1-4. Thereafter, one should go to a great meritorious Tīrtha destructive of sins. It was there that Sage Māṇḍavya became a Siddha. So also did Sage Nārāyaṇa.

Formerly service was rendered to Māṇḍavya who was impaled on a spike by Nārāyaṇa. By taking the holy bath there, O great king, one is rid of the coat of sin.

Yudhiṣṭhira said:

O sage, what has been mentioned by you is a mysterious story in all the worlds. That penance was performed by one impaled on stake has neither been seen nor heard.

Mention all this to me in the company of the sages. Describe the greatness of this Māṇḍavya Tīrtha with eagerness.

Śrī Mārkaṇḍeya said:

5-15. Listen, O king, to what happened on the earth in Tretāyuga. There was a highly intelligent king comparable to the Guardians of the world. King Devapanna was a person who had performed Yajñas and was always engaged in making gifts. He was conversant with all holy rites and fully conscious of what was performed (by all). Like a father protecting his bosom-born children, he assiduously protected his subjects.

Dātyāyanī was the beloved wife of that king. She was always amiable to him. With the sounds of her necklaces and anklets, she made the atmosphere resonant with jingling sound (*Jhaṅkāra*). O king, their mutual love increased day by day. The king ruled the earth full of wealth and equipped with vehicles and filled with elephants, horses and chariots. He possessed all good qualities but had no issues. The king was thus in a state where the perpetuation of the family had stopped.

He was overcome with a great misery. He became distressed in the absence of his own progeny. He performed holy ablution and Homa everyday, O descendant of Bharata, and continued this for twelve years.

He strictly adhered to the restrictions of holy vows and fasts along with his wives and propitiated Goddess Cāmuṇḍā, the destroyer of Muṇḍa, by means of many holy prayers and devout rites of adoration and meditation:

"O Goddess Vārāhī, O Cāmuṇḍā, O three-eyed goddess, be victorious, be victorious! O Brāhmī, O Raudrī, O Kaumārī, O Kātyāyanī, I make obeisance to you! O fierce Bhairavī, O Raudrī of great Yogic powers, proceeding through the sky! In the entire range of the three worlds consisting of mobile and immobile beings there is nothing without you."

Being pleased by the eulogy offered by the king the goddess spoke those words: "Choose a boon as you please, whatever may be in your mind. I have been devoutly propitiated by you. I am pleased and shall grant you the boon."

Devapanna said:

16-22. O goddess of Devas, if you are pleased, if I deserve a boon, do kindly redeem me who has become distressed for want of a male child. Cause the protection, continuation of my family. Save my dynasty.

Indeed houses of men without children resemble a cremation ground. His Pitṛs do not partake of food along with the deities and sages. Though I perform Śrāddha everyday, my ancestors appear to me in my dream as afflicted with hunger.

On hearing these words of the king, the goddess began to meditate. The three worlds consisting of mobile and immobile beings were perceived by her with her divine eyes. With the face beaming with pleasure the goddess thus spoke to the king:

"In the entire range of the three worlds, consisting of mobile and immobile beings, O king, there is no child of thine. Perform a Yajña with the Yajñapuruṣa (Lord Viṣṇu) in view. Otherwise there is no hope of a child unto you. The entire range of the three worlds has been perceived by me with my divine eyes."

After saying thus, the goddess went away and the king returned to his abode.

23-31. He performed the Yajña dedicated to the Yajñapuruṣa and thereupon a daughter was born. She was radiant, beautiful and charming unto all the people.

Such a lovely maiden could be found neither in Devaloka nor in Gandharvaloka. Out of delight she was named Kāmapramodinī by her father.

In due course of time she grew up and stunned the world with her beauty, sportive gait like that of a swan, excellent eyebrows and the downward stoop due to the weight of breasts.

She was dazzling in her earrings and other ornaments. She used to wear red garlands and garments with divine unguent. She used to be guarded duly by her female companions.

The necklace nestled in the middle of her breasts like a garland (series) of lightning streaks. She had curly hairs resembling black bees. She smiled sweetly and her lips sparkled like a Bimba fruit.

With her eyes extending upto her ears, she appeared to drink in the lovers. She seemed to attract Manmatha through the fragrance of the betel leaves mixed with camphor.

Her neck was like a conchshell. Her slender waist was ravishing. The nails of her toes were copper-coloured. The navel was deep and the front part of her buttocks was excellent. Her thighs resembled plantain stems.

She was wholly splendid with excellent rows of teeth.

She increased the delight of her parents, friends and others by her sports. On a certain day she went (to a temple) for the adoration of the goddess, taking with her flowers and incense and other things such as sandalpaste, agallochum, betel leaves, incense, bunches of flowers etc. She was accompanied by groups of her friends.

32-37. All of them took off their garments and ornaments. Placing them on the bank of the lake they went deep into it in the middle of the lake and began their lively water sports.

On seeing her sporting about along with her friends in the clear water, a demon named Śaṁbara came there in the form of a hawk. Kāmapramodinī who was in the middle of the waters was caught hold of by him. The wicked-minded one leaped up into the sky seizing the ornaments too.

O descendant of Bharata, while he was on the aerial path along with the lovely maiden, the earrings and other ornaments fell into the waters of Narmadā where the great sage Māṇḍavya was absorbed in meditation, O great Lord, in the great region of Nārāyaṇa with full control of sense-organs.

His younger brother who attended upon him had become very lean due to his penance and Japa. He meditated upon Lord Janārdana.

CHAPTER ONE HUNDRED SEVENTY

Māṇḍavya Impaled

Śrī Mārkaṇḍeya said:

1-5. On seeing her being carried away by him, all those friends of Kāmapramodinī came out from the water and lamented loudly.

All of them went into the palace and spoke in great sorrow: "O king! Kāmapramodinī has been carried away by a huge bird–a hawk, even as she was sporting about in the lake in the vicinity of the Lord. A search for her should be carried out by you by tracing the path of that bird."

On hearing the words of those girls, Devapanna was extremely distressed. "Alas! Alas!" He cried aloud getting up from his excellent royal seat.

Along with the ministers he went to the lake. Not finding out any clue as to the path taken by the bird he swooned due to great sorrow.

6-15. All the citizens too became miserable due to the king's sorrow. Presently the king was consoled by the ministers and the priests.

"What shall we do? What should be done at this juncture?" He said and had causultations with all of them.

Then he said: "I shall send to all directions the four divisions of the army with the full complement of elephants, horses and chariots."

Drums and other instruments were played and everything was in a chaotic condition.

The king equipped himself and the armies with arrows, iron rods, shafts, swords, axes etc. He was as if swallowing the skies.

Neither Devas nor Gandharvas, neither Daityas nor Rākṣasas could guess what the king would do to vent his anger.

On seeing it the citizens too became dismayed in the mind. There were fourteen thousand elephants with their drivers equipped with goads and hooks. There were eighty thousand cavalry men with weapons in their hands. O leading scion of the family of Bharata, there were sixty thousand chariots. The dust particles kicked up by the hoofs rose up high into the sky along with the sounds of war drums.

O dear one, in the meantime the guard of the city met the king with her ornaments in his hand. All the ornaments of the various limbs were there such as earrings, armlets, bracelets, necklaces, anklets, etc.

He reported to the king: "On searching these were seen by me in the hermitage of the sages where Māṇḍavya surrounded by other sages is present."

16-26. On hearing this report of the chief police officer and seeing the ornaments of the body of the princess clearly produced, the king became angry with reddened eyes. Looking at the ministers and the elite public he said: "Such a Brāhmaṇa is living in my city, who indulges in the activity of a thief! Under the garb of a man of holy vows, he is stealing other people's wealth. He must be a sinner in the guise of a sage by whom my daughter has been abducted.

"Assuming the form of a bird even as he was in the water, he went up into the sky. No sin is incurred if one kills heretics, a perpetrator of prejudicial (prohibited) activities, those who observe Biḍālavratas (hypocrites), rogues, flatterers, thieves and men of evil conduct. This sinner, thief and abductor of a virgin need not be seen (examined) by me in person. Let him be impaled on the stake immediately. There need not be any formal trial in his case. That wicked one is to be killed by me. He is a demon in the guise of an ascetic."

Saying thus in anger he commanded the police officer and went away. Without taking into consideration what should be done and what should not be done, he got the Brāhmaṇa impaled on the stake.

All the citizens and the rural folk were filled with tears in their eyes. "Alas ! Alas!" They said and cried. They told one another thus:

"A despicable act has been committed by the king acting like a Cāṇḍāla. A Brāhmaṇa should not be killed, especially when he is an ascetic. If any of his activities deserved anger he should be banished out of the city. Never should a Brāhmaṇa be killed even if he has indulged in all types of sins. He should be banished from the kingdom along with his entire property intact." O king (Yudhiṣṭhira), none of the citizens took his food at home; there was no fire even in their houses. All of them were gloomy in mind and unmindful of their domestic duties.

CHAPTER ONE HUNDRED SEVENTYONE

Dialogue between Śāṇḍilī and the Sages

Śrī Mārkaṇḍeya said:

1-7. In order to see the said Brāhmaṇa who had been impaled on the stake, all the great sages went to Nārāyaṇa along with ascetics such as Nārada, Devala, Raibhya, Yama, Śātātapa, Aṅgiras, Vasiṣṭha, Jamadagni, Yājñavalkya, Bṛhaspati, Kaśyapa, Atri, Bharadvāja, Viśvāmitra, Aruṇi, Muni and other groups of sages beginning with Vālakhilyas and the members of their family.

The eminent sages saw Māṇḍavya placed on the stake. They said to Brāhmaṇa Nārāyaṇa, "What shall we do to please you?"

All of them became agitated in the presence of the noble-souled Māṇḍavya. They came near him in great agitation and said, "Is he dead? Is he alive?"

On seeing his plight, they became excessively distressed. Unable to bear that sorrow mentally, they said: "Let him be asked. If he consents, reduce the king to ashes:"

On hearing this Nārāyaṇa spoke these words:

8-13. "Even when I am alive my brother has fallen into this plight. Fie upon my life! But yet there is the efficacy of the penance. On seeing my brother impaled on the stake, my mind is torn asunder. Yet I am going to do something wherby the entire kingdom including the king shall be reduced to ashes by me. Let me be pardoned by you all."

After saying this, he took water into his hand and charged it with incantations.

Even as he surveyed in anger there was heard a Huṁkāra sound. The sages were dismayed thereby. They were taken aback by the Huṁkāra sound.

Those excellent Brāhmaṇas went near Māṇḍavya and asked him, "O Brāhmaṇa, do you wish to withold the curse that is sure to kill the king by whom a sinless person has been brought to the verge of death?"

On hearing the words of the sages Māṇḍavyaka said with great pain:

14-22. "O sages, welcome unto you always. I salute you all

with my (bowed) head. Be seated here ye all who deserve Arghya, honour and adoration."

With fully concentrated mind, Māṇḍavyaka spoke to all:

"The terrible misery which I am undergoing is the fruit of what was incurred in the previous life. Do not feel aggrieved over that. Indeed the sin committed has to be borne (by reaping the fruit thereof)."

The sages said:

What is the act which results in one's taking up another birth? As a fruit of what *Dāna* or *Dharma* (charity and pious act) does one go to Svarga?

Māṇḍavya said:

Those who sustain themselves at the expense of other people's fortune and those who do not make liberal donations are reborn.

O excellent Brāhmaṇas, these people fall into terrible hell and are reborn as Cāṇḍālas: those who do not take holy bath regularly; those who do not practise Japa, Homa, worship of Suras, hospitality to other people, performance of Pitṛ Śrāddha during Parvas and also regular Dāna. Again they become very poor and again they commit sins. They stay on in Naraka as a result of the power of the sins. For the same reason they undergo the experience of being born in the transmigratory mortal world that is the primary cause of life. They are reborn as worms and insects.

Those who regularly take the holy bath, those who are devoted to Brāhmaṇas and Devas, those who have conquered the sense-organs, those who invariably take pity on living beings, live in the worlds of Devas. Those who are always pious and who have conquered arrogance and anger live with great delight. Those who are well educated and polite, those who do not harass others, those who utterly exclude other men's wives and remain contented with their own wives need not be afraid of anything in the world. They are innately pure and devoid of sins.

The sages said:

23-33. O great Brāhmaṇa, what was that sin committed by

you in the previous birth? Wherefore was this suffering undergone, the despicable fact of being impaled on the stake?

All of us have assembled here on seeing that you are impaled on the stake. May we see you alive safely taken off from it? Despite the sufferings due to the pain and distress, you seem to be not feeling it at all?

Māṇḍavya said:

What is committed by oneself is to be borne (reaped) by oneself. No one else experiences (the fruits of) either merit or demerit of the previous actions.

Just as a calf finds out its mother from among thousands of cows, so also the previous action comes back to the perpetrator himself.

No one can shake off the actions except by experiencing the good or bad effect thereof. Neither his mother nor his father, neither his brother nor his wife, neither sons nor friends, can be expected to experience them.

I have been asked by you. May my statement be listened to. O Brāhmaṇas, during my earlier years of life, I used to wait long during my baths at the time of removing dirt. Due to my ignorance and puerile nature, the lice were pricked with thorns. When oil was applied over my head and all over the body the lice were not retained by me. I used to comb my hair and prick the lice with thorns. Since sin was committed in regard to them, this result has befallen me.

After spending some more time I will attain unailing liberation. O great sages, you all need not be distressed at all. While experiencing this plight, I shall not curse anyone, nor sin against any one. I shall cause the sin to be wiped off by remaining on the stake for a few days.

O Brāhmaṇas, I shall bear the brunt of the previous action committed by me and experience the result thereof. The king's misdemeanour should be excused. Let the anger be dispelled.

34-44. On hearing the words of Māṇḍavya, the great sages derived great pleasure and esteemed him much and shouted, "Bravo!"

Nārāyaṇa said:

Where shall I drop this Mantra-charged water intended for the king's being reduced to ash along with his priests and the kingdom?

Māṇḍavya said:

Preserve this water which is comparable to Kālakūṭa poison. I shall get it cast off into the ocean. The time for the task of Devas has arrived.

Thereupon all those sages beginning with Kaśyapa bowed down to Māṇḍavya. Taking leave of him, they went back to their abodes with great delight.

Even as they were preparing to leave, they were told, "O ascetics, promise to come back to my presence on the fifth day."

"So, shall it be," promised Nārada and others. When those leading Brāhmaṇas went out of sight, the female ascetic Śāṇḍilī came there on the second day. She was carrying her husband on her head and wandering about at night.

She did not see the sage (Māṇḍavya). O Yudhiṣṭhira, she was staggering due to the excess of burden. The Brāhmaṇa on the stake was not noticed by her. The chaste lady faltered and slipped down against the knees of the Brāhmaṇa on the stake.

Due to the fall of the faltering lady much pain was caused to the sage. Along with the previous predicament caused by fate, the present situation became will-nigh intolerable. He said: "A further infliction of the fruit of sin ! Alas! My pain is great! O sinful lady, I have been further pained by you in a fruitless task. Why? I see you as a wanton woman wandering as you please. Are you a female thief or an ogress?" After saying this and lamenting again and again he fell into a swoon.

45-54. The sages and all the ascetics were agitated in their minds on being aware of the sufferings of the sage (Māṇḍavya). They then asked her, O Yudhiṣṭhira:

"Why do you wander about at night. What is it that you are carrying? Something weighty has been put into this sack. What is the purpose of your arrival here? You have caused pain to this sage, O lady, reeling in misery and going through sorrow after sorrow!

Śāṇḍilī said:

Know ye all that I am neither an Asurī nor a Gandharvī, neither a Piśācī nor a Rākṣasī. Understand that I am a chaste woman loyal to my husband and steadfast in my penance.

I am not overwhelmed with lust or anger, I have no enmity with anyone, nor am I afflicted by jealousy. I did falter and slip down due to ignorance and due to the fact that my eyes could not see properly. It behoves you to pardon me.

For the comfort of my husband, I carry him, as at day time he is troubled by his ailment. Please know that he who is always in the sack is my husband. I bear him, feed him, dress him as he is a patient. Know that this sage is the leader of Śaunaka clan and that I am his wife Śāṇḍilī. Please do not get angry with a chaste woman serving my husband righteously. Treat (us) as guest. It behoves you all to pardon me who have come near saintly persons like you.

The sages said:

Moving about at will, you appear to be unaware of other people's distress and pain. In the morning as soon as the sun rises your husbad will die. O low-born woman, only your own misery you know and not that of any other person.

Śāṇḍilī became chagrined at those terrible words. Afflicted with grief, she was lost in meditation for a short while. Then her eyes became red with anger. Staring at the sages she spoke these words:

55-60. "When a good person visits the house, he should be accorded the adoration due to a guest with gentle and welcoming words. It seems, I have come to the house of you good people in the guise of one committing an offence. This is the type of hospitality accorded to me by you all! The righteous conduct conducive to heavenly pleasures and salvation was not at all noticed by you. I am a Prājāpatyā (the progeny of a patrichal family) but you see me like a barbarous woman. May you and the deities in heaven see women's power in me today. My husband will not die. The sun will not rise. The entire universe will be covered with darkness. The night will not come to an end."

When these words were uttered by her, the sun remained paralysed. Everything fell into gloom. All Vaṣaṭkāras and holy rites remained suspended. There was no Svāhākāra, or Svadhākāra or the rite of five Yajñas. There was no Snāna, Dāna or Japa. All Sandhyā rites stood suspended. For six months the rites of libation and the offer of balls of rice stood unperformed.

CHAPTER ONE HUNDRED SEVENTYTWO

The Greatness of Māṇḍavya Tīrtha

Śrī Mārkaṇḍeya said:

1-7. Then all the sages and Devas with Indra at their head came to the meritorious hermitage of Māṇḍavya on the banks of Narmadā.

The courtesans began to dance to the tunes of the songs of the celestial damsels. Lights shone and conchs and Dundubhi drums were sounded.

Some people began to eulogize narrating the tales of the sage impaled on the stake.

Eighty-eight thousand hermit - householders assembled there with a desire to see everything. Brahmā, Viṣṇu and Maheśāna came there with great pleasure along with the Devas.

The Mothers beginning with Mallikā, Kṣetrapālas, Vināyakas, Dikpālas (Guardians of quarters), the guardians of the worlds, the excellent rivers beginning with Gaṅgā etc., came there.

In that pleasant gathering of sages and Devas, the king too came along with the citizens and the rural folk.

Some came there with great curiosity; some with agitated minds. Their minds were shaken with fear and they stood around.

8-21. In that divine assembly Brahmā, Viṣṇu and Īśa spoke: "O Māṇḍavya of great vitality, along with the Devas we are ready to grant you boons. After a great deal of suffering and austerities, you will now attain spiritual perfection. Request as you please, whatever may appeal to your mind.

Know that the whole world has become devoid of the sun.

It is in a confused state without Vaṣaṭkāras. All the pious rites have become defunct. Make it attain normalcy.

Further, O excellent Brāhmaṇa, we request for your blessings to Śāṇḍilī. See here, the king who has given you much trouble is present before you. O Brāhmaṇa-sage, grace (gratify) the entire group of people including the Devas and Asuras."

Māṇḍavya said:

If the deities are pleased with me and have come here along with Suras, they should stay here in this Tīrtha on all the three Sandhyās along with the sages. May my physical pain and discomfort subside forever with your favour.

The Lords of Devas said: "So be it." O son of Pāṇḍu, even as they said so, the demon came there taking the girl Kāmapramodinī with him.

He said to them: "O holy Sirs, formerly Urvaśī had cursed me and said,'When you abduct a girl, your curse will cease.' My despicable activity is actuated by the curse. This misdemeanour by one who is not highly learned should be excused."

After saying this he disappeared.

After he had gone the lotus-eyed girl was seen carefully by all the Suras. They had mutual consultation and then offered her to the wise Māṇḍavya.

They poured the sacred waters of Narmadā over the Vajraśūlikā (the adamantine stake) and took Sage Māṇḍavya off the stake to the accompaniment of auspicious shouts of "Be victorious" etc. Māṇḍavya the great sage, married the girl and offered obeisance to all of them (Suras).

The king who was nearby and who had been earlier scolded by all the people saying "Fie upon you!" now made all of them delighted. The Brāhmaṇas were propitiated by means of ornaments, garments and food and also with gifts of a crore of gold pieces. They were requested to forgive him.

After the marriage was over Māṇḍavya called Śāṇḍilī and said to her:

22-27. "Honour these Brāhmaṇas. Get the Sun release (from your curse). It is his mercy that dispels the darkness immediately."

On hearing the words of the sage, Śāṇḍilī said in her distress: "O Brāhmaṇas, if the Sun were to rise, my husband will die.

How can I get him released? That will be detrimental to my interest.

O great sages, what do I gain by urging (the Sun) to resume his movement? Is it your idea that I should be without my husband, without anyone to look after me? Ye all stand in darkness. I do not wish that the Sun should rise."

At those words, all the Devas, Asuras and great sages shook their heads and said: "That is all right, but, O highly esteemed chaste lady, O ascetic lady, listen to our words. If you honour all of us, carry out the words spoken (to you)."

Śāṇḍilī said:

28-36. All of you think well and do what will increase happiness. Do that whereby my husband will not die but the words of the sage will be true as well.

On hearing her words, they made the sage fall into a stuporous coma. Even as Śāṇḍilī was watching, he was made to vanish for a short while. All the sages then revived him and made his body free from wounds. That sage was washed with the waters of Narmadā and handed over to Śāṇḍilī.

On seeing her husband refulgent, she became delighted in her mind. She then bowed down to the sages and Devas. The bright Sun then shone all over the world.

All the worldly activities were resumed. The Devas, Gandharvas and human beings were all delighted and they went to their respective abodes and great penance groves.

The chaste lady stayed in that Āśrama along with her husband for a month. On being permitted by Māṇḍavya, she bowed to him and went to her hermitage.

When all those persons had gone, Māṇḍavya installed Lord Acyuta by the name Māṇḍavyeśvara. He was remembered as Nārāyaṇa too.

O descendant of Bharata, he worshipped the deity for a thousand divine years and then he went to Amaraparvata along with the groups of sages. Even today, O descendant of Bharata, the brothers are continuously performing penance and meditating upon the highest station (Being) with their selves under control.

37-48. One should take holy bath there in the Tīrtha and offer libations to Pitṛs and Devatās. By the offer of balls of rice Pitṛs become propitiated for ten years.

At the beginning of a fortnight a person should do the wiping and applying of plaster in the temple. By this smearing and application of plaster one gets twice the benefit derived when a hundred thousand cows are gifted.

By adoration, the benefit shall be fourfold. The merit of lighting lamps is cited as eightfold.

Those who bathe the Lord with curd, honey, ghee, milk or the waters of Narmadā become persons endowed with divine vision in the three worlds including mobile and immobile beings.

Those who adore Virūpākṣa or Lord Nārāyaṇa Hari by means of flower garlands and unguents, sport about in divine aerial chariots for a period of a Kalpa.

One who lights eight lamps on the eighth, eleventh and fourteenth days of the dark half of a month, does not see Yama.

Those who fill the Liṅga with various kinds of fruits move about by means of an aerial chariot and are served by Siddhas and Cāraṇas. There shall be bells and banners in the aerial chariot. So also flower garlands as well as befitting musical instruments. It will pass to the vicinity of Śiva.

He who builds, makes a temple of Viṣṇu, Māṇḍavyeśvara, is a pious-souled devotee and he lives in Svarga until all living beings are annihilated.

The devotee should feed Brāhmaṇas in the shrine named Māṇḍavyanārāyaṇa. If a single Brāhmaṇa is fed, it is as good as a crore of them are fed.

In the month of Āśvina, on the fourteenth day of the bright half, a devotee should observe fast and other restraints and keep awake at night. Rows of lights shall be lit in all the four quarters and the worship shall be performed in accordance with one's capacity.

49-59. Whether the devotee is a man or a woman he or she shall carry on the programme of music, dance and discourses. When the day dawns, O king, he or she should conclude all the rites such as the holy ablution etc. and see the deity thus in silence. The devotee shall be rid of all sins and is honoured in Rudra Loka.

Or in the month of Mārgaśīrṣa, Caitra, Vāiśākha or Śrāvaṇa

or in fact at any time, it shall be as meritorious as Śivarātri. Thus has Śiva told. The benefit shall be like that of a Vājapeya or Aśvamedha. Not otherwise.

A woman may be unlucky, miserable, barren or poor, or her child may have died. If she performs the holy ablution with *Rudraghaṭas* (? eleven waterpots), she shall attain all cherished desires.

Worms, insects and locusts that die in that Tīrtha go to Svarga and assume divine forms, O king.

If those who are afflicted with sickness die by fasting, drowning or by being burnt in fire, they will have that goal from which there is no return. Undoubtedly they go to Rudraloka.

O king, one who bows down to both Śiva and Nārāyaṇa everyday attains the benefit of the gift of a cow by the power of that Tīrtha.

O great king, if one makes a circumambulation of the temple, it is as good as if the entire earth including oceans and mountains has been circumambulated.

Outside the Mallikābhavana there are one hundred fifty Tīrthas. O excellent kings, that is the extent of the Tīrthas.

If a devotee ties round the holy spot, or the temple of Śiva or the Liṅga of Śiva a thread, he attains merit. Listen to it.

60-67. The entire earth has seven continents viz. Jaṁbūdvīpa, Śālmalī, Kuśa, Krauñca, Śāka, Puṣkara and Gomeda. The merit attained by the devotee tying the thread is on a par with that of one who embellishes the entire earth including mountains, parks and forests.

On the southern side of Revā near the Śivakṣetra there is the highly meritorious Devakhāta (a well dug up by Devas) prepared by the Tridaśas (Devas). He who takes his holy bath there, is rid of all sins.

The devotee should perform Śrāddha on a full-moon day, new-moon day, Vyatīpāta, transit of the Sun and Saṁgraha (immediately after the eclipse is over). He shall attain the greatest goal.

All the three deilties, Brahmā, Viṣṇu and Maheśvara, stay in Devakhāta along with sages, Pitṛs, and groups of the Devas. There in that Tīrtha, in the month of Āśvina, especially on the fourteenth day, Śaṅkara stands on the aerial path along with the Devas.

For two days, all the Tīrthas, rivers and oceans all over the earth enter Devakhāta.

In Māṇḍaveśvara, the devotee attains that merit which is normally obtained in Gayāśira, Prayāga, Amarakaṇṭaka and in Somatīrtha.

68-78. On the full-moon day in the month of Āśvina coinciding with Aśvinī constellation, if the devotee offers adoration at Māṇḍaveśvara shrine, he will attain the same merit as by pilgrimage to Lakuleśvara and offering of *Paṭṭabandha* (silk cloth offering).

In the Tīrtha named Māṇḍavya the same merit is eternally obtained as at Mahākāla shrine in Ujjayinī, Tripuṣkara in Vārāṇasī and at Sannihati.

After understanding these facts, O great king, and realizing that this Tīrtha is the most excellent of all Tīrthas, the devotee should adore the Pitṛs and Devas by means of holy ablutions, gifts, adorations etc. He should observe fast on the fourteenth day and remain pure. He shall adore the deity, Śiva, with great devotion and keep awake during the night. The deity is bathed with different kinds of ablutions, and adored with garlands and unguents of agallochum. In the morning of the full-moon day, the rites of holy bath etc., and the libations should be duly performed. The Śrāddha through *Havya* and *Kavya* should be duly concluded. Agniṣṭoma and other Yajñas are performed duly with requisite monetary gifts. The devotee shall wash himself of all sins by these means. The purified soul shall attain the excellent benefit that shall be on a par with the gift of a thousand cows, O descendant of Bharata.

There on that day in the presence of Śiva, after the holy bath etc., the devotee makes the gifts of gold, a bullock, a cow, a plot of land, a pair of bullocks, a horse, a pair of clothes etc. to a good-featured recipient with Śiva in view.

Sandals, shoes, umbrella, pot, red cloths etc. also can be gifted. The Homa, Japa and Dāna rites performed shall bear everlasting benefits.

Sitting in front of the deity the devotee should recite one Ṛk verse, one Mantra from Yajurveda and one Sāman from Sāmaveda. There is no doubt about this that he shall derive the benefit of the (recitation of) entire Veda.

79-90. Merely by repeating the Gāyatrī Mantra, he shall

obtain the benefit of the recitation of all the three Vedas. Through the adoration of Śiva one obtains benefit on behalf of a hundred crores of the members of his family and even more.

By means of the holy bath, Dāna, Śrāddha, keeping awake, singing of songs, playing on the instruments, etc. he will attain the goal of Śivaloka from which there shall be no return at any time. After a great deal of time, he may return to the mortal world. Then he shall become an intelligent king devoid of every kind of sickness. He will live for more than a hundred years with sons, grandsons and adequate wealth. He will remember the same Tīrtha and will get merged into Maheśvara.

One who performs Sandhyā worship in that Tīrtha during Parva days gets the excellent benefit of reciting all the four Vedas along with the Aṅgas and Upāṅgas.

O king, the Sin of Brāhmaṇa-slaughter shall be afraid to move about within a radius of the distance of an arrow-fall all round the Śiva shrine.

A devotee shall stand wherever he pleases and see the trees with eagerness to visit the Tīrtha. Even then he shall be liberated undoubtedly from the different kinds of sins.

There is a Śvabhrī (abysm) seen there, O great king, in the middle of the water. The story is mentioned in the Purāṇa that a female monkey (attained salvation) by resorting to the Tīrtha there.

O great king, there is also a well created by the Devas on the western side of Śiva.

This is an excellent Śivakṣetra. If a devotee performs the rite of Vṛṣotsarga (ritualistic dedication of a bull) at that Tīrtha, his Pitṛs sport about in the heavenly world as they please. If Vṛṣotsarga is performed all these sins perish as that of carnally approaching a prohibited woman, performing Yajña on behalf of an undeserving person, stealing, Brāhmaṇa-slaughter, cow-slaughter and slaughter of the preceptor.

One who attentively listens to the greatness of Māṇḍavya Tīrtha shall be rid of all sins. No doubt need be entertained in this respect.

CHAPTER ONE HUNDRED SEVENTYTHREE

The Greatness of Śuddheśvara Tīrtha[1]

Śrī Mārkaṇḍeya said:

1-5. Thereafter, O great king, a person should go to the highly splendid Tīrtha that destroys all the sins, on the southern bank of Narmadā.

It is well known as Siddheśvara (Śuddheśvara) and is destructive of great sins.

It was here that Maheśvara, the Lord of Devas, attained great sanctity. Earlier, O son of Kuntī, the Trident-bearing Lord of Devas had incurred the sin of Brāhmaṇa-slaughter.

Formerly Brahmā, the grandfather of the worlds, had five heads. For some reason, a lie had been uttered by him.

On hearing it, Parameśvara became furious with him immediately. The Lord then cut off his head with his fingers (nails). The severed head stuck to his hand and never dropped down. Thereupon the Lord of the chiefs of Devas roamed all over the earth.

6-15. Then he went to Vārāṇasī and the head dropped down there. Although the skull fell down, the Sin of Brāhmaṇa-slaughter did not leave him.

Thereupon, Maheśvara, the Lord of Devas, went to the oceans in the east, south, west and north. He wandered over all the Tīrthas. Still the Sin of Brāhmaṇa-slaughter did not leave him.

The Lord reached the excellent Tīrtha on the southern bank of Narmadā. After reaching Kulakoṭi, the self-possessed Lord uttered the prayers. After performing the expiatory rites, he became free from sins.

Then Maheśvara, the Lord of Devas, became rid of all evils. Granting that holy spot to Devas, the Lord vanished there itself.

Ever since then, the Tīrtha was glorified as Śuddharudra. It became well-reputed as the greatest eradicator of the Sin of Brāhmaṇa-slaughter in all the three worlds.

1. The story of Brahmā's head sticking to Śiva's hand is repeated elsewhere in SkP. The credit of freeing Śiva's hand from the skull is given to different Tīrthas in different Purāṇas. Here the author of *Revā Khaṇḍa* gives the credit to Śuddheśvara Tīrtha on Narmadā.

One should duly take his holy bath every month on the new-moon day and in the bright half, O Yudhiṣṭhira, and offer libations to the Pitṛs and Devatās. He should offer a ball of rice to the Pitṛs with the self duly purified, O king. The Pitṛs will become pleased with him for twelve years.

By adoring Parameśvara named Śuddheśvara by means of sweet scents, incense, lights and other things one is honoured in Śivaloka.

Thus, O king, the excellent Śuddharudra has been recounted to you in the manner it was heard by me from the Trident-bearing Lord. One is rid of all sins and one goes to Rudra Loka.

CHAPTER ONE HUNDRED SEVENTYFOUR

The Greatness of Gopeśvara Tīrtha

Śrī Mārkaṇḍeya said:

1-11. Thereafter, a person should go to the Gopeśvara Tīrtha on the northern bank of Narmadā, where, by means of a single bath, men are liberated from their sins.

One who takes his holy bath there in that Tīrtha and gives up his life shall go to the Palace of Śiva by means of a vehicle drawn by peacocks.

After sporting about there in Śivaloka for a long time, O king, he attains human birth here and becomes a powerful king.

The man shall be endowed richly with elephants, horses and chariots and fully equipped with male and female servants. He shall live for a hundred years, adored even by leading kings.

On the ninth lunar day in the bright half of the month of Kārttika, the devotee should observe fast and remain pure. He should then light lamps there.

After adoring with scents and sweet-smelling flowers he shall keep awake in the night. O king, listen to the benefit indicated for him.

He is honoured in Śivaloka for as many thousands of Yugas

as there are lamps. This is the fruit of his merit. Listen to the procedure of Liṅgapūraṇa.

Listen to the fruit of the merit derived by him who, at that Tīrtha, fills up (that is wraps around) the Liṅga with gingelly seeds, lotus flowers, and boiled rice mixed with curds.

O king, he rejoices for as much time as he desires, for as many years as there are gingelly seeds, rice cakes and lotus flowers.

Whatever is given as religious gift at that Tīrtha, O king, shall have crore-times benefit. It cannot be calculated adequately. Thus the most excellent Tīrtha has been recounted to you fully.

CHAPTER ONE HUNDRED SEVENTYFIVE

The Greatness of Kapileśvara Tīrtha

Śri Mārkaṇḍeya said:

1-6. On the northern bank of Narmadā, in the middle of the region called Bhṛgukṣetra, Kapileśvara Tīrtha is well-known as particularly destructive of sins.

The eternal Lord who is cited in the Purāṇa as Vāsudeva, the Lord of the universe, incarnated as Kapila.

There is a Pātāla (nether world) named Sutala. Beneath it is Nitala. Gabhastiga is lower down. Then Andhatāmisra is beneath it. There is the great seventh nether world where the ancient Lord Parameśvara resides.

He is Brahmā. He is Mahādeva. He is the Garuḍa-emblemed Lord (Viṣṇu). He stays there adored by Suras and Siddhas and expounders of Brahman.

O great king, even as Kapila, the preceptor of the universe, stayed there, the sons of Sagara perished in a moment in front of him.

7-11. On seeing them reduced to ashes, Kapila, the excellent sage, was extremely distressed. He thought that he had incurred sin.

'When the mind has been freed from all sensuous objects

and when every contact has been eschewed, it is improper on my part to have destroyed sixty thousand men.

A thing done cannot be undone. I shall, therefore, go to the Kapila Tīrtha that is destructive of all sins and get rid of my sins.'

Thereafter, Kapila, the excellent sage, left Pātāla, settled on the banks of Narmadā and performed a great penance.

Having become extremely disgusted (with worldly affairs), he adored the immutable Rudra by means of different kinds of vows and restraints, holy ablutions, Dāna, Japa etc.

12-19. He who takes his holy bath there in the Tīrtha and worships Parameśvara, shall undoubtedly obtain the merit of gifting a thousand cows.

On the fourteenth day in the bright half of the month of Jyeṣṭha, a person should take his holy bath as per religious formalities there and make gifts devoutly to a deserving Brāhmaṇa, be it very little or much. The benefit has been mentioned as everlasting by Śiva Parameṣṭhin (the Supreme Absolute).

Whether a man or a woman, one should take one's holy bath on a fourth or ninth lunar day coinciding with a Tuesday. With devotion, he should observe fast. For seven births he (or she) always obtains exquisite beauty, unparalleled prosperity, conjugal felicity and good progeny again and again. On new-moon day and full-moon day, one should offer balls of rice after taking holy ablution. The Pitṛs become pleased with him for twelve years and go to heaven.

If with great devotion anyone offers splendid light, O great king, the splendour of his body becomes very great.

In regard to the creatures that die there in the Tīrtha, their departure to Śivamandira (palace of Śiva) shall be without a return from there.

CHAPTER ONE HUNDRED SEVENTYSIX

The Greatness of Piṅgaleśvara Tīrtha

Śrī Mārkaṇḍeya said:

1-5. Thereafter, O king, a person should go to the excellent Piṅgalāvarta Tīrtha which is endowed with all good qualities. It is worthy of being liked and is a very rare (spot) on the earth.

A sin committed earlier, whether verbal, mental or physical, will perish by resorting to Piṅgaleśvara Tīrtha.

Śaṅkara has thus said that a holy bath and *Dāna* performed there at the Devakhāta (holy well dug by Devas) shall be everlasting in benefit.

After digging the well, auspicious water was taken up from all the Tīrthas on the earth and poured into it. Thus it has become the famous Devakhāta.

Yudhiṣṭhira said:

O excellent Brāhmaṇa, how was that Devakhāta formed? How did all the Suras pour the holy waters from (other) Tīrthas therein? O Brāhmaṇa, tell me everything. My mind is eager to hear.

Śrī Mārkaṇḍeya said:

6-11. In order to purify (cleanse) his Śūla (trident) Rudra wandered along with groups of Devas all over the pure earth with a water pot in hand. Then the Suras took their holy bath in Prabhāsa and other Tīrthas. Waters taken out from all the Tīrthas were put into a vessel by them.

Reaching (the Tīrtha called) Śūlabheda, the trident of the Lord became clean and pure. Taking the water from there, they came to Bhṛgukacchaka.

There they saw the tawny-eyed sickly Agni engaged in a severe penance meditating on Maheśvara.

Due to the parts of the Havis offered by Brāhmaṇas and kings, he became dyspeptic and distresssed with many ailments. On seeing Agni, the mouth of Devas, thus the Devas collectively said to Lord Śaṅkara, the benefactor of the worlds:

The Devas said:

12. O Śaṁbhu, may it please you to bless the tawny-eyed, dyspeptic Agni. O Maheśvara, do something whereby his body becomes rid of sickness and capable of receiving Havis offerings again.

Īśvara said:

13. O Suras, I am delighted with his penance. Further, particularly due to your pleading (for him) I shall grant the desired boon.

Piṅgala said:

14. O Lord of Devas, if you are pleased, if the desired thing is to be granted, do stay here with a sixteenth portion after making the Moon and the Sun your eyes.

Further, O Śaṅkara, do that whereby my body will be rejuvenated. O Virūpākṣa, obeisance to you again and again.

Mārkaṇḍeya said:

15. Thereupon Śaṁbhu, Śaṅkara adopted the form of Āditya and removed his ailment.

16-18. Then, when he (Piṅgala) was rejuvenated he addressed Śaṅkara: "O Śaṁbhu, do stay here itself. So also let Bhāskara himself stay here for helping living beings and quelling ailments, for destroying sins and for augmentation of welfare." On being told thus by the noble-souled Piṅgala (Agni), the Lord incarnated and spoke to the Devas thus:

Īśvara said:

19-29. To the north of my shrine dig a splendid well (Devakhāta) and pour into it the water that has been brought from the Tīrthas. Let the water that is capable of destroying all ailments be deposited there. Let this divine water that quells all sins be put there by all the Suras and others.

On being told thus, the thirty-three crores of Devas dug a deep abysmal pit on the north and poured the water from the Tīrthas therein.

All of them with Lord Virūpākṣa (Śiva) as the leader said collectively : "Whoever may he be, a person should take his holy bath after holding a bit of the earth from Devakhāta. On a Sunday, the holy bath is to be performed in the waters of Narmadā. Then he should perform Śrāddha unto the Pitṛs and make monetary gifts in accordance with his capacity. Thus the devotee should adore Piṅgeśa. He will stay in heaven.

What was uttered by the Suras the entire world heard.

"All the ailments of men such as tuberculosis, itching scabies, all types of ailments arising from hiccup, bronchitis and fever, different types of fevers occurring everyday, on alternate days, once in three or four days, fevers arising from attacks by ghosts, cutaneous eruptions, jaundice and other defects perish in seven days due to the holy baths on Sundays. Different kinds of leprosy can be quelled by taking the holy bath on one hundred eight Sundays. After adoring Śaṅkara, the devotee makes the gift of a pot of gingelly seeds to a Brāhmaṇa. Leprosy becomes quelled like serpents by Garuḍa." After saying thus all the Devas went to heaven.

Śrī Māvkaṇḍeya said:

30-33. One should always take one's bath in Devakhātas, lakes, rivers etc. The man becomes rid of sins.

The benefit of the bath in Devakhāta is superior to that of the bath in sixty-six thousand Tīrthas.

O king, one who takes his bath in Devakhātas, offers libations to Pitṛs and worships the excellent Piṅgaleśvara, the Lord of the chiefs of Devas, O descendant of Bharata, obtains the benefit of both horse-sacrifice and Vājapeya. There is no doubt about it.

CHAPTER ONE HUNDRED SEVENTYSEVEN

The Greatness of Bhūtīśvara Tīrtha[1]

Śrī Mārkaṇḍeya said:

1-8. Thereafter, O king, a person should go to the Bhūtīśvara Tīrtha, the most excellent one among all the Tīrthas. Merely by visiting it, all the sins get dissolved.

At that holy spot formerly the Trident-bearing Lord of Devas sprinkled the holy ash on his body. Hence it is called Bhūtīśvara.

On a day of Puṣya or on one's own birthday star, and particularly on a new-moon day, a man should take his holy bath in Bhūtīśvara. Thereby he shall be able to redeem a crore of the members of his family.

O king, listen to the benefit cited as accruing to one who devoutly smears his body with holy ash there in that holy spot.

He is honoured in Śivaloka for as many thousand years as there are particles of ash sticking to his body in the temple of Śiva.

Bhasmasnāna (bathing in i.e. application all over the body of the holy ash) is remembered as the greatest of all modes of baths. It has been so said by ancient sages. It is mentioned in all the Śāstras as the most excellent thing.

This Āgneya (fiery i.e. with holy ash) bath should be taken once, twice or thrice a day forever. The devotee's sin perishes.

O leading scion of the family of Bharata, Vāyavya (pertaining to wind i.e. exposing the body to the dust particles raised by wind) bath is better than Divyasnāna (standing in the sun, divine bath). Brāhmya Snāna (bath within the Brahman–Vedic Mantra) is better than Vāyavya and Vāruṇa (dipping in the ocean) is better than Brāhmya.

9-18. Āgneya is better than the Vāruṇa, since it has been said so by the Self-born Lord. Hence with all effort one should perform the Āgneya bath.

Yudhiṣṭhira said:

I am interested to hear the nature of this Āgneya, Vāruṇa, Brāhmya, Vāyavya and Divya type of bath.

1. This chapter deals with different kinds of baths such as *Āgneya, Vāyavīya, Vāruṇa, Brāhmya* and *Divya* and decides that *Āgneya* bath (smearing holy ash all over the body) is the best bath.

Mārkaṇḍeya said:

Āgneya is the bath in the holy ash i.e. smearing oneself with the ash. Vāruṇa is the bath by plunging into the water of a river, lake or ocean. Brāhmya is the Vedic bath by sprinkling oneself with water while reciting the Mantra *"āpohiṣṭhā"* (RV X.9.1). Vāyavya is exposing oneself to the dust particles kicked up by cows.

The bath when the sun is seen (i.e. sun bath) is on a par with that in the Gaṅgā water. That Snāna is mentioned as the fifth one, the Divya (divine bath), O excellent scion of the family of Pāṇḍu.

Hence one who assiduously bathes in the Bhūtīśvara Tīrtha and adores Lord Īśāna becomes pure internally and externally.

Those who meditate on the greatest Pada (word, region, position) always at that holy spot, the subtlest one beyond the ken of the sense-organs, are undoubtedly blessed. That Tīrtha is the Tīrtha of salvation, the most excellent one of all the Tīrthas. Merely by visiting it, all sins utterly perish.

There, one should eulogize and adore Maheśvara. One gets a kingdom thereby. By *Japa*, the sins are eradicated. By meditation one attains infiniteness.

The Mantra for meditation: "Om, Śiva is the Lord of all Yogas, the Lord of all worlds, free from delusion and grief, can be known through the great knowledge; he is in the form of *Jyotis* (Luminary) with neither a beginning nor a middle; he is never produced. There is no word that can express him. He is immanent in all living beings."

O Lord of men, one who goes there to that Tīrtha and takes the holy bath obtains the benefit of an Aśvamedha Yajña. Men who expect salvation do not, Alas, know the Lord who is thus!

CHAPTER ONE HUNDRED SEVENTYEIGHT

The Greatness of Gaṅgāvāhaka Tīrtha[1]

Śrī Mārkaṇḍeya said:

1-5. Then, O great king, one should go to the excellent and highly meritorious Gaṅgāvāhaka Tīrtha on Narmadā in the vicinity of Bhṛgutīrtha.

There the highly meritorious Gaṅgā performed severe austerities for more than a hundred years observing a great Vrata.

She meditated on the sinless Lord Nārāyaṇa, the source of origin of the universe. O Lord of the world, that river meditated on the greatest splendour, the Supreme Ātman. Thereupon Lord Janārdana came there and said this:

Viṣṇu said:

O river born of the lotus-like feet of mine, I am pleased with your penance. O fair one, what do you wish from me? Tell me, what shall I do for you?

Gaṅgā said:

6-20. O Lord, I have slipped down from your lotus-like feet and naturally begun to flow. O Lord of the three worlds, incidentally I am being saluted by the heaven-dwellers.

King Bhagīratha, therefore, performed a very difficult penance and propitiated Śaṅkara, the Lord of the universe, the benefactor of the worlds. O holder of the earth, he thus caused me to descend down to the earth.

At the instance of both of you, I got down to the earth. Considering that I pertain to Viṣṇu all the people bathed in me. Those who were Brāhmaṇa-slayers in the world, defilers of preceptor's bed, those who abandoned their mothers and fathers, men who take away gold, men who slay cows, those who injure living beings, those who carnally visit prohibited women, those who eat prohibited food, an utterer of falsehood, those

1. Gaṅgā, the most sacred river, gets purified by joining (taking bath in) Narmadā at Śaṅkhoddhāra Tīrtha or Gaṅgāvāha-Tīrtha-syncretism between Śaivism and Vaiṣṇavism attempted here.

who commit breach of trust, those who steal the assets of a deity and Brāhmaṇas, those men who censure Devas, Brāhmaṇas, preceptors and women, those who are burnt by the curse of a Brāhmaṇa, those who commit suicide, destroy themselves, those who swerve from the righteous path but indulge in fasts, renunciation, restraints and Vratas, those who drink prohibited beverages, those who prohibit *Dāna* and those who are averse to the offer of Dāna to deserving persons, those who destroy the Ṛtu-cycle of their own wives, those who are not affectionate towards their parents, those who do not have pity on wretched ones and kinsmen, he who breaks bunds and embankments in fields, one who destroys the earlier pathways, an atheist, one who has given up scriptural studies, a Brāhmaṇa bereft of Sandhyā prayers, one who eats what is not offered in *Homa,* one who is never satisfied, one who indiscriminately eats everything, one who sells everything, misers, atheists, cruel ones, Brāhmaṇas who are ungrateful, those who indulge in calumny, those who sell juices (liquors), those who are deprived of proper occasions, the base Brāhmaṇas who enjoy women of their own Gotras and of other Gotras—all these sinners come to me and are rid of the series of sins accumulated by them. I am distressed as though corroded by the acidity of their sins.

Hence, O Lord of the universe, do something so that I will get happiness which I am denied now."

On being told thus, the Lord of Devas was delighted and he said to Jāhnavī:

Viṣṇu said:

21-29a. I shall always stay here with Gaṅgādhara (Śiva) as my associate. Enter Revā here itself in your own form.

O Triple-streamed One, come to my Sole (of the foot) and flow when you will be carrying the waters of Narmadā at the time of the flood.

In rainy season you will be completely filled with water. You will then overflow both the banks and reach me residing on the northern bank.

Then you will be flooding the conch held in my hand. That

shall be the Vaiṣṇava *Parva,* excelling a hundred other *Parvas* (auspicious occasions).

The holy periods of Vyatīpāta, Saṅkrama etc., cannot be on a par with it. It is more meritorious than the most meritorious. Even the two *Ayanas* (Transits of the Sun) are not like it.

O goddess of Devas, a man who touches the conch on that *Parva* and takes his holy bath in the mixed waters of Gaṅgā and Narmadā shall certainly effect the destruction of clusters of his sins. It is the most meritorious of all meritorious things; It is the most auspicious of all auspicious things, because it has been held by Viṣṇu. Hence peace emanates. The man should take his holy bath in Śaṅkhoddhāra and offer libations to Pitṛs and Devatās.

29b-32a. The Pitṛs will be pleased for twelve years. They will attain the fulfilment of all cherished desires.

If a devotee offers Śrāddha in Śaṅkhoddhāra in Gaṅgāvāha the Pitṛs dance in full appreciation of that offer of the ball of rice.

O Jāhnavī, a man should take his holy bath in Śaṅkhoddhāra and worship Bala and Keśava. By keeping awake at night he becomes pure.

What you consider as unbearable sins committed by the people of the world they can be eradicated fully by taking holy bath on that *Parva.*

After saying this, O most excellent one among men, Viṣṇu vanished.

32b-35. Ever since then that Tīrtha is known as the excellent Gaṅgāvāhaka. It is honoured by Brahmā and others as well as by the sages following the tradition thereof O descendant of Bharata, he who devoutly bathes in that Tīrtha is on a par with one who has taken the holy bath in the Gaṅgā Tīrtha.

In regard to the men of purified souls who die there in that Tīrtha, there is no return from Viṣṇuloka at any time. Their departure is ultimate.

CHAPTER ONE HUNDRED SEVENTYNINE

The Greatness of Gautameśvara Tīrtha

Śrī Mārkaṇḍeya said:

1-8. Thereafter, O great king, one should go to the excellent Gautameśvara Tīrtha that destroys all sins and is well-known in all the three worlds.

O Yudhiṣṭhira, penance was performed there at that Tīrtha by Gautama for a period of one thousand divine years. Thereafter Maheśvara was pleased.

Gautama bowed down his head and installed Parameśvara. Since Īśa was installed by Gautama, the deity is called Gautameśvara.

By propitiating Parameśvara there, excellent Siddhi has been achieved by Devas, Gandharvas, sages, Pitṛs and Devatās.

One who takes his holy bath there in that Tīrtha and worships the Pitṛs and Devatās and adores the great Īśāna is liberated from all sins.

Deluded by the Māyā of Viṣṇu many do not know that the trident-bearing Lord Maheśvara is present there.

O Lord of men, one who remains celibate, takes his holy bath there in the Tīrtha and adores Mahādeva shall obtain the benefit of an Aśvamedha (horse-sacrifice).

One who remains celibate and offers libation to the Pitṛs and Devatās and adores the great Īśāna is absolved of all sins.

9-16. The *Dāna* offered with devotion to Brāhmaṇas in that Tīrtha shall be of everlasting benefit. No doubt need be entertained in this respect.

O king, in the month of Aśvayuja on the fourteenth day in the dark half, a person should take his holy bath duly and offer a hundred lights, after worshipping Mahādeva with sweet scents, flowers etc. The man is liberated form all sins. After death he goes to Śiva's City.

On the eighth and fourteenth lunar days, particularly on the full-moon day in the month of Kārttika a devotee should observe fast, remain pure and bathe Śiva with ghee, Pañcagavya, honey, curd or cold water. That man obtains the benefit of all Yajñas.

Afterwards he should worship (Śiva) with devotion. He shall get the excellent benefit.

A man who worships Gautameśvara, with Kuśa, Apāmārga, Kadaṁba and Droṇa, Mallikā and Karavīra of red, yellow, white and black flowers obtains all desires.

One who worships with other flowers, according to their availability, regularly for six months shall obtain all desires. On death he shall go to Śiva's City.

CHAPTER ONE HUNDRED EIGHTY

The Greatness of Daśāśvamedha Tīrtha

Śrī Mārkaṇḍeya said:

1-8. Thereafter, O king, a person should go to the great Tīrtha Daśāśvamedhika endowed with all good features. It is destructive of all great sins.

After going there, taking the holy bath and worshipping Īśvara, a man derives the benefit of ten horse-sacrifices.

Yudhiṣṭhira said:

Aśvamedha is a great Yajña requiring many requisite things and much wealth for distributing monetary gifts. It cannot be performed by ordinary men. How can they get the benefit thereof? What has been mentioned by you is very astonishing. Do tell me in such a way as to create credence in me and impart to me longevity of life.

Śrī Mārkaṇḍeya said:

This is indeed astonishing. The Three-eyed Lord was asked the same by Gaurī. Even as you have cleverly put the question, I shall recount it to you.

Formerly, seated on his bull, Śaṅkara, the Lord of Devas, accompained by Umā, was roaming about on the earth. He reached the banks of Narmadā.

On seeing the Daśāśvamedhika Tīrtha the three-eyed Maheśvara reverently joined the palms facing the Tīrtha and made obeisance.

On seeing the Lord with palms joined in reverence, the goddess said thus:

The Devī said:

9-18a. What is this, O Lord of the chiefs of Devas bowed down to by mobile and immobile beings? You appear to be endowed with great devotion with palms joined in reverence and head bowing down. This is a great surprise without a parallel. O Lord, tell me everything.

Īśvara said:

See the benefit from the Tīrtha directly. Do not be surprised. Even as I remain on the ground watch me steadily remaining in the air itself.

After saying this, the Lord of Devas became a fair-complexioned Brāhmaṇa. He was completely dried up with the veins visible on the body everywhere. He had matted hair and he appeared emaciated due to hunger with the throat parched.

He sat on bare ground and repeated Vedic Mantras in a sweet tone. Mahādeva, fond of Krama Pāṭha (a mode of Vedic recitation) delighted everyone with the sweetness of his voice.

On hearing that sweet voice of the Deva Brāhmaṇas who had all come there for their baths became agitated and confused.

Everyone forgot his own daily routine due to the confusion created by what they heard. On seeing him going on with his recitation though afflicted by hunger and thirst, a certain Brāhmaṇa, invited him for food with great devotion: "O Brāhmaṇa, may you be pleased to take your food in my house. Today my life has become fruitful. Today all my sacred rites have become fruitful. All my delighted grandfathers will grant me my cherished desires if you take food, O excellent Brāhmaṇa. Be pleased with me certainly."

18b-28. On being told thus, Mahādeva who was in the guise of a Brāhmaṇa laughed and replied in sweet words to the Brāhmaṇa:

"Penance was performed by me for a thousand years without food. Now, O excellent Brāhmaṇa, I will take food in the house of that person by whom ten horse-sacrifices have been performed and Pāraṇā (ritualistic breaking of the fast) as well."

On being told thus by the Lord of Devas, the Brāhmaṇa became surprised. He shook his head and went away to his house.

Thus when the invitation was not accepted many Brāhmaṇas turned away. Many *Nāstikas* (non-believers) who did not know the implication of the Purāṇa, went away.

Ultimately a certain Brāhmaṇa who was highly learned and conversant with the sense of the Purāṇa and the reality thereof, invited Śiva in the form of a Brāhmaṇa.

He was also told the same thing by the Lord. He mentally reflected on the meanings of the Purāṇa. The excellent Brāhmaṇa decided thus: 'What has been mentioned in the Smṛtis, Vedas and Purāṇas should be really so' and said to the Brāhmaṇa laughingly: "O Brāhmaṇa, wait till I return." Saying this, the Brāhmaṇa went to the great Daśāśvamedhika Tīrtha. Holy bath, *Mahālambhana* (the great seizing, touching, killing etc.) rite etc. were performed by that Brāhmaṇa. Japa, Śrāddha, Dāna etc. were performed in accordance with the pious rites. He then performed the Saṁkalpa of a Kapilā (tawny cow intended for Dāna) and hastened to the place where the other Brāhmaṇa was waiting.

29-38. After coming there he said to the Brāhmaṇa: "The horse-sacrifice has been performed by me. Get up. Let us go to our beautifull house for taking food."

On being told thus by that Brāhmaṇa, Śaṅkara became surprised. The Lord said to the Brāhmaṇa: "You went from this place just now, O excellent Brāhmaṇa: How were the stipulated ten Yajñas involving great amount of money performed?"

The Brāhmaṇa said:

You need not worry. Undoubtedly the Yajñas have been performed.

If the Vedas are valid and also Brāhmaṇas are Devas on the earth, if the Daśāśvamedhika Tīrtha is real, O excellent Brāhmaṇa, if what has been stated in the Vedas and Purāṇas shall happen undoubtedly, then everything has been attained by me. No doubt need be entertained in this respect.

* * *

On being told thus, the Lord of Devas pondered over his faith and belief in his mind but did not say anything by way of reply.

He went to his beautiful house reciting the eternal Vedic passages. On reaching the house, the local Brāhmaṇa adored the other Brāhmaṇa (Śiva) devoutly with *Pādya* and *Arghya*. Afterwards a good meal with dishes of all the six tastes was also given by him duly.

Then when Mahādeva, identical with all the Devas (Śiva wholly consisting of all the Devas) finished his meal, a shower of flowers fell on his head from the firmament. On observing his faith and belief, Śaṅkara became pleased and said:

Īśvara said:

O excellent Brāhmaṇa, tell me, I am the bestower of boons. What shall be done for you? Certainly even that which cannot be given ordinarily, I shall give you who are single-minded.

The Brāhmaṇa said:

39-49. O Lord, if you are pleased with me, if a boon has to be granted to me, O Mahādeva, you will have to stay in this Tīrtha always for helping (the world). O Lord of Devas, this shall be an ideal boon unto me.

After saying so, the excellent Brāhmaṇa climbed on to an aerial chariot that could grant all desires (that could be loved by all) and that was fully crowded with Gandharvas and Apsarās. Being eulogized he went to that place where all the people were free from ailments.

Mārkaṇḍeya said:

On seeing this unprecedented miracle, the goddess was extremely surprised. With the eyes beaming with wonder, she asked Śaṅkara:

Pārvatī said:

How can this be true? Why, this is unreasonable? O Maheśvara, many do bathe here. Do they go to Svarga like this Brāhmaṇa who has gone to heaven now? How did this happen? Tell me, great is my surprise.

On hearing this, the Lord of Devas laughingly said to her: "None should express incredulous surprise in regard to a Vedic passage, the meaning of the Purāṇa, the idea conveyed by a Smṛti and the utterance of a Brāhmaṇa. It is a valid means of testimony. If some people take up only one of the sides (regarding it doubtful) and consider what is sung about in the Purāṇa as impossible, O Pārvatī, they will not get Siddhi. There is nothing surprising.

If the people are non-believers, if they break the bounds of decorum and convention, they will never have Siddhi. If there is belief, if there is faith, it will certainly happen."

After hearing this narration, the goddess bowed down to the excellent Tīrtha that is established on Narmadā, that is meritorious and destructive of great sins.

Śrī Mārkaṇḍeya said:

50-59. O great king, Daśāśvamedha is the most excellent one of all excellent Tīrthas. It possesses all good qualities. It is destructive of great sins.

Sarasvatī is a meritorious river. It is the foremost one of all meritorious rivers. It is the most excellent one among all rivers.

Merely by means of its name one is rid of all sins. Those who take their holy bath in it, go to heaven. Those who die therein, are not reborn.

That river Sarasvatī too comes to Daśāśvamedha with a desire to have the holy bath. O king, she observes the vow of Brahmacarya. By propitiating the Lord of Devas, she attains the greatest relief in salvation.

In order to wash off the sins accumulated in the course of a year, the river born of Brahmā comes here on the tenth day in the month of Āśvina.

After observing fast for the night and worshipping the Slayer of Tripura, she becomes free from sins and on the morrow attains the eternal region.

Yudhiṣṭhira said:

Sarasvatī, the most excellent one of all the rivers, the highly meritorious river, comes once a year to Daśāśvamedha in order to bathe. Will the Tīrtha have some special effect on Daśamī (tenth) day?

Śrī Mārkaṇḍeya said:

O king, in the month of Aśvayuja on the tenth day, it becomes augmented (in sanctifying power). In all the Tīrthas of the earth, it is the most perfect one.

In Daśāśvamedhika, O king, Daśamī (tenth lunar day) is always auspicious. Especially in the Āśvina month, the tenth day of the bright half is destructive of great sins.

On that day, a devotēe should be engaged in the observance of fast after taking the holy bath and worship Devas. After performing the Śrāddha rite in accordance with the injunctions, he should worship Śiva.

60-70. He should also adore the divine river Sarasvatī present there and desirous of taking the holy bath (and address): "Obeisance, obeisance to you, O goddess of Devas, born of the body of Brahmā! O divine river, destroy the sins. Redeem me from the worldly existence."

He should adore with sweet scents and incense again and again. After circumambulating ten times, he should encircle it with a thread. (A Kapilā cow should be encircled?) Without any ill feeling, the devotee offers the Kapilā to a Brāhmaṇa.

After gifting the Kapilā possessing all good features and offered along with the appurtenances to Brāhmaṇas, the devotee need not repent for his omissions and commissions.

Thereafter, he should light the lamps with ghee and keep awake for the night reading the Purāṇas, dancing and singing. He should worship the Moon-crested Lord by means of *Jāpyas* mentioned in the Vedas.

When the Sun has dawned clearly, he should take his holy bath in the Narmadā water and devoutly feed Brāhmaṇas and Yogins who are devotees of Śiva.

By doing thus, O king, he shall obtain the benefit of the Tīrtha perfectly.

A man who takes his holy bath there in the Tīrtha and worships Śaṅkara, obtains the excellent merit of the Avabhṛtha (valedictory bath) of ten horse-sacrifices.

With the soul purified by that merit, he goes to Rudraloka riding on a great (aerial) vehicle that is very splendid and that can go wherever it desires to.

There, the divine Apsarās fan him with chowries and raise auspicious sounds of 'Be victorious' etc. He thus sports for a long time.

In due course of time, he comes down to the earth here and certainly becomes a king who will scorch his enemies, enjoy great pleasures and be richly endowed with elephants, horses and chariots.

71-81. The *Dāna* made over to Śivayogins at the Daśāśvamedha Tīrtha shall undoubtedly be on a par with ten Aśvamedha sacrifices.

Of all Yajñas, Aśvamedha is the most excellent one. It is inaccessible to men of meagre wealth and more so in the case of men of sinful activity.

Śaṅkara has said, O great king, that though it is inaccessible to Suras and Asuras, it shall be attained through the holy bath and offering of *Dāna* in that Tīrtha.

Whether he is desirous of it or not, O Lord of men, one who dies there shall attain the status of a Deva. No doubt need be entertained in this respect.

O excellent one among men, one who enters fire there at the Tīrtha shall stay in Agniloka until the annihilation of all living beings.

O Lord of men, one who meditates on Mahādeva and gets drowned there in the Tīrtha, shall attain Varuṇaloka.

This is the statement of the Śruti that if anyone were to cast off his body in Daśāśvamedha in a heroic activity, his goal shall be everlasting.

Neither those who fall off precipices nor the staff-bearing Daṇḍin Sannyāsins nor Sāṅkhyas and Yogins obtain that goal obtained by persons dying in a great battle reverberating with the sounds of Dundubhi drums and conchs and having the banners chaotically fluttering therein. A heroic man who is encircled by enemies and killed by them but never utters a pathetic cry, will attain everlasting worlds as reward.

If one adopts life of a recluse (Sannyāsa) at the Daśāśvamedha Tīrtha, he will never ruturn from Rudraloka. O Yudhiṣṭhira, the merit accruing from Daśāśvamedha has been succinctly recounted with devotion (by me). It is destructive of all sins.

CHAPTER ONE HUNDRED EIGHTYONE

The Creation of Bhṛgukaccha (Broach)

Śrī Mārkaṇḍeya said:

1-9. Henceforth, I shall recount the details of the Bhṛgutīrtha, on hearing which a Brāhmaṇa-slayer and a man guilty of cow-slaughter are liberated from all sins.

In the Tīrtha there is a well well-known as Vṛṣakhāta. O great king, formerly a penance was performed by Bhṛgu there.

Yudhiṣṭhira said:

Tell me the reason why that eminent Brāhmaṇa lived in Bhṛgukaccha and attained great Siddhi after performing an elaborate penance.

What is it that is called Vṛṣa? Who dug the *Khāta* (abyss) there? O sinless one, narrate all this in detail to me.

Śrī Mārkaṇḍeya said:

O king, listen with concentration of mind. I shall recount everything in reply to this question, O great king, asked by you.

The sixth mental son of Brahmā, the excellent Bhṛgu, performed an elaborate penance in the excellent holy spot Śrīvṛta for a thousand divine years.

The excellent sage abstained from food and pleasure and stood emaciated like a dry piece of wood and a steady rock.

Once the glorious Lord of Devas came by that path there, riding in an excellent aerial chariot and accompanied by Umā.

On seeing the highly esteemed Bhṛgu standing there like an anthill, the goddess asked the Lord of Devas thus: "O Lord, what is this that appears here?"

Īśvara said:-

10-20. O great goddess, the sage named Bhṛgu meditates upon me and has been performing a very severe penance for a thousand divine years.

Once in a month he drinks a drop of water by means of the

tip of a Kuśa blade. O lady of excellent countenance, he is in this standing posture for more than a hundred years.

On hearing this the eyes of Gaurī rolled in anger. The goddess spoke to the trident-bearing Maheśvara, the Lord of Devas: "O Bull-emblemed One, truthfully you have been made well-known all over the world as Ugra (the fierce one). You are bereft of mercy, very difficult to propitiate and extremely terrifying to all living beings.

Tell me why you do not grant any boon to this Brāhmaṇa who has been meditating on Śaṅkara for a thousand divine years."

On being told thus, O tiger among men, the Lord of Devas laughed and said to the Daughter of the Mountain in a tone as majestic as the rumbling sound of a cloud:

"A woman is doomed through pride; a penance perishes due to anger; bulls and cows die by traversing long distances; and an excellent Brāhmaṇa perishes by partaking of cooked food from a Śūdra.

O Gaurī, this Brāhmaṇa is highly irascible. Hence he gets no Siddhi (achievement of perfection), nor will he get it in the course of ten thousand or hundred thousand years. O dear, there is no other reason. Anger has wrought a great havoc in him, though he is of such a (laudable) nature."

After saying thus, Śaṁbhu thought of his bull for a moment. Indeed this Vṛṣa (Bull, Nandin) is Lord Brahmā and Maheśvara in the form of a bull.

When remembered (by Śiva) within a moment he reached there and began to bellow frequently and said: "O Parameśvara, O most excellent one among Suras, what can I do? Why have I been thought of? Whose premature death shall I bring about?"

Īśvara said:

21-33. Go and infuriate the excellent Brāhmaṇa Bhṛgu, so that, Gaurī, the most beautiful woman in this world, may be convinced.

On hearing this, the bull went to the beautiful bank of Narmadā near the hermitage of Bhṛgu for attacking the excellent Brāhmaṇa.

By means of his horns Bhṛgu was held by the Vṛṣa and hurled into the waters of Narmadā. Bhṛgu became very angry. The great sage seized a big stick with his hand (and said), "I will hit your head with the stick in the manner you deserve as a beast."

O lady of excellent countenance, the tuft, the sacred thread and the cloth he wore were set right by him. Then Bhṛgu ran behind him and said:

Bhṛgu said:

O bull of wicked activities and sinful deeds, how can you go away after insulting me by making a deep pit with your hoofs?

The Vṛṣa bellowed loudly and made the Brāhmaṇa fall down.

On realizing that he had been felled on the ground by the all-powerful Vṛṣa, Bhṛgu blazed with anger like fire after an *Āhuti* (ghee offering) has been put into it.

O Yudhiṣṭhira, he took up the huge stick in his hand as though it was another Brahmadaṇḍa. The sage then rushed at the bull with the intention of killing him.

Seeing him rushing at himself that excellent Vṛṣa went to various places (to escape). In the eastern ocean he went from continent to continent, such as Jaṁbūdvīpa, Kuśa, Krauñca, Śālmali, Śāka, Gomeda and Puṣkara. From the east he turned to south. He travelled from island to island in the northern and western oceans. Then he went to the nether worlds, viz. Pātāla, Sutala, Vitala, Talātala, Tāmisra and Andhatāmisra. Then he went to the seventh nether world. Seeking the safety of his life, the Vṛṣa went to Bhūr Loka, then Bhuvaḥ, Svaḥ, Mahaḥ, Satya and Jana Loka followed by the Brāhmaṇa. He did not get relief anywhere.

34-43. After committing a sin, being induced and tormented by the force of lust and anger, no man can have relief or peace.

Thereafter, he sought refuge in Brahmā and Viṣṇu. He sought refuge in Indra, Candra and others. When he was rejected by all, the Guardians of world, the leaders of Suras such as Ādityas, Yama, Varuṇa and Māruta, then he bowed down to the Lord and said: "O Mahādeva, save me. I am being killed by Bhṛgu, the powerful one. O Lord, I am abandoned by all the people."

On seeing him fallen before his feet like a helpless orphan, the Lord spoke these words smilingly:

Īśvara said:

O highly esteemed fair lady, O beautiful one, see the state of the mental control of the Brāhmaṇa:

Pārvatī said:

If you wish to do something pleasing to me, do grant him a boon immediately so long as the Brāhmaṇa is not furious with us, O Parameśvara.

Then the Lord adopted his original form as the Trident-bearing One with the Moon for his crest jewel, Umā constituting a half of his body.

He said: "O excellent Brāhmaṇa, your anger has not yet subsided. Hence, O dear one, this shall be a spot of anger."

On seeing the excellent Three-eyed Lord, Bhṛgu knelt down on his knees and recited this prayer:

Prayer by Bhṛgu:

44-55. O Lord of the universe, I am afraid of Saṁsāra. I wish to submit something after making my obeisance to you, the Lord of spirits and goblins (or all living beings), the source of origin of the world, the bestower of prosperity and one transcending all fears.

What power has this mortal being to recount your good qualities? Even Vāsuki who has a thousand mouths cannot recount them.

Still, O Śaṅkara with the Moon as your crest-jewel that has rendered everything white with its clusters of rays, O Maheśvara, be pleased with me who am eloquent in my eulogy and am devoutly engrossed in meditating on your feet.

O Lord, you are Sattva, Rajas and Tamas capable of creating, sustaining, and destroying (the world). I am eagerly devoted to the refuge in you, O Lord of the universe. O master of the worlds, I am afraid of the worldly existence.

Yama, Niyama, Yajña, Dāna, recitation of the Vedas, retention of breath, Yogic practice—all these do not merit even a thousandth fraction of your devotion (devotion unto you).

The sign of those who have prostrated to you are seen clearly here in this birth, viz. the excellent Siddhis of Rasa (Mercury), Rasāyana (chemical product), Khaḍga (sword), Añjana (collyrium, showing hidden treasures), cavity and sandals (capable of travelling anywhere).

Even to that person who bows to you roguishly, you bestow prosperity, O Lord, as much as he wishes. The devotion unto you, O Lord, is destructive of worldly existence. Devotion (unto you) has been evolved for the sake of salvation.

O Parameśvara, save me, (although) I am involved with other men's wives, and assets, engaged in looking upto other people's faces and distressed due to the grief and misery occurring due to the harassment of others.

O Śaṅkara, save me who am elated due to excess of arrogance, who flaunt the momentary and transient affluence, and who have turned towards the wrong path ruthlessly. Hence I have sought refuge in you.

I am a wretched Brāhmaṇa. In seeking the boon my hope has not been fulfilled by kinsmen. O Maheśvara, destroy my thirst (for worldly things). Why do you deceive me who am already deluded?

Take away my thirst for worldly things. Grant me Lakṣmī (fortune) quickly who resides in your own heart. Sever the noose of pride and delusion. O Lord of Devas, redeem me from the worldly bondage.

This prayer is divine in origin and is termed *Karuṇābhyudaya* (Rising up of Compassion). It can yield all Siddhis. One who reads this and remembers Bhṛgu goes to Śivaloka when the body dies."

56-65. On hearing this eulogy (hymn) uttered by Bhṛgu, Mahādeva in the company of the goddess, spoke to the most excellent devotee, "I am the bestower of boon."

Bhṛgu said:

O Lord of the chiefs of Devas, if you are pleased, if a boon has to be given to me, may this holy spot be a Siddhikṣetra (a sacred spot granting excellent achievement and perfection) named after me.

All of you should be present along with Umā. Let this meritorious region be a Devakṣetra whereby everything will take shape.

In this spot I shall make a great shrine, O Lord of the universe. O Lord of Devas, let my desire be fulfilled with your favour.

Īśvara said:

This has been already done by Śrī formerly. Was it not known to you, O Brāhmaṇa? After getting the assent of Goddess Śrī and if she so desires, you may do whatever you please. What has been done by you cannot be otherwise.

After saying this, the Lord went away. Bhṛgu then had his holy bath and went towards Śrī. After breakfast the Brāhmaṇa stayed there with her i.e. Śrī. In due course of time, he said:

Bhṛgu said:

O fair lady, if this appeals to you, if it will not disturb your seat, I shall make myself an abode in the holy spot chosen by you.

Śrī said:

O Brāhmaṇa-Sage, make a splendid spot as you deem fit. I have nothing against it. It shall be in your name or in my name.

Bhṛgu said:

This Kṣetra stands on Kacchapa (Lord Viṣṇu in the Tortoise form). It is on his back, O Ramā. Invoke him and in consultation with him, make (the spot) splendid.

CHAPTER ONE HUNDRED EIGHTYTWO

The Greatness of Bhṛgukaccha Tīrtha

Śrī Mārkaṇḍeya said:

1-9. Thereafter, Bhṛgu went to the Kacchapa (Tortoise) accompanied by Śrī. After the customary obeisance and courtesies, he spoke these splendid words:

"The entire earth as well as the mobile and immobile beings are supported by you. Further, O highly intelligent one, you remained there with meritorious feelings.

I shall establish an institute of the four lores with the help and collaboration of Śrī. O Lord, if you consent to this, then give me the necessary directions."

Kūrma said:

Thus, O excellent Brāhmaṇa, there will be a city named after me. It will be well-established on me for a long time. It will be immovable and steady. O dear one, O fair-eyed one, you need not be afraid.

On hearing these splendid words coming out from the mouth of the Kacchapa, Bhṛgu, the son of the Lotus-born One, became delighted and contented. So also was Śrī. When it dawned he dressed himself auspiciously. O descendant of King Bharata, in the year called Nandana, on the fifth lunar day in the month of Māgha, in the splendid conjunction of Uttarā, when the lunar sphere was in Kumbha (Aquarius), on the majestic northern bank of Revā, the excellent Sage Bhṛgu made that holy spot filled with hundreds of palaces. It faced the west and the region extended to the north and east. It had a crore of Tīrthas and the holy spot altogether extended to a Krośa (3 Kms.). The sage who was endowed with the power of penance thought of Viśvakarmā (for assistance) and completed it without any delay in a short while.

10-22. The Brāhmaṇas were learned in the Vedas, the Kṣatriyas were protectors of the kingdom; the Vaiśyas were engaged in their avocations and the Śūdras attended upon the other three castes.

Thus the holy spot chosen by Śrī was highly delightful and pleasant. O dear one, this holy spot that is destructive of sins was made by Bhṛgu.

Thus is the origin of Bhṛgukaccha.

Śrī Mārkaṇḍeya said:

After a long time, for some reason Lakṣmī quickly went to Devaloka. She handed over the apartments along with the key to Bhṛgu, the expounder of Brahman in the assembly of sages.

(She said:) "Keep the place safely. O sage of good vows, keep this spot of mine."

After completing the tasks of Devas, Śrī came back once again. Goddess Ramā came to Bhṛgukaccha hurriedly.

Her own house with all the apartments and the things therein and the keys thereof were demanded by her. O son of Kuntī, Bhṛgu falsely denied everything.

O King, thus a great dispute arose, each claiming "This is mine", "This is mine." After a long time, Bhṛgu gathered a great congregation of the Brāhmaṇas well-versed in the four Vedas (four lores) for the sake of authorisation.

He said, "O fawn-eyed beautiful lady, this entire city is mine. The Brāhmaṇas well-versed in the four Vedas know it."

Śrī said:

O eminent Brāhmaṇa, undoubtedly all the four castes are my authority. Let the excellent Brāhmaṇas say whether it is mine or yours.

Thereafter, all the scholars discussed with one another, after surveying the place under dispute. Among all those eighteen thousand Brāhmaṇas, all those eighteen thousand abstained from making any decisive answer.

As they were afraid of the anger of Bhṛgu, ultimately this was said, "He who has the key in his hand possesses this."

On hearing this decision made by the Vedic scholars, the goddess was overwhelmed with great anger. She cursed those leading Brāhmaṇas:

Śrī Devī said:

23-33. Since with minds overcome by greed you have completely rejected the truth and my legitimate seat has been denied to me, listen to my words:

Learning will extend only to three generations. Wealth will not go over to the third generation. O Brāhmaṇas, a second Veda will not be yours even if read (your knowledge will be limited to one Veda). The houses will not have two storeys. O Brāhmaṇas, prosperity will not be steady; your pious rites are based on partiality and not on feelings for welfare.

One member of the family whose mind is overwhelmed with greed has been made the favourite. One cannot be true by setting aside the claim of the two.

"From now onwards, arrogance will be predominant in the case of all Brāhmaṇas. Neither father is pleased with the words of son nor son is pleased with the activities of father. Undoubtedly all will be swayed with arrogance."

After cursing thus, Goddess Ramā immediately went to heaven. When Lakṣmī had gone, the Devas and pure (sinless) Brāhmaṇa-Sages said: "This place is vitiated by anger and avarice."

On seeing that the goddess, the sages and the ascetics had gone, the highly powerful Bhṛgu was much distressed.

Once again he propitiated Śaṅkara, the slayer of Tripura, by means of great penance. O son of Kuntī, Maheśvara became pleased thereby.

In due course of time, he spoke thus to the delight of the excellent Sage Bhṛgu: "O eminent Brāhmaṇa, why are you distressed? What is the cause of your grief? Even when I am pleased, O sinless one, why should you have this state? Tell me".

Bhṛgu said:

Earlier Lakṣmī cursed all the Brāhmaṇas and went away. Thereupon, the Devas pronounced this spot unholy and went away too.

Īśvara said:

34-45. As has already been said by me, and it cannot be

otherwise, this is the place of anger. Listen to another point too.

The Brāhmaṇas hailing from that holy place with my favour, will hereafter be devoid of great fear. They will be masters of all scriptural texts. They will conclude the valedictory baths after observing the vows connected with Vedic learning. Even those hundreds and thousands who came here hurriedly (will do so). O excellent Bhṛgu, if a fool does not learn and gets involved in various miserable states to him even Śakra is not capable of granting anything.

This spot will be Koṭiitīrtha (having a crore of Tīrthas), destructive of all sins from now onwards, O great Brāhmaṇa, undoubtedly.

By my grace, it will be one frequented by groups of Devas. With my favour, even worms and insects that die in Bhṛgukṣetra will take up residence in Śivaloka.

A man who takes his holy bath in Vṛṣakhāta and adores Maheśvara, will undoubtedly get the benefit of a sacrifice called Sarvamedha (a Yajña without Soma[1]). If a man takes his holy bath in Bhṛgutīrtha and offers libation to Pitṛs and Devatās, they become propitiated and enjoy peace for twelve years.

Those who bathe Virūpākṣa by means of curds, milk, ghee, honey or water shall have their residence in heaven.

O excellent Brāhmaṇa, with my favour this Bhṛgukṣetra will be resorted to by all the Devas and will be on a par with Kurukṣetra etc.

If at the time of a solar eclipse a devotee makes a golden barley, places it on the head and takes his holy bath in Bhṛgukṣetra, O excellent Brāhmaṇa, know without worry that he is one who has taken his holy bath in Kurujāṅgala.

46-57. I will stay here. My beloved Aṁbikā, the goddess who destroys all miseries, will stay here under the name Saubhāgyasundarī (the beautiful goddess of conjugal felicity). I will stay with that goddess in Bhṛgukaccha.

After saying thus, the Lord as well as Aṁbika stayed there at Bhṛgukaccha.

Bhṛgu went to his city that reverberated with the chanting sound of the Vedas. Along with the sounds of Ṛk, Yajus and Sāman, it reverberated with that of Atharva Veda.

1. Monier Waliams (1186)

He who takes his holy bath there in the Tīrtha and ritualistically (leaves off a Vṛṣa, bull) attains Sāyujya (Identity) with Śiva. So said Śaṅkara.

One who takes his holy bath there in the Tīrtha and performs all rites in the month of Caitra, worships Saubhāgyasundarī and offers salt to a Brāhmaṇa or cows, plots of land and gold to many Brāhmaṇas uttering the Mantra, "May Lalitā and Śiva be pleased", does not become miserable or wretched. A woman does not get separated from her husband, O great king, by taking the bath in Bhṛgutīrtha.

O excellent king, listen to the benefit that one obtains, O son of Pāṇḍu, who daily visits Lord Bhṛgu along with the deities established there upto *Brahmasadana* (abode of Brahmā). He gets certainly the benefit of offering to a Brāhmaṇa who has observed all vows, an excellent, young, tawny-coloured milch cow of good nature and gilded horns accompanied by her calf.

O Lord of men, a mortal being who casts off his body by heroic act or dies by drowning (in the Tīrtha) gets the hospitality of Śakra for seven thousand years. If he dies in fire (by self-immotalion) he gets it for twelve thousand years.

This narrative is always conducive to fame, heavenly pleasures, wealth, progeny and long life. One who listens to this always during festivals with devotion attains everything. He will become like Ajamīḍha (a king of Pūru dynasty). One who adopts Sannyāsa (life of a recluse) in Bhṛgutīrtha, in accordance with the injunctions, will, after death attain the highest place which is extremely difficult to get."

58-65. On hearing this uttered by the Lord of Devas, the excellent Brāhmaṇa Bhṛgu became delighted with a beaming face and stayed there itself.

When the Lord vanished, the excellent Brāhmaṇa Bhṛgu left his *Mūrti* (idol) there itself and went to Brahmaloka.

O great king, O son of Pāṇḍu, the story of the origin of Bhṛgukaccha, the destroyer of all sins, has been succinctly recounted to you.

This holy spot has been proclaimed by the Lord as meritorious and destructive of sins. A day of Pitāmaha is remembered as being constituted by a thousand sets of four Yugas. O Brāhmaṇa, when a day of Brahmā begins the Yugas start. Rudra himself has mentioned that he who listens to this with devotion, whether a man or a woman, attains to the greatest world.

The holy rites a man performs after taking the holy bath in Devakhāta, such as offering balls of rice etc., O excellent king, are everlasting.

There is no doubt about this that he who devoutly listens to the description of Bhṛgukaccha attains the benefit of a crore of Tīrthas.

CHAPTER ONE HUNDRED EIGHTYTHREE

The Greatness of Kedāreśvara Tīrtha

Śrī Mārkaṇḍeya said:

1-8. Thereafter, O great king, a person should go to the Tīrtha called Kedāra. After going there he should perform Śrāddha and drink water after worshipping the Lord of the chiefs of Devas. He will obtain the benefit arising from (such pious acts performed at) the Kedāra shrine.

Yudhiṣṭhira said:

O excellent one among Suras (on the earth?), how did the Tīrtha named Kedāra itself come to the northern bank of Narmadā? Recount this in detail.

Śrī Mārkaṇḍeya said:

Formerly at the beginning of Kṛtayuga, Śaṅkara was propitiated by Bhṛgu at Bhṛgukacchaka. It was cursed by Śrī saying, "This spot is devoid of sanctity. It will be bereft of all Vedas." After saying this, O excellent king, the Beloved of Hari went away.

Bhṛgu performed an elaborate penance for a thousand years without taking any food. He took in air alone. He was reduced much and the veins were visible spreading over his body.

Thereupon Maheśvara appeared before him in the form of a Liṅga. Piercing through the seven nether worlds, he suddenly came before him. Bhṛgu saw the Lord like a bud of lotus.

He eulogized the three-eyed Lord Sthāṇu. On being eulogized thus, the Lord laughingly said again and again, "O sage, what for do you wish to request me?"

Bhṛgu said:

9-17. O Lord, this holy spot extending to five Krośas (5 x 3 Kms.) has been cursed by Padmā (Lakṣmī). After saying "This holy spot will become unholy and bereft of all the Vedas", the goddess went to heaven. O Maheśāna, please do see to this that this excellent holy spot becomes sacred once again, if you are pleased, O Śaṅkara.

Īśvara said:

O Brāhmaṇa, this Liṅga named Kedāra shall be the first one; including this there will be ten primordial Liṅgas. The eleventh one shall be invisible and it will be in this Kṣetra.

The all-pervading Lord Himself, the eleventh one, will sanctify the Kṣetra.

Similarly, by my grace the twelve Sun-gods (Ādityas) who remove ailments and miseries shall stay at Bhṛgukṣetra.

(In addition to them) there will stay eighteen Durgā-goddesses and sixteen Kṣetrapālas (Guardians of the Kṣetra), Vīrabhadra and Mother-deities at Bhṛgukṣetra. This Kṣetra shall become permanently sanctified.

One who conquers his sense-organs, takes his holy bath early in the morning in the month of Māgha and worships Kedāra for a whole month shall go to Śiva's place. O descendant of Bharata, one who takes his holy bath in that Tīrtha and performs Śrāddha with the Pitṛs in view, in accordance with the injuctions, makes his grandfathers pleased.

Thus the holy spot named Kedāra has been described to you in full details. It is meritorious and destructive of all sins. It dispels all miseries.

CHAPTER ONE HUNDRED EIGHTYFOUR

The Greatness of Dhautapāpa Tīrtha

Śrī Mārkaṇḍeya said:

1-5. Thereafter, a person should go to Dhautapāpa Tīrtha. It is in the vicinity of Bhṛgutīrtha. It was there that Bhṛgu was shaken (thrown in the Tīrtha) frequently by the bull (Nandin).

Hence it became well known in all the worlds by the name Dhautapāpa. For the sake of the pleasure of the excellent Bhṛgu, Mahādeva stationed himself there.

O king, even if one takes his holy bath roguishly at that place, he is rid of all sins. No doubt need be felt in this connection.

One who duly takes his holy bath there in accordance with the injunctions and worships Śiva, Devas and Pitṛs are rid of all sins.

The Sin of Brāhmaṇa-slaughter and cow-slaughter, O Yudhiṣṭhira, is always afraid (of the Tīrtha) and hence it does not enter there. Even if it enters, it is duly destroyed.

Yudhiṣṭhira said:

6-15. O excellent Brāhmaṇa, do explain this, that appears to be very wonderful in this world, that the Sin of Brāhmaṇa-slaughter cannot have access to the Dhautapāpa Tīrtha. There will not be a sin like that of the slaughter of a Brāhmaṇa. O Brāhmaṇa, how does it perish on entering Dhautapāpa? Do tell me in detail. I eagerly ask.

Śrī Mārkaṇḍeya said:

In the course of the earlier first creation, on seeing the distorted fifth face resembling that of a horse, of the all-powerful Brahmā, Śaṁbhu clipped it off with his thumb in conjunction with one of the fingers. As soon as the head was severed, he incurred the sin of Brāhmaṇa-slaughter.

Possessing the sin of Brāhmaṇa-slaughter, he remained on the northern bank of Narmadā. There the bull in the form of piety shook off everything and installed the goddess as Dhauteśvarī venerated by all the deities. Lord Śaṁbhu visited Goddess Durgā,

Dhauteśvarī, the destroyer of the Sin of Brāhmaṇa-slaughter. After the visit Śaṅkara, the slayer of Tripura, rested there.

He considered himself rid of Brahmahatyā by the power of the Tīrtha. Seeing the Brahmahatyā far away from the Tīrtha, the distinguished Lord of Devas was surprised.

He thought thus: 'The Hatyā is afraid of the goddess. Thanks to the power of her piety, the Hatyā will not enter Vidhautapāpa Tīrtha that is very much honoured. Brahmahatyā is like a dark-complexioned woman wearing red garments and red garlands and attracted by red garland-strings. She is desirous of catching hold of my shoulders secretly but remains far off due to the power of the excellent Tīrtha.' Thinking thus mentally, the Enemy of Smara decided to stay there in the Tīrtha.

16-24. After reflecting upon it many times, he remained there himself. He has become famous as Vidhautapāpa on the earth. He became a permanent resident of the place in the vicinity of Vidhautapāpa.

Ever since then, O great king, that Tīrtha Vidhautapāpa became established on Narmadā as a Tīrtha destructive of Brahmahatyā.

The ninth lunar day in the bright half of the month of Aśvayuja is of special significance there at that Tīrtha. In fact the three days beginning with the seventh day are important, O great king.

There is no doubt about it that he who observes fast and recites the Vedas called Ṛgveda, Yajurveda and Sāmaveda along with their ancillaries, during day and night, shall be rid of the sin of Brahmahatyā.

One who is guilty of cohabiting with a Vṛṣalī or wife of preceptor, becomes rid of the sin by taking bath in the excellent Brahmasaras with a potful of water.

A barren woman, a woman who gives birth only to girls, a woman having only one progeny and a woman whose child is dead, should take bath with potfuls of water. She will have living children and sons as well.

An illiterate Brāhmaṇa should observe fast and utter a single Mantra from Ṛk, Yajus or Sāman in the course of a Parva day. He should observe fast and repeat Gāyatrī, the mother of the Vedas, without repeating any other Ṛk Mantra. The great Brāhmaṇa should repeat the Mantra on the ninth day. He shall be rid of a group (series) of sins. Thus, O dear one, it is mentioned in the Purāṇas by great sages.

25-31. That Dhautapāpa is extremely meritorious, has been told to me by Śiva. One who casts off one's life in water or on the ground by means of fire, shall have the lustre of Fire-god and Sun. He shall be served by groups of Apsarās even as he rides an aerial chariot fitted with swans and peacocks and goes to the great place of Śiva inaccessible even to Suras. He sports about there as he pleases as long as the moon, the sun and the stars shine.

A woman who gives up her life in Dhautapāpa, O son of Kuntī, will attain manhood at the same moment.

Of what avail is too much of talk? Whether auspicious or inauspicious, whatever is done in Dhautapāpa has everlasting benefit, O king.

One can invariably give up food and sensual pleasures and (eating) fruit, roots etc., but one should not give up water.

One who does so, goes to R̃udraloka, Õ son of Kuntī. After enjoying all pleasures there, he is reborn on the earth as a king.

CHAPTER ONE HUNDRED EIGHTYFIVE

The Greatness of Eraṇḍī Tīrtha

Śrī Mārkaṇḍeya said:

1-3. Thereafter, O king, a person should go to the excellent Eraṇḍī Tīrtha. Merely by taking his holy bath therein Brahmahatyā is dispelled.

On the fourteenth lunar day in the bright half of the month of Aśvayuja (Āśvina), a devotee should observe fast and remain pure. After bath he should offer libations to Pitṛs and Devatās.

He will be blessed with sons, prosperity and handsome features. He will live for a hundred years. On death he goes to Śivaloka. No doubt need be entertained in this respect.

CHAPTER ONE HUNDRED EIGHTYSIX

The Greatness of Kanakhaleśvara Tīrtha

Śrī Mārkaṇḍeya said:

1-5. Thereafter, O king, one should go to the excellent Kanakhala Tīrtha.

As soon as Garuḍa was born, he worshipped Maheśvara and performed a penance for a period of a hundred divine years, O descendant of Bharata.

He was seen by God Śaṁbhu as having become emaciated by austerities and Japa. Thereupon, the delighted Lord Mahādeva spoke these great words to Garuḍa, the delighter of Vinatā, whose speed was like that of mind:

"O blessed one, I am pleased with you. O devotee of excellent vows, choose your boon. Even if it happens to be the most inaccessible thing in the three worlds, O bird flying in the firmament, I shall grant it to you."

Garuḍa said:

I wish to become the vehicle of Viṣṇu, O Lord of Suras, and also to have the status of being the chief *(Indratva)* of birds. It is my opinion that when you are pleased everything will come to me.

Śrī Maheśa said:

6-15. O dear, O sinless one, the boon requested for by you is very difficult to be acquired by living beings. The ability to carry the Lord of Devas, and the status of being the king *(Indratva)* of birds is very difficult to get.

The entire range of the three worlds is in the belly of Nārāyaṇa. All mobile and immobile beings are there. How can that preceptor of the universe, the Lord of Devas, be carried by you?

Indra was established by him alone (as the Lord) in the vast expanse of the three worlds consisting of mobile and immobile beings. How can Indrahood be accessible to another? Hence the extreme difficulty of achieving it.

Yet at my instance you shall become the vehicle of the Lord who has the conch, discus and club in his hands and who carries the three worlds. Undoubtedly among birds you will be the Indra (King).

After granting him this boon, Hara vanished.

After Mahādeva had gone, O king, the younger brother of Aruṇa propitiated Cāmuṇḍā embellished with skulls, the goddess who being the resident deity of cremation ground, was accompanied by many goblins. She was a Yoginī, perfect in the practice of Yogic exercise. She was fond of suet, flesh and wine.

Immediately after being meditated upon by him, she appeared before him.

The same Siddhi goddess as is present at Jālandhara (in Punjab), Kaulīna and the great Uḍḍiśa tract (Orissa) was wholly present in Bhṛgukṣetra, the holy Siddhakṣetra. 'Goddess Cāmuṇḍā remained stationed there in the Siddhakṣetra (holy spot of Siddhas).

She was regularly eulogized by sages and Devas for the purpose of *Yogakṣema* (acquisition and preservation of what is acquired). The delighter of Vinatā devoutly propitiated the Yoginī, O king, by means of Vedic and non-Vedic hymns.

Garuḍa said :
(*Eulogy of Cāmuṇḍā:*)

16-32. Oṁ. May the goddess Śrī Vīramātā Carmamuṇḍā resembling the pure spotless moon protect you all! Her throat is parched with thirst and hunger, (but) mouth is splashed with fresh blood. She is seated in the lotus-pose on dead bodies. Armed with a trident, she plays with various groups of goblins in her abode of cremation ground and has for her upper cloth a garland of skulls, dripping the blood of great heroes killed with her weapons.

May that Carmamuṇḍā protect you all. Her throat is parched with thirst and hunger. She is deformed and terrifying. She strikes terror into those who commit evil deeds. She chews the flesh of the departed (corpses), gnashing her teeth emanating a series of sparks of fire. Her tawny-coloured tresses of hair are tied upwards. Her body resembles the Sun. She wears hide of a tiger as the upper garment. She is bowed down to by leading Daityas, Yakṣas, Rākṣasas, Apsarās and Suras.

May that Carmamuṇḍā protect you all! She holds in her

fierce baton-like arms, Ḍamarus and bells that produce '*raṇa-saṇa*' and '*ṭam*' sounds. She, as the mother of goblins, bounces and leaps and generates wild gusts of winds like those produced at the time of the close of a Kalpa, which strike the loud Paṭaha drums. She is emaciated due to hunger, and her belly is dried up. She shatters and powders the flesh of ghosts with her sharp nails and produces boisterous laughter with the sound of '*ghura-ghura*'.

May that Carmamuṇḍā residing in cremation ground protect you all! She is refulgent with the belly caving in. She terrifies the fear of the distorted worldly existence. She is armed with a trident. She is Cāmuṇḍā crushing the necks. She appears beautiful causing the sounds of Jhallarī (big cymbals) generating jingling sound, when the skulls dash against one another. She terrifies all the three worlds with diverse awful sounds of '*kakahakahakaha*' and dances in the middle of the Mothers.

May that Kanakeśvarī protect me! She is absorbed in (smelling) the Kanakaprasava flowers; she is excessiviely refulgent and supports the entire universe by means of a part of her power.

May that Kanakeśvarī protect me! She is the goddess born of Himālaya. She reveals her form out of mercy. She is the beloved of Śiva and is attached to him (Śiva).

May Kanakeśvarī protect me! She is in the form of Padmā along with the Discus-armed Lord. She holds jewels within herself and is fond of Vasus. She is beginningless and is the cause of the universe.

May Kanakeśvarī protect me! She bestows happiness on those who remember her. She is Sāvitrī, Gāyatrī, Mṛḍānī (Pārvatī), Vāk (Sarvasvatī) and Indirā (Lakṣmī).

May Kanakeśvarī protect me! She is the supreme power and the greatest intellect. She creates and protects the universe always with her gentle and non-gentle forms.

May Kanakeśvarī protect me! She is the mother of the universe, the Māyā of the universe. She is the greatest creative power at the time of the creation of Brahmā.

May Kanakeśvarī protect me! She is the chief goddess that maddens and elates. She is the protective power of Viṣṇu engaged in the protection of the universe.

May Kanakeśvarī protect me! She is the power of Rudra,

who is the infinite one and blissful one. She is the chief goddess in the matter of the annihilation of the universe and is resorted to by Rudra.

May Kanakeśvarī protect me! She was earlier taken away by Bhasmaka along with the goddess of the Svarṇaketakī plant growing on the ridges of Kailāsa.

May Kanakeśvarī protect me! She displays the single emotional fervour as an *Abalā* (one of weaker sex). She appears to be afraid without her husband and longs for the powerful influence of her Lord.

May Kanakeśvarī protect me! She is interested in the protection of the universe. She is guarded by Kanaka (God). She is the mother of everything from Brahmā to a blade of grass.

May Kanakeśvarī protect me! She is the first power and she as Śakti enabled Brahmā, Viṣṇu and Īśvara to take up physical forms.

On hearing her own four-fold activity mentioned by Garuḍa, the goddess became pleased. Appearing in front of him she spoke these words:

Śrī Cāmuṇḍā said:

33-41. O devotee of excessive inborn strength, I am pleased with you. Choose a boon desired by you. O excellent one among birds, I shall grant you whatever appeals to you.

Garuḍa said:

With your favour, let me be immortal, devoid of old age, incapable of being assailed by Suras and Asuras and by others as well. I should be unconquerable. Further, you must stay here always, O goddess, in the vicinity of the Tīrtha.

Śrī Mārkaṇḍeya said:

After saying, "It will be so", the goddess who was eulogized by Devas went through the firmament accompanied by a multitude of goblins.

O excellent king, when the excellent city was established by Lakṣmī, it was dedicated to the goddess after getting her permission and assent.

Lakṣmī said[1]:

O goddess, my city should always be protected by you like a mother for the purpose of the achievement of *Yoga* and *Kṣema* (acquisition and preservation of what is achieved) and for the guarding through me.

Garuḍa too took his holy bath and adored Kanakeśvarī. After establishing the Tīrtha too there itself, he went to the excellent firmament.

He who takes his holy bath there in the Tīrtha and worships Pitṛs and Devatās, attains the benefit of a Yajña fully equipped with everything desirable.

One who adores Kanakeśvara with sweet scents, flowers etc. achieves Yogic power in Yoga Pīṭhas. Upon death, he goes to the Yogeśvara Loka with all auspicious things like the sounds of "Be victorious" etc. There is no doubt about it. He will be accompanied by the groups of Yoginīs.

CHAPTER ONE HUNDRED EIGHTYSEVEN

The Greatness of Kālāgnirudra Tīrtha

Śrī Mārkaṇḍeya said:

1-9. Thereafter, a person should go to Jāleśvara, the first Liṅga of the Self-born Lord. It is well-known as Kālāgnirudra and it is well-established in Bhṛgukaccha.

It suppresses all the sins. It destroys all calamities. It has sprung up for the destruction of sins in holy spots.

It has sprung up out of the compassion (of the Lord). In an earlier Kalpa, all the three worlds were overrun by groups of Asuras. Dharma (piety) became extinct, since all the Vedic rites became defunct. Celestial sages, ascetics and Siddhas, of course, retained their greatest faith. At that time a column of smoke originated from Kālāgnirudra as though issuing from the god of Death himself.

1. The portion hereafter is obscure.

From the column of smoke issued forth the Liṅga piercing through the seven nether worlds. Making a depression in the south, the Liṅga stood there itself.

There in the Tīrtha, O excellent king, there is a Kuṇḍa (Pit) from which sparks of fire arose. It was here that the sparks fell even as Śiva was burning the city (of the Tripuras). There the *Avaṭa* (depression) occurred. Thereafter there arose a spiralling column of smoke therefrom.

He who takes his holy bath there in the Kuṇḍa in the waters of Narmadā, performs Śrāddha unto the Pitṛs and worships the Three-eyed Lord attains the greatest goal in the world of Kālāgnirudra.

Any rite with some cherished desire, or an Abhicārika rite (of black magic), or a rite bringing about destruction of enemies or any rite for the acquisition of a progeny, becomes fruitful ere long provided it is performed in this Tīrtha here.

CHAPTER ONE HUNDRED EIGHTYEIGHT

The Greatness of Śālagrāma Tīrtha

Śrī Mārkaṇḍeya said:

1-6. Thereafter, O great king, one should go to the Śālagrāma Tīrtha at a distance of forty paces therefrom. It is adored by all the Devas.

It is there that the primordial god Vāsudeva, Trivikrama, the immanent soul of the world, stays himself with a desire for the welfare of all.

On coming to know that Bhṛgukṣetra is the holy spot of spiritual perfection, penance was performed by Nārada himself on the banks of Revā and a Śālā (large assembly-hall) was made for Brāhmaṇas.

The Lord of Brāhmaṇas named Śālagrāma was installed. Vāsudeva was installed for the sake of rendering help to the good.

In order to help Yogins, Janārdana, worthy of being meditated upon by Yogins, resorted to the banks of Narmadā in the form of Śālagrāma.

On the eleventh lunar day in the bright half of the month of Mārgaśīrṣa a devotee should take his holy bath in the meritorious waters of Revā and observe fast for the whole of the day.

7-13. He should keep awake at night after worshipping Janārdana. When the day dawns on the twelfth day, he should take his holy bath in the waters of Narmadā. He should then offer libations to Pitṛs, Mātṛs (Mothers) and Devas. Thereafter he should perform Śrāddha to Pitṛs according to injunctions. He should honour Brāhmaṇas in accordance with his capacity through gift of gold, cloth and food. He should then crave the forgiveness of those Brāhmaṇas and the bird-emblemed Lord (Viṣṇu).

Listen attentively, O excellent king, to the merit one attains by doing thus: During his life here he will never meet with grief and misery. On death he attains equality with Lord Murāri. He will dispel all great sins. Never again will he drink the breast milk of a mother.

One who visits Śālagrāma everyday after taking the holy bath in the waters of Narmadā that dispels series of sins, is liberated from sins such as that of the Brāhmaṇa-slaughter by the recollection of Nārāyaṇa.

Those who adopt the way of life of a recluse and stay there with miseries dispelled and contacts abandoned and meditate upon the fourth Pada of Murāri (Viṣṇuloka) through the Sāṅkhya way go there alone.

CHAPTER ONE HUNDRED EIGHTYNINE

The Greatness of Udīrṇa Vārāha Tīrtha

1-7. Thereafter, O great king, the person should go to an extremely splendid Tīrtha, where the divine Boar rose up holding the Earth.

Holding this Earth and shaking the terribly sharp-edged, curved fangs, he rose up. He alone is called the fifth Varāha[1], the bestower of salvation.

1. The five Varāhas are mentioned in vv 14 onwards.

Yudhiṣṭhira said:

How was Varāha the holder of the Earth, in the form of one rising up? Why did he adopt the form of a boar? Why is he termed "the fifth"?

Śrī Mārkaṇḍeya said:

In the primordial Kalpa formerly, O king, Lord Hari was lying on his serpent-couch in the Milk Ocean. He was deeply lost in his Yogic slumber. The pair of his feet were being rubbed and massaged by the two lotus-like hands of Lakṣmī. While the Lord of Devas was asleep, the Earth was distressed due to the excess of burden, O excellent king. She went to the presence of Devas and said, "I am distressed due to the overload. I (fear that I) will sink down into Rasātala."

On seeing this, the Devas too became sad. They went to the place where Janārdana was present. Through pleasing words, they eulogized Keśava, the Lord of the universe:

The Devas said:

8-17. Obeisance, obeisance to you, O Lord of Devas, O omnipresent Lord, O dispeller of the distress of Suras. O Viśvamūrti (having universal forms), obeisance to you! Save us all from the great fear.

On being told thus by the Devas, the Lord said: "What has befallen you? What is my task? Say, O Devas, do not delay."

The Devas said:

The Earth, the support of living beings, is sinking down, highly distressed due to the excess of burden. O Hṛṣīkeśa, raise her up. Stabilise the worlds in her steady position.

On being told thus by all the Suras, Keśava, the great Lord, adopted the form of a boar, consisting of all the Yajñas. He was terrifying due to the curved fangs. The eyes were tawny-coloured and the hair curly. Making Ananta (the serpent of that name, Śeṣa) his foot-rest, he lifted up the Earth by means of the tips of the curved fangs.

Lifting up the Earth with the ocean as her girdle, along with the mountains and forests, Lord Viṣṇu became *Udīrṇa* (rose up). He revealed himself in five forms on the northern bank of Narmadā. The first one was in *Korala* and the second in *Yodhanīpura.* The third one was of the form of a Liṅga deluding the Asuras. He is glorified as *'Jaya'* in the holy spot named 'Jayakṣetra'. (The fourth one) is called *Śveta,* O tiger among kings. He stationed himself for the purpose of sanctifying the universe. Since he has the lustre of the moon, he is termed Śveta. After lifting up the goddess of the worlds, he rose up from Bhṛgukaccha. Hence the term *Udīrṇa Varāha* for the fifth one.

18-29. Thus, O son of Pāṇḍu, the five Varāhas have been described to you. Seeing all these simultaneously dispels the sin of Brāhmaṇa-slaughter.

The eleventh lunar day in the bright half of the month of Jyeṣṭha is specially significant here.

On the tenth day itself a devotee goes to Ādivarāha. Haviṣya rice should be eaten as a light meal when the sun is about to set in the evening. He should keep awake at night in the shrine of Ādivarāha.

When the day dawns, he should take his holy bath in the waters of Narmadā. After offering libations to the Pitṛs and Devatās with gingelly seeds mixed with barley grain, he should make the gift of a cow embellished with all ornaments to a deserving Brāhmaṇa.

The devotee should be free from *Mamatva* (sense of possession) and from *Ahaṁkāra* (egotism) when he makes the gift to Brāhmaṇas.

He should then adore Lord Varāha named Ādi (the first). After adoring in this way, he should go to the Jaya shrine quickly.

Hastening to Jaya shrine he should repeat the procedure as in the first case. A horse should be given as a gift to an eminent Brāhmaṇa at the shrine of Jaya.

Gingelly seeds should be gifted at the Liṅga (third shrine) and gold at the Śveta shrine.

At the Udīrṇa shrine a plot of land should be gifted.

The previous procedure should be adopted.

O son of Kuntī, listen with mental concentration to the

benefit acquired by one who visits all the five Varāhas before the sun sets.

All the following sins will, O most excellent one among the descendants of Bharata, perish immediately like a heap of cotton in fire; the sins of Brāhmaṇa-slaughter, imbibing liquor, theft, intercourse with the wife of preceptor, associating with those sinners mentioned before, breach of trust of those who had confided, taking as wife a sister, a daughter or a member of sister's family, in fact all the sins committed from birth to death. All these sins of a Vaiṣṇava sanctified by all the five Tīrthas perish.

30-38. Sins may be as big as peaks of mountains, still these perish if Nārāyaṇa is remembered, and specially so if *Japa* and *Dhyāna* are performed.

The devotee should, showing great manliness, take his plunge into the waters of Narmadā. After visiting the five Varāhas and performing the Śrāddha duly, he should visit Loṭaṇeśvara between sunrise and sunset. He shall be rid of (future) physical bodies. So said Śaṅkara.

He immediately attains salvation called *Parameśvarī,* the one which is ordinarily inaccessible. If Siddhi is not achieved even after great manly endeavour, they say that the sinner may go to heaven.

If a person proceeds elsewhere but happens to be in the vicinity of the five Varāhas on the eleventh lunar day in the month of Jyeṣṭha, he should certainly stay there wherever he may be. The five Varāhas, Ādi, Jaya, Śveta, Liṅga and Udīrṇa should be visited by him.

It was on the eleventh day in Jyeṣṭha that the powerful Lord Viṣṇu assumed the Varāha form and lifted up the Earth. Hence it is more meritorious than the most meritorious and destructive of all the masses of sins.

After visiting the five Varāhas, the *Kroḍa* (Boar) in the form of Udīrṇa should be adored in accordance with the injunction and then he should keep awake.

39-43. At the time of the *Jāgaraṇa* (keeping awake) the devotee should with devotion, light five-wicked lamps filled with ghee. Purāṇas should be listened to and auspicious songs and dances performed. The night should be spent with the

Japa of Vedic Mantras. O Ajamīḍha[1], listen to the merit that a man obtains thereby:

The waters of Revā are highly meritorious on the earth. So also Lord Hari, the ruler of all worlds. O Lord of men, the Ekādaśī is destructive of sins. It is obtained (and benefited) by men through many strenuous efforts.

Each of these is capable of destroying a series of sins like Brahmahatyā, O king. Then tell me, will they not be able to destroy if they are united together?

O son of Dharma, this has been told to you in the same manner as it was heard from the moon-crested Lord Śaṅkara. After listening to this willingly and reciting it, one is rid of all sins and goes to the region of the Enemy of Vṛtra.

CHAPTER ONE HUNDRED NINETY

The Greatness of Candrahāsa Tīrtha

Śrī Mārkaṇḍeya said:

1-7. Thereafter, O king, a person should go to the excellent Somatīrtha which is well known as Candrahāsa and adored by all deities. It is there that the kingly Soma, the most excellent Sura, attained the greatest Siddhi.

Yudhiṣṭhira said:

How did the kingly Soma, the Lord of the universe, attain Siddhi? I wish to listen to everything. O sinless one, do tell me.

Śrī Mārkaṇḍeya said:

O descendant of Bharata, it is said that he was cursed by Dakṣa, the learned sage:

"Since you do not stay (as a husband) with all the (other) wives impartially, you will be a victim of the wasting disease."

1. A descendant of Pūru, Yudhiṣṭhira.

O excellent one among men, listen to the ultimate fate of those who do not resort to their wedded wives (like a husband). By properly courting women (wives after their monthly course) a son is born. It is the exhortation of the Śruti that Svarga and salvation can be obtained through a son.

Those men who do not court her through activities befitting the occasion incur the sin of Brāhmaṇa-slaughter. There is no doubt about it.

8-17. Enveloped by that sin, he (i.e. such a man) will fall into Raurava. (Other) sinners drink his blood for a period of time they like.

In due course of time, he comes down and is born in different types of wombs. In all those wombs that evil-souled one becomes unlucky.

The lust of women is always stronger. Particularly at the time of monthly course, a woman is pierced by the darts of the god of Love.

Slighted by her husband, a woman thinks of other men as her husband. A son born to her roams about and makes the excellent family swerve (from the correct path). The moment he (such a son) is born, his Pitṛs who were in Svarga before slip down. Hence he is called *Kulaṭa.*

The Moon became a victim of the consumptive disease as a result of his Karma. Leaving off the world of leading Suras, he came down to the mortal world. After wandering over many holy spots and shrines, he came to Narmadā, the destroyer of all sins. For twelve years, he observed fasts, performed holy rites, observed restraints and made gifts. Thereupon, he was rid of the sins.

He installed Mahādeva, the destroyer of all sins. Becoming fully endowed with his original lustre, he went to the excellent Somaloka.

By adorning the Lord installed, a devotee enjoys his world for as many thousand Yugas as the number of years he worships the Lord.

18-26. Hence men instal deities on the earth in accordance with the injunctions whereby the benefit becomes everlasting and unmutilated.

A man who takes his holy bath in Somatīrtha and worships Lord Īśvara becomes pleasing like the Moon to look at, and beautiful when reborn.

One who goes to Candraprabhāsa and duly takes his holy plunge, shall never be assailed by any sickness. If one is afflicted with the consumptive disease he should take his bath in Candrahāsya on the twelfth day.

On the fourteenth day, he should observe fast and perform Homa with milk *Caru*. He should adore the Three-eyed Īśana with five Mantras. After taking in the remnant of Havis offering, he should visit Candrahāsyeśa.

By this procedure Lord Maheśvara becomes pleased. He is rid of the consumptive disease through this association with the Tīrtha. A devotee who takes the holy bath on seven (consecutive) Mondays and worships Śiva is rid of afflictions in the ears.

So also, O king, an ailment of the eyes is removed. A devotee who goes to Candrahāsya at the time of a lunar or solar eclipse and devoutly takes the holy dip, is rid of all sins.

O excellent king, everything performed in Candrahāsya, the holy bath, Dāna, nay all types of auspicious and inauspicious activities, yields everlasting benefit.

27-33. Men who take their bath in Candrahāsya and view the eclipse are blessed noble souls. Their life is excellent. Merely by taking the holy bath there in that Tīrtha, O great king, the verbal, mental and physical sins incurred earlier become dissolved.

Many persons afflicted with great delusions do not know it like the supreme Ātman immanent in the body of everyone.

Undoubtedly one obtains in Candrahāsya the entire benefit of those who go to the Somatīrtha in the western ocean.

A man who bathes in Candrahāsya during Saṁkrānti (transit of the Sun), Vyatīpāta, Viṣuva and Ayana becomes rid of all sins.

Those who do not know Candrahāsya situated on Narmadā are deluded and wicked in conduct. Their life is aimless.

If anyone adopts the life of a recluse in Candrahāsya, his departure to Somaloka is never followed by a return.

CHAPTER ONE HUNDRED NINETYONE

The Greatness of Dvādaśāditya Tīrtha

Śrī Mārkaṇḍeya said:

1-6. Thereafter, one should go to the Siddheśvara Tīrtha very near it. That is the first Liṅga of the Self- born Lord. It exudes nectar. Immediately on being seen, the man becomes free from indebtedness.

Formerly the twelve Ādityas propitiated Parameśvara for more than a hundred years and acquired the greatest Siddhi. Hence the deity is called Siddheśvara. He is the bestower of Siddhis on those who yearn for them.

Yudhiṣṭhira said:

O excellent Brāhmaṇa, I have become excessively surprised on hearing that the Ādityas have attained Siddhi. How did they attain it in the Siddheśvara Tīrtha? What was the purpose for which the Ādityas were engaged in the severe penance? O excellent Brāhmaṇa, they attained their desired Siddhi. I have put the question briefly, O Brāhmaṇa. Do recount it in detail.

Śrī Mārkaṇḍeya said:

7-17. The twelve Ādityas beginning with Śakra were born of Aditi. They were Indra, Dhātṛ, Bhaga, Tvaṣṭṛ, Mitra, Varuṇa., Aryaman, Vivasvān, Savitṛ, Pūṣan, Aṁśumān and Viṣṇu. All these twelve Ādityas desired the position of Bhāskara (the illuminator). So they came to the banks of Narmadā and established themselves in severe penance. O great king, the noble-souled sons of Kaśyapa collectively known as Dvādaśāditya attained great Siddhi at Siddheśvara Kṣetra. Divākara, the supporter of the universe, was installed with their respective parts in that Tīrtha by them.

Ever since then, O king, that Tīrtha became renowned in the world. At the end of the (four) Yugas when dissolution becomes imminent, twelve suns issue from Dvādaśāditya.

Indra blazes in the eastern part, Dhātṛ in the south-east, Gabhastipati (i.e. Bhaga) in the south, Tvaṣṭṛ in the face (direction) of the south-west, Varuṇa in the western part, Mitra in the north-west, (Viṣṇu) in the north and Vivasvān in the north-east.

Savitṛ blazes above and Pūṣan below, drying (everything). Aṁśumān and Viṣṇu burn the universe issued forth from the mouth. They all wandered here and there so that they burn the entire universe, O great king.

So also the twelve Ādityas facilitate the fulfilment of the desires of devotees. Listen to the benefit of that person who gets up early in the morning, takes his holy bath and visits the Lord of the chiefs of Devas, named Dvādaśāditya.

18-24. All the sins committed earlier, whether verbal, mental or physical, perish instantly, as soon as Dvādaśāditya is seen.

O descendant of Bharata, if a devotee circumambulates that Lord, then undoubtedly the whole earth is circumambulated by him.

The benefit one derives through a fast on the seventh lunar day in that Tīrtha may or may not be obtained through the same for seven Saptamī days elsewhere.

If a devotee, after visiting Dvādaśāditya on a Sunday coinciding with the sixth lunar day, circumambulates the deity, his sin perishes. He will be free from ailments for seven births.

One who circumambulates devoutly a hundred times every day, all scabs, white patches, tumours, nay all skin diseases, perish like serpents at the sight of Garuḍa. He will beget a son by resorting to the Tīrtha for sixty days.

CHAPTER ONE HUNDRED NINETYTWO

The Birth of Śrīpati

Śrī Mārkaṇḍeya said:

1-7. Thereafter, O dear one, one should go to the excellent Devatīrtha. After seeing Śrīpati, the man on the earth is rid of all sins. Lord Janārdana was the son-in-law of the great sage Bhṛgu.

Yudhiṣṭhira said:

Who is this Lord, the Consort of Śrī, the overlord of Devas? How did he come into being? O sage, is he one of the three deities Brahmā, Viṣṇu and Śiva? How did Keśava become a relative of Bhṛgu? O Brāhmaṇa, O descendant of Bhṛgu, it behoves you to recount this in detail.

Śrī Mārkaṇḍeya said:

I shall succinctly narrate the great story of Sādhyā. All the great sages are incapable of recounting it in detail.

The Four-faced Lord was born of the lotus arising from the navel of Nārāyaṇa. O king, Dakṣa was his son, having been born from his right thumb.

Dharma was born from the tip of his breast. Hence he became his son. Even Aja (Brahmā), O bull among the descendants of Bharata, had the assistance of Nārāyaṇa.

8-17. The following ten daughters of Dakṣa became the wives of Dharma. They were highly lustrous. They were: Marutvatī, Vasu, Jñānā, Laṁbā, Bhānumatī, Satī, Saṁkalpā, Muhūrtā, Sādhyā, Viśvavatī and Kakup.

Among them the blessed Sādhyā gave birth to sons, O king, namely Nara, Nārāyaṇa, Hari and Kṛṣṇa. These four sons of Dharma were the parts of the parts of Viṣṇu.

Nārāyaṇa and Nara identified their Ātman with the Supreme Ātman and performed a great penance on the Gandhamādana mountain.

They meditated on that which has nothing comparable to it, which was their cause and which has no other cause. They meditated on Vāsudeva who cannot be pointed out, who is beyond comprehension and is undifferentiated.

The two noble souls were fully engaged in Yogic exercise. They maintained themselves as great ascetics. On account of the power of their penance, the Sun stopped blazing.

The wind blew hesitatingly. Undoubtedly it was pleasing to the touch. Even burning fire became very cool. Lions, tigers and other wild animals moved about mildly on the mountain along with deer. O Lord of the Earth, the Earth distressed by their weight appeared like a cow. Mountains shook and the great ocean became agitated. The Devas lost their lustre in their own lustreless abode in the sky. O king, they became much agitated.

Śakra, the king of Devas, became scorched and furious by their penance. With a desire to cause obstacles to them, he engaged the celestial damsels there.

Indra said:

18-29. O Rambhā, O Tilottamā, O Kubjā, Ghṛtācī, Lalitā, O splendid Pramlocā, O Sumlocā of excellent eyebrows, O haughty Saurabheyī, O Alambuṣā, O Miśrakeśī, O Puṇḍarīkā, O Varuthinī, assume very charming personality that awakens Manmatha (erotic urge) and go to Gandhamādana. There act according to my instructions.

The two Brāhmaṇas, Nara and Nārāyaṇa, are performing penance with the requisite initiation. The sons of Dharma are performing penance which is extremely difficult for others to practise. O beautiful women, if they continue to perform the great penance, they are likely to give us great misery and agony through their all-surpassing activities. They may destroy our future prospects.

Hence go. Do not be afraid. All of you should carry out this instruction. O excellent ladies, Smara and Vasanta shall be your associates.

At the sight of beauty and youth that excessively excite love, which submissive man does not come under the influence of *Kandarpa* (god of Love)?

Śrī Mārkaṇḍeya said:

On being told thus by the king of Devas, O king, all those celestial damsels and Vasanta went off along with Madana.

They reached Gandhamādana which Mādhava (Spring) turned into a beautiful park with blossoming trees and parks agitated by the cooing male cuckoos.

The wind from Malaya mountain blew from the southern direction. The whole forest became excessively charming on account of the humming sounds of the swarms of bees.

The fragrant scent arising from the groves of trees delighted the noses of Kinnaras, Uragas and Yakṣas.

All those ladies of exquisite bodily features set about in

their task of tempting the sages, Nara and Nārāyaṇa, through their words, graceful movements of their limbs and smiles.

One of them sang sweetly; another celestial damsel danced; O king, another played on the musical instruments in a fascinating manner.

30-39. For the purpose of agitating them mentally the slender-limbed ladies made various efforts through their coquetish manners, emotional displays and sweet words.

Still, O Lord of the earth, they were the least affected mentally as they had reached the climax of their spiritual practice and mental discipline.

O king, they stood without any excitement or movement like a lamp in a windless spot. Their minds maintained steady equilibrium as it was dedicated to Vāsudeva.

Just as the great ocean on being filled with waters does not get excited, nor does it overflow into another world, so also their minds remained steady.

Meditating on the great Brahman in the form of Vāsudeva, conducive to the welfare of all living beings, they did not become the victims of either *Rāga* (attachment) or *Dveṣa* (hatred).

Smara too did not find it possible to enter their heart illuminated by perfect knowledge like darkness that does not gain entry into an apartment illuminated with lamps.

O bull among men, those great sages saw as an aspect of Brahman, everything such as the excellent trees shining well in their full bloom, the spring season, the southern breeze, all those celestial damsels, Kandarpa (god of Love), the penance begun by themselves, their own selves and Gandhamādana.

Fire does not burn fire nor does water wet water. It is so because the self-same object does not cause any aberration in itself.

After realizing again and again Brahman in its essential form, no effect or adverse influence of the spring season, Kandarpa and his women occurred to them.

40-48. Thereafter, O king, Vasanta, Madana and those slender-limbed ladies made further and stronger efforts to excite them both.

Then Nārāyaṇa of exalted mind took up courage and created a woman of excellent limbs from his thighs.

O Lord of the earth, the jewels of beautiful ladies of all the three worlds will become insignificant in their qualities verily at her very sight.

On seeing her, O Lord of the earth, the Wind became mentally shaken, Vasanta became dismayed and Smara could not remember anything.

The celestial young women beginning with Raṁbhā and Tilottamā became embarrassed as their hearts and eyes becoming the target of her sight ceased to shine.

Thereupon, O king, Kāma, Vasanta and the celestial damsels bowed down to the excellent holy sages and eulogized them.

Vasanta, Kāma and the celestial damsels said:

May the creator and supporter of the universe be pleased. We have been deluded by the Māyā of that Lord and so do not know the difference between the two.

May that Lord be pleased with us, the Lord whose form is twofold. He is the abode of all the worlds; he is beginningless; and he is without an end.

May the two Lords Nara and Nārāyaṇa wielding weapons like the conch and the discus be favourable with a benign face, to us all, though we are guilty.

49-58. He is the storehouse of all lores. He is like fire unto the forests of all sins. Hence may Lord Nārāyaṇa with the Śārnga (bow) as his weapon dispel all sins.

May the glorious, sinless Nara, the knower of self, dispel all the sins. He is the Ātman unto all embodied beings.

He has tucked up the clusters of matted hair. May the gentle face and sight of these two, who will pardon us, dispel all the sins incurred in the whole of this life.

Further a great crime has been committed by us, due to the defect in the learning we had. That is why we came here to tempt the Lords worthy of being respected by all the three worlds.

O Lord, O one full of pure knowledge, be pleased with us of deluded visions. Good people always keep up their righteousness.

Just as this excellent jewel of a lady came into being on

seeing us, so also, O Nārāyaṇa, the excellent intellect has originated in you, the intellect that facilitates getting across to the other shore of Saṁsāra. Hence, O eternal Lord, of a great soul, of a truthful soul, O Nārāyaṇa, be pleased. You are the greatest ultimate resort of all people by means of that truth.

O Nara, of clear intellect, of quiescent soul, O Lord having pleasant face and eyes, be pleased, O Lord of Yogins. O Lord, O omnipresent and unswerving one!

We bow down to Lord Nara; and also to Hari Nārāyaṇa. Obeisance to Nara worthy of being bowed to! Obeisance to Nārāyaṇa too!

O Lord, we were helpless before. But we have a Lord who helps us. We are pleased. May Nara bring about our welfare. O Nārāyaṇa, grant us welfare.

Śrī Mārkaṇḍeya said:

59-68. On being adored thus by means of the eulogy in the presence of all living beings, O king, Lord Nārāyaṇa devoid of *Rāga, Dveṣa* (attachment and hatred) said:

Nārāyaṇa said:

Welcome unto Mādhava, Kāma and the celestial damsels. May this be said as to what is to be done by us unto you who have come here.

Certainly you have been deputed by the enemy of Bala for overpowering us. Hence this display of the combination of dance etc.

We are not allured by songs, dances, movements of the limbs, utterances etc., nor by sensual objects. I consider these sensual objects terrible.

O splendid ones, when our senses are not defiled by contact with sounds etc., how can then things like dances etc., offer temptation to us?

We are Siddhas and not Sādhyas (conquerable) by you all, Smara and Mādhava. Let Śakra be free from suspicions, composed and at ease.

The supreme being, the greatest Puruṣa, Parameśvara, the Supreme Ātman, is the cause of the origin of mobile and immobile beings. It is in him that everything gets dissolved. In view of his being the immanent Lord, he is termed *Sarvavāsī* (the abode of all) and *Vāsudeva.*

We are the parts of the parts of that honourable Lord having four *Vyūhas.* (emanations).

We follow the path indicated by him for the enlightenment of embodied beings. We see the Lord of all abiding in all beings. We see all impartially everywhere. How can we having discrimination entertain attachment (*Rāga*) and hatred?

69-75. That same Bhūtātman (the Ātman) is present in me, Vasanta, Indra, in you all the celestial damsels and in Smara. How can there be hatred etc.?

Viṣṇu is the Lord of the Lords of all. All creatures are identical with him. That being the case, how can there be *Rāga* etc.?

All the things and beings of the universe are born from that single Supreme Ātman–beings such as Brahmā, Indra, Īśāna, Āditya, Maruts, Viśvedevas, sages, Sādhyās, Vasus, Pitṛs, Yakṣas, Rākṣasas, spirits etc., Nāgas, serpents, reptiles, men, birds, cows, elephants, lions, aquatic beings, flies, mosquitoes, bees, butterflies, water-worms, hedges, trees, creepers, bamboos, grasses, whatever can be seen or cannot be seen. Know that this is so, O celestial damsels.

Born thus, O celestial damsels, who can have attachment, hatred and greed, because Viṣṇu is his own greatest Ātman?

76. Viṣṇu is identical with all living beings, omnipresent and supporter of all. How can there arise the qualities of Rāga etc., after belittling that Viṣṇu who is different from ordinary living beings?

77. Thus, O women, when we all, you all and all the living beings have become identical with him, where is the occasion for Rāga etc.?

78. The eye that comprehends the unity of all is called *Samyagdṛṣṭi* (right eye). Knowing as different is a popular usage.

79-80. This entire universe consists of the elements, sense-organs, inner mind, Pradhāna (Prakṛti) and Puruṣa. Then of what nature is difference?

The waves come into being and get subsided in the waters of the ocean. But they are not different since they are only water. Similar is the universe, due to the identity.

81-88. Just as the sparks of fire are yellow, tawny, pink and grey in colour but are not different from fire, so also the universe is not different from Brahman.

That Purandara (Indra) makes you all cause excitement in us is improper as our minds are inclined towards good conduct and true knowledge.

You all, the Lord of Devas, all the people including Suras and Asuras, along with oceans, mountains and forests—all these are within my body.

Just as this lady exquisitely beautiful in all the limbs is shown to you all, I shall show the entire universe too in a similar manner.

Let not Indra be arrogant. Whose Indra-hood is permanent? You too do not become proud. There are many women with extraordinary beauty.

When the difference itself does not exist, what is beautiful? What is ugly? If there is comparison in regard to beauty of form, it is always due to the view of discrimination.

I correctly conjectured that your pride originated from such qualities as exalted physical beauty. Hence this slim lady was shown to you. Therefore, you are likely to be quiescent.

Since this lady of excellent limbs and blue lily-like eyes has come out of my thighs (Ūru), she will become an excellent Apsarā named Urvaśī.

89-95. Just as you have been sent by him to us with a desire for our pleasure, so may this lady of exquisite complexion be taken to Devarāja.

That thousand-eyed Indra should be told thus: "Our austerities are not motivated by a desire for enjoyment or of getting some benefit not yet acquired.

I Shall point out the righteous path to the wide world. I along with Nara shall carry out the protection of the universe. I am bent upon it.

O Lord of Tridaśas (Devas), if anyone is to harass you, I shall restrain him. O Vāsava, you abstain from (such attempts).

If you fail to chastise any wicked one, I shall surely chastise him. This I shall bring about undoubtedly.

Being aware of all these, you need not experience any distress on my account. O Vāsava, I have taken the incarnation to render help unto the worlds.

O Purandara, this lady Urvaśī who originated from me shall be the cause of Tretāgni (three sacrificial fires)."

CHAPTER ONE HUNDRED NINETYTHREE

The *Greatness of Śrīpati Tīrtha*

Śrī Mārkaṇḍeya said:

1-6. When this was spoken (by Nārāyaṇa), all the Apsarās bowed down to Nārāyaṇa repeatedly with a desire to have his vision and said:

Vasanta, Kāma and Apsarās said:

O holy Sir, this advice tendered by Your Holiness with a desire for our welfare has been understood and your greatness is comprehended.

You were kind enough to say with a delighted mind, "This wide-eyed beauty has been shown; I shall show you the universe too." Now, O Lord of the universe, we have surrendered to you in all respects. Hence reveal yourself in the same manner as Ūrvaśī has been shown.

If you have no anger towards us despite our guilt, do reveal your own self directly. O Lord of the worlds, we offer obeisance to you!

Nārāyaṇa said:

O ladies of Suras, see here in my person all the worlds, Vasanta, Madana and yourselves, as also whatever besides you wish to see.

Śrī Mārkaṇḍeya said:

7-15. After saying this, the holy Lord Nārāyaṇa laughed loudly and the entire universe came into being there, viz. Brahmā, the lord of the subjects (the patriarch), Śakra, all Rudras, the Pīnaka-bearing Lord, Ādityas, Vasus, Sādhyās, Viśvedevas, the great sages, Nāsatya, Dasra, Wind-god, the Fire-gods everywhere, Yakṣas, Gandharvas, Siddhas, Piśācas, Serpents, Kinnaras, all the celestial damsels, the lores, the Vedas with their ancillaries, expressions (utterances) (of scriptural texts), human beings, beasts, worms, birds, trees, reptiles, subtle beings, all other beings called *Jīva* (living organism), all the oceans, mountains, rivers, forests, all the islands and continents, all the lakes, the entire earth full of cities and villages. All these were seen by the celestial ladies in the body of the great Soul.

Within the Cosmic-formed Lord those ladies of beautiful limbs saw the entire firmament filled with stars, planets and constellations.

No limit or end was seen above, below, or at the sides of that being. Hence they eulogized the Lord, the infinite and beginningless Being.

All the excellent ladies became terrified along with Madana and Madhu became dismayed and praised the lord devoutly.

Vasanta, Kāma and the Apsarās said:

16-25. O Lord, we do not perceive your beginning, end or middle. Your enormous physical form is *Avyakta* (unexpounded, not comprehended). We bow down to you, O Nārāyaṇa, O ultimate resort of the worlds, O infinite one, O immanent Soul.

O supreme Soul, not inferior to anyone else! You are identical with *Śabda* (sound) and other sense objects.

The *Mahābhūtas* (great elements): earth, firmament, wind, water and fire constitute your form.

All these originate from you, O imperishable one. O Lord, O (great) Soul, difference too constitutes your form.

O Hari, you alone are the seer of colour or form, the knower of the greatest; (you alone are) the hearer of sound. You are omnipresent and the creator of all, the enjoyer of fragrance, and a separate individual soul.

There is no one among all the Suras, there is no one in the human world, there is no one among beasts and other classes of beings who does not form a part of yours, O Lord of Devas.

O gentle one, Brahmā, ocean, the Moon, Śakra and others are your excellent forms. Among those possessing courage your form is the sea. Among the refulgent forms, you are the Sun as well as fire.

Among those with forbearance as their asset (i.e. virtue) the most excellent form is *Kṣiti* (Earth). Among the quickest and the most powerful ones (your form) is the rapid-moving wind. The human form is the royal guise. O Lord of all, among the deluded ones you are the tree.

O imperishable one, you are Dānava among all those who are unjust. Among those with great discrimination you are Sanatsujāta. You abide in water in the form of taste. Fragrance is your form. You are Hutāśana (fire) in the form of the visible.

You are of the form of touch in the wind. Sound etc. of thine is the form in the firmament. O Lord, in mind you are of the form of thought.

In intellect, you are of the form of knowledge and understanding. You are the only one everywhere, O Lord of all, immanent in all.

In the middle of the lotus in your navel I see Lord Brahmā and in your eyebrows I see Hara. The Aśvins are in your ears. All the Guardians of the world are stationed in your arms. Your nose is Anila (wind or breath) and the Sun and the Moon are in your eyes. Your tongue is Sarasvatī, O Lord.

26-35. O Hṛṣīkeśa, we see the earth as your feet and all the worlds in your belly. We constitute your calves and the multitudes of Piśācas, Yakṣas, Uragas and Siddhas are in the toes of your feet.

The Lord of all subjects (Patriarchs) is established in your manliness. All the Kratus are established in the pair of your lips. O Lord, all of us are in your teeth and curved fangs. The Devas have become your teeth.

All the groups of the Devas are your hair. O Lord, Vidyādharas are the lines in the soles of your feet. All the Vedas along with the Aṅgas (ancillaries), O Lord, are stationed in the joints of your arms.

The form of the Boar holds up the Earth; the form of the Manlion is always highly terrible. Your lofty equestrian head we find in Trivikrama. It is incomprehensible.

These oceans are in your body. These mountains constitute the place of your girdle (waist). So also these rivers with Gaṅgā as the chief one, and also all the continents and the regions of forests etc.

O Lord, these sages stationed in your body eulogize your exalted greatness. These performers of Yajñas worship you, the Lord of all the worlds, the infinite one.

Whatever is gentle here in the world originates from you alone. O *Samastamūrti* (one whose form is constituted of everything), there is nothing more hideous than you. O Keśava, there is nothing colder or hotter than you. You alone surpass all the other forms.

Be pleased, O Lord of all. O Lord identical with all beings, O eternal Ātman, O great Īśvara, O Īśa, pardon our offence because our minds are deluded by your Māyā.

Or, what offence has been committed by us, O Lord of Devas, because our hearts (as well as yours) have originated from your Māyā? O destroyer of the distress of those who bow down, our mind, suspicious of your Māyā, has become confused.

We have not committed any offence against you. If at all, any offence has been committed by us traversing the wrong path, let that be pardoned. O Lord, the offence is thine because as a creator you created our indiscretion too.

36-47. Obeisance, obeisance to you, O Govinda, O Nārāyaṇa, O Janārdana! May all our sins perish by the recitation of your names.

Obeisance, O infinite one, obeisance to you, O Soul of the universe, O conceiver of the universe! May all our sins perish by the recitation of your names.

O most excellent one, O Yajñapuruṣa, O protector of the subjects, O Vāmana! May all our sins perish by the recitation of your names.

Obeisance to you, to the Lotus-navelled one, to the patriarch! O Hara, may all our sins perish by the recitation of your names.

O Adhokṣaja (Viṣṇu), we offer obeisance to you, the boat for crossing the ocean of worldly existence. May all our sins perish by the recitation of your names. Obeisance to the supreme Lord of Śrī, to Vāsudeva the creator, who voluntarily combines himself with the Guṇas, to the cause of creation, sustenance and dissolution (of the world)!

O immanent Soul of the universe, withdraw this eternal form of yours. O Īśvara, our eyes are incapable of looking at this ever increasing form (of yours). O imperishable one, this dazzling lustre of yours is on a par with that of thousands of fires at the time of ultimate annihilation. With its enormous extent, the quarters, the earth and the firmament have been enveloped.

We do not know where we are stationed. O Lord, you alone

are seen. We see the entire world dumped here, heaped into a lump.

Can we extol adequately your form? O Hari, what is the extent of this form? What is your greatness, O Lord? How can we describe it when it does not fall within the ken of the tongue?

A clear description of your exquisite features and your extent, cannot be effectively carried out, O Lord, even by ten thousand propounders and ten thousand times ten thousand intellects. Well, the form has been displayed. Great favour has been shown. O Lord of the worlds, withdraw this at your will (when it pleases you).

Śrī Mārkaṇḍeya said:

48-56. On being eulogized thus by those celestial damsels, Lord Janārdana, the conceiver of all living beings entered all those beings through his own partial aspects in the full view of those ladies now endowed with divine knowledge.

On seeing Lord Adhokṣaja getting merged into those beings, all those celestial damsels were surprised much.

The Lord of all entered the mountains, trees, oceans, earth, water, fire, wind and firmament. The Ātman of all entered the Kāla and Diks (quarters) by himself as well as otherwise.

He revealed the universe stationed in the form of himself by his own greatness. With regard to the Devas, Dānavas, Rākṣasas, Yakṣas, Vidyādharas, Uragas, human beings, animals, insects etc., beasts, the beings in the space above, on the earth, in heaven and those having water as their abode or the Ātman of the universe entered all these by assuming their forms. He merged thus along with Nara.

O suppressor of enemies, all those ladies of the Devas became surprised much with what had been seen by them before. On account of awe and fright, their faces became pallid, O excellent king, and they bowed down.

Lord Nārāyaṇa spoke to those celestial ladies:

Nārāyaṇa said:

57-63. May the fair lady Ūrvaśī be taken to the place where the Lord of Devas lives. For the sake of the welfare of ye all, the knowledge that this being is within all living beings has been imparted by me who have merged myself again into all those living beings. Hence do go now, you all. The entire group of Bhūtas (living entities) is a part of mine. I am a part of Vāsudeva, the Yogin, whose existence is within the Ātman. There is nothing other than this which is cited as Ananta (Infinite). Know ye all that he is unborn, Lord of all living beings and the greatest region. I myself, you the ladies, Devas, human beings, beasts—all these are the creations of Vāsudeva, the infinite one. After realizing this, O ladies of Devas, Asuras and human beings along with the flocks and herds of cattle should be seen impartially as equals.

Śrī Mārkaṇḍeya said:

On being told thus by that Lord, all those Sura-damsels bowed down to them both. O king, accompanied by Madana and Vasanta, they took Ūrvaśī with them and went back to the king of Devas. To the king of Devas they recounted everything in the manner it had happened.

Śrī Mārkaṇḍeya said:

64-71. Similarly, O great king, you too, comprehending Keśava within all the Bhūtas achieve equanimity and impartiality which alone is conducive to salvation.

Realizing this in particular, i.e. that Vāsudeva the great Īśvara is immanent in all the Bhūtas, how can you not eschew covetousness and other defects?

When all the Bhūtas have come out from Govinda, O king, and when they are not different, the emotions of enmity etc. too are likewise, O dear son. They should not be entertained.

Thus, O king, see the entire universe as having Vāsudeva for its Ātman. This form alone has been exhibited by Kṛṣṇa. The form that is Parameśvara has been recounted to you. It is the greatest form of Viṣṇu devoid of all states such as birth etc.

O king, what I mention succinctly may be listened to. By knowing this, a person attains the greatest salvation. Everything is on a par with Viṣṇu. Bhāva (existence) and Abhāva (non-existence) are identical with him.

This Īśa is both *Sat* (manifest) and *Asat* (unmanifest); Mahādeva is the highest state.

Viṣṇu alone is the refuge and raft unto men immersed in the ocean of worldly existence, who are assailed by the squall of Dvandvas (like pleasure- pain), who are burdened with the succour of sons, daughters and wives, who get drowned in the dangerous waters of sensual pleasures without a boat.

CHAPTER ONE HUNDRED NINETYFOUR

The Marriage of Śrīpati

Śrī Mārkaṇḍeya said:

1-8. On hearing that the Cosmic Form was revealed by the Infinite Being, the Lord, Devas and their king became excessively surprised.

On seeing Ūrvaśī, the splendid Apsarā with lotus-like countenance, Indra surrounded by royal glory became surprised and dismayed.

He kept quiet without saying anything in reply. Thus the activities of Nārāyaṇa became the current news.

On hearing about the great form, the Cosmic Form (of Nārāyaṇa), Lakṣmī born from the Khāti (abyss) of Bhṛgu, O king, became surprised and thought thus:

'By what means shall this Lord Nārāyaṇa be my husband? Is it through Vrata, penance, Dāna or some restraints? Can it be through attending upon the old people or by propitiating Devatās?' O Yudhiṣṭhira, Satī (Śiva's consort) knew that the girl was thinking thus and she said: "It is through austerities that Śaṅkara was obtained by me as my husband. So also Prajāpati (Brahmā) was obtained by Gāyatrī. Desired husbands were obtained like that by other women too. O lady of good Vratas, it is only through penance that the husband should be obtained by you. Hence perform penance, great and fierce, which will give you all that you desire."

Śrī Mārkaṇḍeya said:

9-15. O conqueror of the cities of enemies, Lakṣmī went to the outer limit of the oceans and performed an elaborate penance extremely difficult (for others) to perform, for a long duration.

She stationed herself steadily like a lamp-post for a period of one thousand divine years. Thereupon Indra and other Devas holding conch, discus and the club (like Viṣṇu) went there for her sake. She asked the Suras, "Be quick, manifest the Cosmic Form of Viṣṇu."

Abashed and perturbed thereby the Devas went to Nārāyaṇa and said, "We were not able to reveal the Cosmic Form."

Thereafter they went away as they pleased. Viṣṇu thought, 'The fair lady stays there in a dreadful form. This Bhārgavī is burning her body. Hence I shall go there to her. After granting her the desired boon I shall perform penance once again or display once again the Cosmic Form belonging to Viṣṇu, which ordinarily cannot be seen by either Devas or Dānavas.'

Śrī Mārkaṇḍeya said:

Then Hṛṣīkeśa went to Śrī staying at the outer limit (shore) of the ocean. He said, "O fair lady, I am pleased with you. Choose a boon as desired by you."

Śrī said:

16-25. O Lord Janārdana, if you are pleased with me who have dedicated myself to and sought refuge in you, O sinless one, show me what was seen by the celestial damsels.

O Keśava, O conceiver of the living beings, your Cosmic Form is infinite. O Lord Viṣṇu, do recount to me the details of the penance performed by you on Gandhamādana, if it is not false. I am not convinced with this form at all, the form I see before me.

Even though they have come to know my mental attachment to Hari, I have been freely wooed by many Yakṣas and Rākṣasas moving about employing their magical tricks.

They had assumed the form of Viṣṇu adopting four arms and wielding the discus. But all of them went away fully abashed and chagrined since they were unable to display the Cosmic Form.

Śrī Mārkaṇḍeya said:

On being told thus by her, Lord Nārāyaṇa gave up that form

holding the conch, discus and club, the form adored by Suras, and displayed the great Cosmic Form as mentioned before.

After showing it, he spoke these words in accordance with the injunctions in the Pāñcarātra text: "He who adores me always is worthy of adoration. After being adored, he will become possessor of wealth and foodgrain and all means of pleasurable enjoyment.

Brahmacarya (celibacy) is the very root of all pious activities. Therefore I will stay there with the title *Mūlaśrīpati* (Consort of original Śrī). Mūlaśrī is called Brāhmī. She is in the form of Brahmacarya. She is meritorious, Yoga incarnate, auspicious, and destructive of all sins.

26-37. I am her Lord and consort, O my beloved, the bestower of boons on living beings. A man who bathes in the waters of Revā and adores me named Mūlaśrīpati with due performance of Vratas and maintenance of restraints, shall attain the desired benefit. If he offers Dāna and Mahādāna there, O my beloved, he obtains the merit thousand times more than elsewhere.

It was seen by you there in that region and perfectly comprehended. Adoring it, you will undoubtedly obtain great desires.

O goddess of Devas, choose a boon desired by you (even if it be) inaccessible to the Suras who have fallen into the impassable forest of worldly existence, O great goddess."

Śrī said:

O Nārāyaṇa, O supporter of the universe, O Lord of the universe, O great Brahman, O ultimate great resort! Be pleased with me for my devotion. Save me perfectly. Employ me in the perfect creation. You are my lover. Manage everything so that I can be your beloved.

The stage of householder is the root cause of Dharma, Artha and Kāma. It has been approved by Devas. Adopt that meritorious Āśrama (stage of life) and employ me in the rites for welfare.

Nārāyaṇa said:

O fair lady, since you addressed me (submitted to me) uttering the word Nārāyaṇa, my name here will be Nārāyaṇagiri.

At the recollection of Nārāyaṇa the sins incurred in the course of crores of births vanish. It is termed Giri because it swallows (sins). The *'Giri'* (mountain), the supporter of all, shall be the king of all mountains! O fair lady, just as I am the supporter of Suras, Asuras and human beings.

Those who adore this divine form of mine named Nārāyaṇagiri, O lady of splendid eyes, after placing it in the mystic Maṇḍala (diagram) become richly endowed with divine knowledge and divine physical form as well as divine activities. (They) will attain the divine Loka enjoying divine pleasures.

Śrī Mārkaṇḍeya said:

38-43. Even as they were having the dialogue thus, Devas with Indra as their leader and great sages came to that forest region at the outskirts of the ocean.

After knowing that she was Bhṛgu's daughter, the king of Devas requested him for what Nārāyaṇa had been thinking of. He, the righteous soul, gave her readily. Dharma performed the rites of marriage in accordance with the injunctions. O sage-king, he performed the rites of marriage of the Lord of Devas with due consideration for the sake of the Devas.

Yudhiṣṭhira said:

It has been told by you that Dharma performed the rites of marriage in accordance with the injunctions. What was the *Vidhi* (Procedure)? What Dakṣiṇā was offered by Bhṛgu in the Yajña of that Vivāha (marriage)? Who became the holder of the *Sruk* and *Sruva* (sacrificial ladles and vessels)? Who were the Ṛtviks and who were the members of the sacrificial assembly, O excellent Brāhmaṇa? Was there an Avabhṛtha (the valedictory bath thereof)? Mention everything in detail. I am not fully satiated by imbibing the nectar of your words.

Śrī Mārkaṇḍeya said:

44-52. Neither Brahmā nor Parameśvara is capable of describing the good features of the marriage of Nārāyaṇa, the Yajña and the Tapas of that Lord and his perfect conduct. O Yudhiṣṭhira, yet I shall recount in a general way. Listen with careful attention.

Brahmā and the Seven Sages were engaged in holding the *Sruk* and *Sruva* there. They performed the Homa in the sacrificial fires, O king. The entire earth along with the oceans was the altar.

The oceans gave jewels to the Brahmarṣis, O excellent king. Dhanada (Kubera) too gave the monetary gift as desired by all the Brāhmaṇas.

Viśvakarmā built houses of wonderful varieties fully embedded with all jewels and showed them to the glorious Lord of Devas.

Then, O great king, Śatakratu asked the various Brāhmaṇas assembled there to choose whatever they desired. They were the Brāhmaṇas including Śaunakas etc., Bāṣkalas, Chāgalas and Ātreyas with Kāpiṣṭhala as their leader.

On seeing those wonderfully variegated jewels, they said to the Lord of all chieftains: "This (joint) assembly of Devas and sages is highly meritorious. O Lord of Suras, we wish to stay forever in this meritorious assembly."

Śatakratu said again, "Your residence shall be here as long as you please, while all of you are engaged in true Dharma."

Śrī Mārkaṇḍeya said:

53-61. O tiger among kings, in answer to your question as to who were the priests offering sacrificial oblations in the sacrifice, I shall describe it. Listen to it with concentration.

Those with Sanatkumāra as their chief were the *Sadasyas* (members of the sacrificial assembly). Atri, Aṅgiras and Marīci officiated as *Udgātṛs*. Dharma and Vasiṣṭha did the job of *Hotṛs* (reciters of the Vedic Mantras). Sage Sanaka was the *Brahmā* (Presiding priest in the sacrifice). Śatakratu (Indra) gave them thirty-six thousand vallages.

The Lord did everything and so Lakṣmī was united with her husband. Even as Brahmā was performing the Homa, his forehead was visible to the Suras seated all round. The region where such view was possible is called *Lalāṭadeśa* and that spot became the meritorious spot of Śrīpati and was resorted to by Devas and sages.

It is full of miracles, divine and efficacious. Then Lakṣmī endeavoured to establish the row of the Brāhmaṇas. She spoke these words to the Lord named Śrīpati.

Śrī said:

I wish to duly establish these Brāhmaṇas of excellent Vratas and restraints. They are the disciples of Bhṛgu and others. O Adhokṣaja, with your favour I wish to establish them. O Garuḍa-emblemed One, Marīci and others have been established by the Lord of Suras.

There are many Brāhmaṇas here of steadfast Vratas and restraints. Some of them are engaged in the Prājāpatya Vrata of Brahmā. O Adhokṣaja, I shall establish them with your favour.

Śrī Mārkaṇḍeya said:

62-71. Thereupon the enthusiastic Bull-emblemed Lord asked the Vratins who were all allotted different avocations.

Nārada approached Mahādeva, the consort of Satī, and said, "These Brāhmaṇas of steadfast Vratas wore deer hides. These excellent Brāhmaṇas should be made to cover their nakedness by means of excellent clothes. O Lord of Suras, there are twenty-four thousand Prājāpatyas. O Bull- emblemed One, there are twelve thousand members of those who follow Brahmacarya Vrata and propound those Vratas."

On hearing the words of Nārada, Devas and celestial sages considered the suggestion good but none of them said anything.

Thereupon, Lakṣmī devoutly called those Brāhmaṇas, touched their feet and said: "Favour may be done to me. There are thirty-six thousand houses constructed by Viśvakarman. All of you, do stay there."

They were delighted in their minds. They promised, "So will it be". They became rich owners of money and food-grain, the fulfilment of their desire. There being no necessity to begin their activities, they were fully satisfied with their desires fulfilled.

After establishing those Brāhmaṇas thus, Lokṣmi stood there and protected them. Viṣṇu, interested in doing what pleased Goddess Śrī, stood there in four forms.

Thus, the Yajña of the marriage rites was concluded and the sages asked, "O Janārdana, where will we take the Avabhṛtha (valedictory) bath?"

72-80. On hearing these words, Śrīpati released the waters of Jāhnavī from his lotus-like feet. The pure waters flowed into the middle of Revā.

On seeing the waters issuing forth from the feet of Hari and being fully aware of its worth and weightiness, those sages who knew its greatness, became wonder-struck.

All the Devas along with Rudra and the sages too began to shake their heads. They were surprised and talked about it in their dialogues.

The sages said:

Do tell us, O Śaṁbhu, what is this sudden outflow of water arising from the lotus-like feet of Viṣṇu. It is greatly fascinating.

Īśvara said:

O Suras, I know fully well that this is the water from the feet of Viṣṇu. Bath in this water surpasses the valedictory bath to be taken after ten horse-sacrifices. Śrīpati (Lord of Śrī) is adorable to you. Whence can you have the Avabhṛtha bath? Hence he has quickly created the (Gaṅgā) water for your sake.

No one is competent to explain fully, O Lord of Devas, the benefit that can be attained by taking the holy ablution here. Hence why talk more?

Śrī Mārkaṇḍeya said:

O eminent one, O Bull among the descendants of Bharata, after saying thus and taking their holy ablution, the Devas with Maheśāna as their leader went away in the manner they had come.

Thereupon, all the Brāhmaṇas resorted to their own houses, O great king, in the Devatīrtha destructive of all sins.

CHAPTER ONE HUNDRED NINETYFIVE

The Glory of Śrīpati

Yudhiṣṭhira said:

1-7. O sage, what is said to be the greatness of Devatīrtha? What is the benefit acquired by those who perform holy ablution, *Dāna* etc. there?

Śrī Mārkaṇḍeya said:

O mighty-armed one, all the Tīrthas on the entire earth, resorted to by Devas and groups of sages, were thought about by Viṣṇu and they arrived there together, O Yudhiṣṭhira. That Tīrtha is the well-known Devatīrtha, a meritorious Vaiṣṇava holy place.

Kurukṣetra is the greatest Tīrtha on the earth, and Tripuṣkara in the firmament. Puruṣottama is the greatest Tīrtha in heaven. Devatīrtha is greater than the greatest.

O Yudhiṣṭhira, there is no Tīrtha on a par with Devatīrtha in this world as well as in the next one. On attaining it , a man ceases to become distressed.

All the Tīrthas were told by Devas: "If a man takes his holy bath here in Devatīrtha, it is as good as though he has taken his holy bath everywhere."

"So be it", the Tīrthas told the Devas and the groups of sages. They adored Śrīśa and went to their respective places fully contented.

8-19. O king, if one takes his holy bath here (in Deva Tīrtha), adores Śrīśa and observes holy fast in accordance with the injunctions, and gifts gold pieces duly at the time of a solar eclipse, he will obtain the benefit of the holy bath here.

Śatakratu has said: "Gifts of plots of land, cows and gold have endless benefit. So also gift of diamond gives infinite benefit. Soma attained endless benefit, due to gift of clothes, Bhārgava due to gift of pearls; the Sun and Dharmarāja made a gift of gold and attained endless benefit. Bṛhaspati of a generous mind says: "Whatever Dāna is offered in Devatīrtha by one with full faith has infinite benefit."

Devatīrtha in Bhṛgukṣetra is superior to all the other Tīrthas.

A man who takes his holy bath in Devatīrtha and visits Śrīpati at the time of a lunar eclipse, redeems a hundred members of his family and enjoys heavenly pleasures.

Those men by whom gifts were made to eminent Brāhmaṇas in Devatīrtha, O Lord of men, will enjoy great pleasures after death.

With Hari in view, if a person feeds out Brāhmaṇas, O Yudhiṣṭhira, he enjoys all types of pleasures in Svarga Loka.

A man or a woman should take a holy bath in Devatīrtha with mind in full control. He or she shall observe fast on the eleventh day with complete devotion and adore the Consort of Śrī devoutly. He should light a lamp with ghee and keep awake during the night. He should get up early in the morning on the twelfth day, take bath in the waters of Narmadā and duly propitiate a Brāhmaṇa couple (or couples) with clothes, ornaments, betel leaves, flowers, incense and unguents. He or she will rejoice in Viṣṇuloka as a result of the satisfactory completion of the Vrata.

20-30a. One who takes holy bath on the eleventh lunar day, observes fast, worships Hari and keeps awake at night in accordance with the injunctions in the Veda and scriptural texts, never faces the torturous and accursed harassment meted out by Dharmarāja.

One who adores Śrīpati in accordance with the injunctions in the Pāñcarātra system, after duly receiving the Vaiṣṇava initiation that annihilates sins, bestows heavenly pleasures and salvation, also accords worldly delight and wealth, kingdom, sons, good fortune, excellent wife, devotion to Viṣṇu, will cross the ocean of worldly existence, O highly esteemed scion of the family of Kuru.

One who worships the Consort of Śrī there in Devatīrtha, or Viśvarūpa, or Mūlaśrīpati, or Nārāyaṇagiri in the house with devotion and faith, on the eleventh lunar day gets great benefit. He should make use of the following material in the course of the worship: milk, water, unwashed cloth of fine texture, silk cloth of various colours, woven silk garments, incense, agallochum, sandalpaste, Guggulu mixed with ghee and various kinds of food offerings like milk pudding etc., O Yudhiṣṭhira, O Lord of men.

A man who adores the Lord with lamps made of *Piṣṭa* (flour-cakes with wicks fitted in) that charm the mind and glow increasingly, goes to Viṣṇuloka. On how he goes listen, O descendant of Bharata. He will be equipped with conch, discus, club and lotus and will have the form of the Garuḍa-emblemed Lord. He passes through Devalokas and reaches Viṣṇuloka.

30b-41. One who devoutly, sees the lotus-like feet of Śrīpati established in four forms as well as Śrī, the mother of the three worlds, while offering entertainment by dances and songs is certainly rid of sins.

One who is always engaged in waving lamp as *Nīrājana* lights to the Lord at dawn, mid-day and evening and adores and worships Hari, shall cross impassable dangers. He will never get distress and misery.

The rite called *Nīrājana* (showing of lights) of Hari is conducive to the lengthening of life expectation and enhancement of glory. It is highly pleasing to the eyes and destroys minor sins. He is blessed who recites the prayer to the Lord of Devas at the time of Hari's Nīrājana.

One who waves his inverted palms over the remnant of Hari's *Nīrājana* and wipes his eyes and face therewith, becomes free from *Timira* (blindness) and other eye diseases. His face becomes bright. Lighting of lamps in front of Śrīpati is efficacious in destroying all defects, O best of men. A devotee engaged in Vratas should take his holy bath in the meritorious Revā water and offer the same ritualistically (i.e. water is held in the joined palms cupped together, Mantra is recited and the water is thrown up). It is as good as the entire earth with seven continents, oceans and rivers circumambulated. So said Śaṅkara.

One who listens to this narrative or reads this shall at the time of death recollect Hari and become sinless to Hari.

It is conducive to renown, longevity, heavenly pleasure and delight of the groups of Pitṛs.

One who reads the greatness of Śrīpati before Brāhmaṇas at the time of a Śrāddha, has the same benefit as though he has propitiated the Pitāmahas (ancestors or grandfathers) with ghee and honey.

CHAPTER ONE HUNDRED NINETYSIX

The Greatness of Haṁsatīrtha

Śrī Mārkaṇḍeya said:

1-6. Thereafter, O king, a devotee should go to the excellent Haṁsatīrtha where a swan performed penance and attained the status of the vehicle of Brahmā.

A man who takes his holy bath in Haṁsatīrtha and makes gift of gold becomes rid of all sins and goes to Brahmaloka by means of a vehicle fitted with swans and having the lustre of the sun and richly endowed with all desirable things. He will be attended upon by groups of celestial damsels.

After enjoying all pleasures as he pleases, he will be reborn as a human being where he will be able to remember previous births.

He then renounces and casts off his body when, O descendant of Bharata, he will attain salvation. Thus, O son of Kuntī, has been recounted to you, what the merit of visiting Haṁsatīrtha is. It is meritorious, destructive of all sins and capable of destroying all miseries.

CHAPTER ONE HUNDRED NINETYSEVEN

The Greatness of Mūlasthāna Tīrtha

Śrī Mārkaṇḍeya said:

1-11. Next to that, one should go to the excellent Sūrya Tīrtha which is well known as Mūlasthāna (the original holy spot).

It is a splendid shrine established by the Lotus-born Deity. The goddess was told by Mūlaśrīpati, "Instal Bhāskara." On hearing what was told by the Lord, the goddess installed Bhāskara.

It is mentioned as 'Bhāskara designated Mūlasthāna' on the banks of Narmadā.

A man who controls his mind, takes his holy bath there in the Tīrtha, offers libations of water and rice-balls to Pitṛs and deities and thereafter visits Mūlasthāna attains the greatest goal. A special feature there has been heard by me.

It is a greater than the greatest secret. I heard it in the assembly of sages from the Moon-crested Lord Śaṅkara.

On the seventh lunar day, the Mūla constellation or Sunday, a devotee should go to the river Revā, take the holy bath in the waters, propitiate Devas and Pitṛs and offer Dāna in accordance with his capacity, O most excellent one among the descendants of Bharata.

He should carry on the adoration with Karavīra flowers and the water of red sandalpaste. He should instal Bhāskara devoutly and in accordance with the injunctions.

Then he should fumigate with incense along with Aguru (agallochum) and Kundara grass in particular. The Lord of the chiefs of Devas is adored with incenses and lights should be kindled illuminating the ten quarters.

He should observe fast and keep awake at night, and there should be a special arrangement for vocal and instrumental music. If this is performed, O Lord of the earth, he shall never be a victim of acute misery.

O excellent king, he will stay in Sūryaloka for a period of three hundred Kalpas and he will be served and attended upon by Gandharvas and celestial damsels there.

CHAPTER ONE HUNDRED NINETYEIGHT

The Greatness of Śūleśvara Tīrtha

Śrī Mārkaṇḍeya said:

1-9. Thereafter, O Lord of the earth, one should go to the Bhadrakālī Saṅgama well known as Śūlatīrtha. It was created by the Lord himself.

The Trident-armed great Lord Parameśvara who is adored by all Devas, stands in the middle of Pañcāyatana (five shrines).

That *Saṅgama* (confluence) is always resorted to by Devas, O excellent king.

By visiting that Tīrtha, and more particularly by taking the holy bath and offering gifts evils like ill-luck, bad omens, curses, imprisonment by king etc. are destroyed. So said Śaṅkara.

Yudhiṣṭhira said:

How did Goddess Śūleśvarī and Hara Śūleśvara come to be well established and well reputed on the banks of Narmadā? Do recount this in details.

Śrī Mārkaṇḍeya said:

There was a certain Brāhmaṇa well known by the name Māṇḍavya. He was conversant with all types of pious rites and pursued his avocation while engaged in truthfulness and penance.

The radiant sage of arduous penance observed the vow of silence. He stood at the foot of a tree in the middle of a grove of Aśoka trees with hands lifted up.

For a long period he thus engaged himself in the severe penance when some thieves carrying a great deal of booty reached that hermitage, closely pursued by a number of king's officers of law. O scion of the family of Kuru, they deposited the stolen goods in his abode.

10-21. After depositing the stolen goods, the thieves remained hidden in the hermitage itself. Even as they remained hidden, a posse of police officers came there immediately, closely following the thieves. The pursuers of the thieves spoke to the sage and asked him the details.

"O excellent Brāhmaṇa, do tell us which way did the thieves go? If we know it, we can quickly follow them."

Despite their repeated queries in these words, O king, the ascetic did not say anything good or bad.

The royal officers made a search of the hermitage, found the goods lost and bound him and the thieves. They produced them before the king.

The pious sage was impaled on a stake and remained there for a long time meditating on Śaṅkara, the consort of Umā and the Lord of the three worlds. He meditated on Maheśāna mentally for a very long time. The Brāhmaṇa-sage did not take in food. Yet he did not die.

A bull among Brāhmaṇas, he meditated on Hari in his heart. A penance was performed by him though he suffered much at the top of the stake.

On hearing this, all the sages became excessively distressed. O descendant of Bharata, they took the form of birds and came to him at night.

After noticing the power of the sage they asked the excellent Brāhmaṇa: "O Brāhmaṇa, we wish to hear. What sin was committed by you?"

Śrī Mārkaṇḍeya said:

22-31. Thereupon, the tiger among sages said to those ascetics: "Can I escape from my own faults? No one else has committed any offence against me."

After saying thus (to himself), the sage said so to all of them. Thereupon, the sages submitted this to the king the next day.

On hearing that it was a sage (who had been impaled) the king came out along with his kinsmen. He craved the indulgence of the excellent sage impaled on the stake.

The king said:

O dear one, it was due to ignorance that a great offence has been committed by me. I request you to become pleased. It does not behove you to be angry with me.

On being requested thus, the sage became pleased. The king got him brought down from the stake. The sage had become pleased.

On being brought down the flesh of the sage got entangled on the stake. The Brāhmaṇa became highly distressed. He meditated on Śaṅkara mentally.

Śaṅkara had been meditated upon by him after a long period of fast. Mahādeva appeared before him and cut off the stake.

Standing at the foot of the stake, the delighted Śaṁbhu said again and again: "What should be done, O Brāhmaṇa who are abiding by your Sāttvika nature? I am pleased and so also is Umā. I shall grant you something that cannot be (ordinarily) granted. But (one thing kindly note) the achievement of truthful persons in the world may not be (necessarily) much. Creatures enjoy the benefit only in accordance with their own actions. Prosperity results from good actions and misery from evil acts."

32-43. (Past) Actions bear fruit in diverse forms for human beings. To some it gives poverty; to others it gives suffering due to loss of wealth. To some the suffering may arise from absence of progeny. To some it is due to the contrary. They may be distressed due to misbehaviour of children. To some persons the distress may be due to the death of sons or separation of dear friends. To some misery may be due to tyranny of a king, to a thief or to a fire accident brought about by adverse fate.

The distress due to evil action may manifest in the bodies of certain persons. Old age sets in at various stages of life. Ailments are also to be seen.

One is subjected to slander and calumny through sins incurred in the course of the actions of previous births. Some (apparently) sinless now, fall into the most miserable situations.

In the same way, as a result of the previous Karmas some continue to be pious and abiding in performing austerity. Many are self-controlled, devoted to their own wedded wives, munificent and ready to give liberally and eager to worship (deities). Others are endowed with many good qualities such as bashful modesty, tactfulness etc.

There are some men who do not get excited or distressed due to insuperable calamities as a result of their own Karmas. They do not censure pious behaviour and religious activity. They consider this as a form of penance. On the other hand, some stupid persons censure it as torture. Good men do not lament during sufferings saying, "Alas, my brother ! Mother ! Son ! etc." They remember me or the lotus-eyed Lord Viṣṇu. They get ready to reap the fruit of evil actions. Thereat, certainly it gets subdued.

If good men continue to meditate on Lord Īśa and endure the sufferings, their (past) acts become milder, O Brāhmaṇa. It is emphasized by Śrutis. O Brāhmaṇa, this is since I have been mentally remembered and worshipped by you in the midst of your sufferings, that I have come here in the company of Gaurī. Tell me, O Brāhmaṇa, what should be done by me."

Māṇḍavya said:

44-56. O Śaṅkara, if you along with Umā are pleased and if you are going to grant me a boon, then do clarify my doubt which occurred while I was on the stake.

When all my limbs were impaled on the stake, I did not have

any pain at all. That Śūla (Stake) appeared to exude nectar. Do tell me to what power it was due.

Śūlapāṇi said:

It was due to the fact that I have been mentally remembered by you, O Brāhmaṇa. I am the destroyer of injustice and evil actions. I dispel miseries.

As soon as I was meditated upon, O Brāhmaṇa, when I was stationed in the nether worlds, I, Śaṁbhu came to the foot of the Śūla and the Goddess herself stationed herself on the top. Goddess Ambikā, the mother of the universe, flooded you with nectar.

Māṇḍavya said:

Since you along with Umā had already pervaded the Śūla and stationed yourself there, even now you in her company are inclined to do me favour.

Merely by remembering her all *Daurbhāgya* (ill-luck) will get dissolved. There is nothing more miserable than the greatest misery of ill-luck.

O excellent one among Suras, this traditional verse is being sung in the Purāṇas: While you were burning the three worlds, all *Saubhāgya* (conjugal felicity) gathered into one unit and getting to the chest of Viṣṇu settled down there. This is already heard by us.

As it dripped down from his chest it was imbibed by Dakṣa the Parameṣṭhin (Patriarch). Therefrom was born this lady with eyes like blue lotus in the form of Satī.

O Lord of Devas, when he performed a Yajña he insulted you. Hence, that goddess consigned herself, her Prāṇas, into the fire. After reducing herself to ashes, O Lord, she was born of Menakā (Menā) as the daughter of the Himālaya Mountain. She is now named Umā.

O Lord of Suras, that Goddess has neither beginning nor end. She is beyond comprehension and guess, O Lord of Devas, if you are pleased and if Umā is pleased to grant me a boon, both of you shall become stationed in this spot, i.e. the foot and the top of the Śūla. Your incarnation may be here and there but the permanent stay shall be here.

Śrī Mārkaṇḍeya said:

57-63. When this was requested by him, the ground was suddenly split into two and from the foot and the top of the Śūla they came out in the form of replicas of Linga and idol.

The Liṅga was seen at the foot illuminating all the quarters. To the left was the Goddess Śūleśvarī stationed as the idol.

She shone filling up all the quarters and fascinating the entire universe. On seeing her, the excellent Brāhmaṇa joined the palms in reverence and began to eulogize.

Māṇḍavya said:

You are the mother of this world; the deity presiding over the fortune of the universe. O lady of excellent countenance, there is nothing without your presence in the whole of the Cosmic Egg.

O goddess expert in the knowledge of Dharma, do favour me. It behoves you to command me.

Where are the different spots where you are stationed in the forms similar to this? O great goddess, be favourable to me and mention them.

Śrī Devī said:

I should be seen as present everywhere in all living beings, everywhere on the earth. In all the worlds there is nothing that is created without me.

I shall, however, truthfully recount to you the places where I should be visited by people desirous of Siddhi and remembered by those desirous of prosperity.

64-75. The deities in various shrines are: Viśālākṣī in Vārāṇasī, Liṅgadhāriṇī in Naimisa, Goddess Lalitā in Prayāga, Kāmukā in Gandhamādana, the deity named Kumudā in Mānasa, Viśvakāyā in Apara, Gomatī in Gomanta, Kāmacāriṇī in Mandara, Madotkaṭā in Caitraratha, Hayantī in Hastināpura, Gaurī stationed in Kānyakubja, Raṁbhā in Amalaparvata, Kīrtimatī in Ekāmraka, Viśvā in Viśveśvara, Puruhūtā in Puṣkara, Mārgadāyinī in Kedāra, Nandā on the tableland of Himālaya, Bhadrakarṇikā in Gokarṇa, Bhavānī in Sthāneśvara, Bilvapatrikā in Bilvaka, the deity named Mādhavī in Śrīśaila, Bhadreśvarī in Bhadra, Jayā on Varāhaśaila, Kamalā in Kamalālaya, Kalyāṇī in Rudrakoṭī, Kālī in Kālañjara,

Kapilā in Mahāliṅga, Mukuṭeśvari in Makoṭa, Mahādevī in Śāligrāma, Jalapriyā in Śivaliṅga, Kumārī in Māyāpurī, Lalitā in Santāna, Utpalākṣī in Sahasrākṣa, Mahotpalā in Hiraṇyākṣa, the deity named Vimalā in Gayā, Maṅgalā in Puruṣottama, Amoghākṣī in Vipāśā, Paṭalā in Puṇḍravardhana, Nārāyaṇī in Supārśva, Bhadrasundarī in Trikūṭa, Vipulā in Vipula, Kalyāṇī on Malayācala, Koṭavī in Koṭitīrtha, Sugandhā in Gandhamādana[1], Trisandhyā in Godvāśrama, Ratipriyā in Gaṅgādvāra, Sabhānandā in Śivacaṇḍa and Nandinī in Devikātaṭa.

76-85. Rukmiṇī in Dvārāvatī, Rādhā in Vṛndāvana forest, Devakī in Mathurā, Parameśvarī in Pātāla (nether world), Sītā in Citrakūṭa, Vindhyanivāsinī on Vindhya, Ekavīrā on the Sahya Mountain, Caṇḍikā in Hariścandra, Ramaṇā in Rāmatīrtha, Mṛgāvatī on Yamunā, Mahālakṣmī in Karavīra, Rūpādevī in Vināyaka, Ārogyā in Vaidyanātha, Maheśvarī in Mahākāla, Abhayā in Uṣṇa Tīrtha, Mṛgī in Vindhya caves, the deity named Māṇḍukī in Māṇḍavya, Svāhā in the city of Maheśvara, Pracaṇḍā in Chāgaliṅga, Caṇḍikā on Amarakaṇṭaka, Varārohā in Someśvara, Puṣkarāvatī in Prabhāsa, Vedamātā on Sarasvatī, Pārā on the banks of Pārā, O Sage, Mahābhāgā in Mahālaya, Piṅgaleśvarī on Payoṣṇī, Siṁhikā in Kṛtaśauca, Śāṅkarī in Kārttika, Lolā in Utpalāvartaka, Subhadrā in the Śoṇa confluence, Lakṣmī considered (the deity) in Siddhavaṭa, Taraṅgā in Bharatāśrama, Viśvamukhī in Jālandhara, Tārā on Kiṣkindhā mountain, Puṣṭi in Devadāruvana forest, Medhā in Kāśmīra Maṇḍala, Bhīmādevī[2] on the Himālaya mountain, Puṣṭi in Vastreśvara (but in verse 84 Devadāruvana is named), Śuddhi in Kapālamocana and Mātā in Kāyāvarohaṇa.

86-98. The deity named Dhvani in Śaṅkhoddhāra, Dhṛti in Piṇḍāraka, Kālā on Candrabhāgā, Śaktidhāriṇī in Acchodā, the deity named Amṛtā on Veṇā, Urvaśī in Badarī, Oṣadhī in Uttarakuru, Kuśodakā in Kuśadvīpa, Manmathā on Hemakūṭa, Satyavādinī in Kumuda, Vandinīkā in Aśvattha, Nidhi in Vaiśravaṇālaya, Gāyatrī in Vedavadana, Pārvatī in the vicinity of Śiva, Indrāṇī in Devaloka, Sarasvatī in Brahmāsya (face of Brahmā), the deity named Prabhā in Sūryabimba (Solar disc), (I am) considered Vaiṣṇavī among the Mothers, Arundhatī among Satīs (chaste ladies), Tilottamā among Ramās (beautiful ladies), the deity named Brahmakalā in Citra, Śakti of all

1. Also Kāmukā in v 64.
2. In v 68 Nandā is associated with Himalaya.

the embodied beings, Śūleśvarī in Bhṛgukṣetra, Saubhāgyasundarī in Bhṛgu.

Thus the excellent one hundred eight names (of the deities) as well as the holy spots have been cited on the whole.

O Brāhmaṇa, this alone shall be the greatest (resort) of everyone. A man who reads the one hundred eight names in the presence of Śiva, shall be liberated from all sins. He will get the covetable and coveted woman.

A woman who takes her holy bath on the third lunar day and worships me devoutly shall never meet with misery, O excellent Brāhmaṇa, by my power.

A woman who invariably comes and visits me will never have misery brought about by her sons or husband.

In my shrine, a woman devotee shall adore the Tulāpuruṣa. She should then worship and decorate the Devas and the Guardians of the worlds, along with Fire-god. Thereafter she should honour Brāhmaṇas along with their wives by giving them garments and ornaments.

Then oblations are offered to the spirits. She should then circumambulate the Tulā and the Ṛtviks and the preceptor repeating this Mantra:

99-110. (She shall be pure and wear red garments and hold a palmful of flowers.) "Obeisance to you. You are the Śakti of all the Devas stationed supreme as witness. You are the mother of the universe created by the source of origin of the universe. O Tulā, you are glorified as the authority unto all living beings."

The devotee then closes both the fists and looks at the face of Umā. While placing herself on a pan of the weighing instrument (Tulā), eight things are to be placed on the other pan, O eminent Brāhmaṇas, in accordance with his monetary capacity. These eight things are my own parts fixed on the earth. They are: gold, Niṣpāva rice, black mustard, safflour, Tṛṇarāja (sugarcane), Indu (camphor), salt and saffron as the eighth one.

One of these should be used in accordance with the money that one can command. Gold and other things may be more than one's weight or exactly equal, O Brāhmaṇa, and the woman or man devotee should wait till the weighing is over. Then the following is to be repeated: "Obeisance, obeisance to you, O Lalitā termed Tulāpuruṣa. O Umā, redeem us from this mire of worldly existence." Then the devotee gets off the weighing machine. One half is gifted to the preceptor and the other half to the Ṛtviks while water is ritualistically poured. After taking the formal leave from them, the devotee should gift other things to other suppliants. The preceptor and his wife should be given red clothes to wear. So also to other Ṛtviks according to capacity. The preceptor is adorned with armlets and bracelets. Saying "May Lalitā be pleased"; a white milch cow too should be gifted.

A woman who performs this rite thus in my temple, shall be on a par with me. With royal glory she will shine. She will be like Sāvitrī in beauty for another fifteen births.

Śrī Mārkaṇḍeya said:

111-117. On hearing these words of Gaurī, the most excellent Brāhmaṇa bowed down and quickly went to (his) abode, O Dharmarāja.

Ever since then that Tīrtha became well-known as Śūleśvarī. A devotee should take his holy bath there in that Tīrtha and offer libations to Pitṛs and Devatās.

Brāhmaṇas should be propitiated through food and clothing and the Pitṛs and Pitāmahas through balls of rice. Śaṅkara, the Lord of Devas, should be propitiated along with Umā through the usual offerings of a devotee such as incense, Guggulu and bright lights.

Rid of all sins, he will go to the presence of Śiva. An indicted and cursed man who takes his holy bath there for three days, becomes liberated, O Lord of men.

The man who has become pure (by taking bath) and who has observed fast shall keep awake in the night on the fourteenth lunar day in the dark half. He shall then worship Śiva. Dispelling the delusion caused by sins, he goes to Rudraloka. He will acquire the form of Rudra with three eyes and four arms. He will sport about with celestial girls as long as the moon, sun and stars shine.

CHAPTER ONE HUNDRED NINETYNINE

The Greatness of Āśvina Tīrtha

Śrī Mārkaṇḍeya said:

1-7. Next to it is the excellent Āśvina Tīrtha, O king. It is the most desirable among all the Tīrthas. It is the bestower of Siddhis on all living beings.

It was at this Tīrtha that the Āśvina Devas, the most excellent ones among physicians, the very handsome ones performed an elaborate penance and became sharers in the offerings of Yajñas.

They became the most honoured ones to all the Devas. These two sons of Āditya, called Nāsatyas, were fully endowed with inherent power. They are the most excellent ones among the destroyers of all miseries.

Śrī Yudhiṣṭhira said:

For what reason did the sons of Āditya become Nāsatyas. O dear Brāhmaṇa, I wish to hear your best assessment.

Śrī Mārkaṇḍeya said:

In the Bhāskara (i.e. Āditya or Saura) Purāṇa, the behaviour and action of the noble-souled Mārtaṇḍa, the Lord of Devas, has been heard in detail by me.

Though I have become emaciated on account of old age, O descendant of Bharata, I shall undoubtedly recount this to you in brief, since you are endowed with devoted feelings.

On observing the excessive refulgence of Ravi, O excellent one among men, (His) queen, the goddess, assumed the form of a mare and performed very severe austerities in the forest on Meru.

8-14. After many days, the venerable Lord Ravi saw her galloping about briskly here and there according to her physical capacity. He became a victim to the mind-born god of Love. He cast off his supremely refulgent form and high splendor. He became a nimble-footed horse.

Neighing loudly he began to indulge in copulation with the mare. The light-footed goddess (mare) turned towards him face to face. So the excellent semen penetrated her nostril.

From the seed (semen) that entered the nostrils, an excellent foetus developed. O son of Kuntī, the sons born thereof became well known as Nāsatyas. Their limbs were symmetrical and well-formed like a duplicate drawn from an image.

They excelled all the Devas in their handsome features and masterliness. They came to the banks of Narmadā. They performed very difficult penance at Bhṛgukaccha and attained great Siddhis.

He who takes his holy bath there in that Tīrtha and offers libation to Pitṛs and Devas becomes fortunate and handsome, O son of Kuntī.

CHAPTER TWO HUNDRED

The Greatness of Sāvitrī Tīrtha

Śrī Mārkaṇḍeya said:

1-6. Next to it, O son of Kuntī, is the excellent Sāvitrī tīrtha where the highly esteemed Sāvitrī, the mother of the Vedas, attained Siddhi.

Yudhiṣṭhira said:

Who is this Sāvitrī, O excellent Brāhmaṇa? How is she propitiated by the learned? On being pleased, what boon does she grant? Do tell me.

Śrī Mārkaṇḍeya said:

Padmā, the Yoginī of lotus, presided over by the Lotus-seated One, resembles the Sun-god in her splendour. Hence she is called Sāvitrī.

The lotus-complexioned, lotus-faced Sāvitrī with the eyes resembling lotus-petals should be always meditated upon duly by Brāhmaṇas, Kṣatriyas and Vaiśyas.

She should never be meditated upon by Śūdras for fear of incurring the sin of Brāhmaṇa-slaughter. If it is uttered or retained in the mind by a Śūdra he certainly falls in Naraka.

It has been decided that for merely pronouncing the Veda

(Vedic text by a Śūdra) the tongue of that Śūdra should be cut off by Kṣatriyas who are the protectors of Dharma.

7-18. In the course of the excellent Sandhyā meditation early in the morning, Sāvitrī is to be imagined and meditated upon in the form of a girl resembling the crescent moon, with red garments and red unguents.

At midday Sāvitrī should be imagined and meditated upon as a sweet-faced, auspicious-looking, young woman with large and protruding breasts, richly adorned with all ornaments and wearing white garlands and unguents. She is wearing white clothes and has white Yajñopavīta (sacred thread). She bestows worldly pleasures and salvation.

At dusk, O son of Kuntī, she should be remembered as white-complexioned with grey hair. She protects like a mother in a forest of impassable tracts.

O great king, the excellent Sāvitrī Tīrtha is of special excellence and efficacy. After holy bath, a devotee should duly perform the Ācamana (ritualistic sipping of water). By means of Prāṇāyāma he will destroy many of his sins incurred in the course of seven births mentally, verbally and physically. He should thereby burn all defects.

A person should sprinkle his body with water while uttering the Mantra *āpohiṣṭhā,* nine, six or three times in that Tīrtha, O excellent king. If the Mantra *āpohiṣṭhā* etc. is repeated thrice, one is not defiled by the sin of *Pratigraha* (acceptance of gift from undeserving persons).

If the Mantra of *Aghamarṣaṇa* consisting of three Ṛks or one from one's Veda of special study is repeated, one is not defiled by minor sins, like a lotus leaf which is not wetted by water.

Usually the Ācamana is performed three times by a Brāhmaṇa. He shall perform three *Ullekhas* (scrubbing). He who performs the fourth one dispels the sin of Brāhmaṇa-slaughter.

The Mantra called *Drupada* from the Vājasaneyaka Veda (i.e. Vājasaneyī Saṁhitā, Śukla Yajurveda) should be repeated while in water. It destroys all sins.

One should adore Divākara (the Sun-god) with the Mantra beginning with *udutyam* and then perform the Japa of the holy Gāyatrī, the mother of the Vedas. A Brāhmaṇa who performs the Japa of Goddess Gāyatrī uninterruptedly after the Sandhyā prayers, shall be rid of all sins. He goes to Brahmaloka.

19-27. Gāyatrī quells a sin incurred in the course of ten births if repeated a hundred times. If it is repeated a thousand times, it quells the sins committed before in the course of three Yugas.

A Brāhmaṇa who has only repeated the Gāyatrī and exercises self-control is far superior to a Brāhmaṇa who has learnt all the four Vedas but has no self-control, who eats everything indiscriminately and sells everything indiscriminately.

A man bereft of Sandhyā prayers is always impure. He is disqualified in all sacred rites. If at all he does anything (religious), he does not derive the benefit thereof.

A Brāhmaṇa who does not perform the Upāsti (adoration) of the Sandhyā (twilight) is dull-witted. In this very life, he is on a par with a Śūdra. On death he is reborn as a dog.

A Brāhmaṇa, after reaching the Sāvitrī Tīrtha should perform the Japa of Sāvitrī. Undoubtedly he gets the benefit of studying the three Vedas.

If the devotee takes his holy bath with the Pitṛs in view and offers balls of rice, O king, his grandfathers become satisfied for twelve years.

If after reaching Sāvitrī Tīrtha a person castes off his life, he shall stay in Brahmaloka until the annihilation of all living beings. On the completion of that period he is reborn as a human being. O king, he is reborn in a pure family of a Brāhmaṇa learned in all the four Vedas.

He will be endowed with plenty of money and heaps of grain and have sons and grandsons. Free from ailments and grief, he shall live for a hundred years.

CHAPTER TWO HUNDRED ONE

The Greatness of Deva Tīrtha

Śrī Mārkaṇḍeya said:

1-4. Thereafter one should go to the excellent Deva Tīrtha, O king. O Yudhiṣṭhira, it was there that the highly esteemed Devas including Indra attained Siddhi.

Holy bath, Dāna, Japa, Homa and study of the Vedas as well as adoration of deities performed there become everlasting in their benefit by the power of the Tīrtha.

Especially the thirteenth day in the dark half of Bhādrapada is of great importance because the deities of all the Tīrthas gather together there.

A person should take his holy bath on the thirteenth day, perform Śrāddha in accordance with the injunctions and worship the Bull-emblemed Lord established there by Devas. He shall be free from all sins and go to Rudraloka.

CHAPTER TWO HUNDRED TWO

The Greatness of Śikhitīrtha

Śrī Mārkaṇḍeya said:

1-7. Next to it a person should go to another excellent holy spot called Śikhitīrtha. It is the most important of all the Tīrthas. It has five excellent shrines.

For the sake of his flames (and sparks) Havyavāhana (Fire-god) performed a penance and got it. Thereby he came to be called Śikhin ('one having flame'). He installed Śiva named Śikhā.

On the first lunar day in the bright half of Aśvayuja, O king, a person should go to the excellent Tīrtha and bathe in the waters of Narmadā. With gingelly seeds and water, he should offer libation to Devas, sages and Pitṛs as well as others.

After propitiating Hutāśana (Fire-god), he should make a gift of gold to a Brāhmaṇa. Thereafter, he should adore Śiva with scented garlands and incense.

After worshipping Maheśvara with this procedure in the Śikhitīrtha, the devotee becomes eligible to go to Rudraloka. Surrounded by groups of celestial women and sung about by Gandharvas, he travels by an aerial chariot having the lustre of the Sun. His enemies get destroyed and he becomes brilliant, if he is reborn on the earth.

CHAPTER TWO HUNDRED THREE

The Greatness of Koṭi Tīrtha

Śrī Mārkaṇḍeya said:

1-6. Thereafter, O Lord of the earth, a person should go to the excellent Koṭitīrtha where great and highly esteemed sages, a crore in number, became Siddhas.

After performing an elaborated penance, the sages installed Śiva as well as goddess Koṭīśvarī, Cāmuṇḍā who killed the demon called Mahiṣa.

O king, it was on the fourteenth lunar day in the dark half of the month of Bhādrapada that the sages invited crores of Tīrthas and installed Śiva. If the constellation Hasta coincides with that lunar day, it is destructive of all sins. One should go there at that time and take his holy bath with mental concentration and purity. Thereby he redeems twenty-one generations of members of his family from Naraka. Merely by offering libations with gingelly seeds and water, this is achieved. All the more so if the man performs Śrāddha. Holy bath, *Dāna, Japa, Homa,* study of the Vedas and worship of deities performed, become a crore times more effective through the contact of that Tīrtha.

CHAPTER TWO HUNDRED FOUR

The Greatness of Paitāmaha Tīrtha

Śrī Mārkaṇḍeya said:

1-9. Thereafter a person should go to the excellent Bhṛgu Tīrtha, the king of all the Tīrthas. It is highly meritorious and destructive of all sins. It pertains to Pitāmaha (Creator).

For some reason, formerly, the propitiation of Śaṁbhu was carried out by Brahmā, there at that Tīrtha for three hundred years.

Yudhiṣṭhira said:

O tiger among sages, why did Brahmā, the grandfather of the worlds, propitiate Maheśvara, the Lord of Devas, with great devotion?

He himself is worthy of being propitiated by all living beings. He is the Lord of the universe. I wish to listen about this great and excellent miracle worthy of being heard.

On hearing the words of Dharmaputra, Mārkaṇḍeya, the leader of sages, recounted the old legendary story.

Śrī Mārkaṇḍeya said:

Formerly, the Grandfather wished to approach carnally his own mental daughter, O excellent one. He was then cursed by the angry Lord of Devas: "O Lotus-seated One, the Vedas will cease to be with you and your knowledge will come to an end. Undoubtedly you will never be worthy of the adoration of all the worlds."

When this curse was uttered, Brahmā became overwhelmed with sorrow. He went to the northern bank of Revā. Taking regular baths, he propitiated the Lord of Devas for three hundred years. Śaṅkara was ultimately pleased and said: "During *Parvas* (days of religious festivity) you shall become worthy of being worshipped. I too shall stay here along with the Devas and Pitṛs."

Śrī Mārkaṇḍeya said:

10-16. Ever since then, thanks to Pitāmaha, that Tīrtha became famous. It is meritorious and destructive of all sins. It is the most excellent one among all the Tīrthas.

On a new-moon day (or) any day in the dark half of the month of Bhādrapada, one should take holy bath and offer libations to Pitṛs and Devas.

O kings, even if it is only a single ball of rice or water mixed with gingelly seeds, the Pitṛs undoubtedly become satisfied for twelve years.

When (the Sun) is in Virgo, a person should offer Śrāddha everyday. The ancestors derive delight therefrom and begin to laugh and jump (joyously). Undoubtedly, one gets through a single Śrāddha performed on a new-moon day that benefit which accrues by performing Śrāddha in all the Pitṛtīrthas.

A man who takes his holy bath in Paitāmaha Tīrtha and worships the Consort of Pārvatī becomes rid of major and minor sins. There is no doubt about it.

Men who die there in that Tīrtha become purified in their souls, O king. They undoubtedly go to Rudraloka from which they never return.

CHAPTER TWO HUNDRED FIVE

The Greatness of Kurkurī Tīrtha

Śrī Mārkaṇḍeya said:

1-5. Thereafter, O king, a person should go to the highly splendid Tīrtha well known by the name Kurkurī. It is destructive of all sins.

The goddess of Devas, Kurkurī, is the presiding deity of the Tīrtha. She grants whatever one prays for such as cattle, sons, wealth etc.

The Kṣetrapāla (guardian of the holy spot) residing there is named Dhaundheśa. A devotee, man or woman, who propitiates him and then bows down (to the deity), O great king, gets his ill-luck destroyed thereby. One without a son gets a son. One without wealth gets excellent wealth. Men and women realise the excellent wishes cherished by visiting and taking bath in that Tīrtha in accordance with the injunctions.

CHAPTER TWO HUNDRED SIX

The Greatness of Daśakanyā Tīrtha

Śrī Mārkaṇḍeya said:

1-5. Thereafter, O king, one should go to the highly splendid and meritorious Tīrtha that destroys all sins. It is well-known as Daśakanyā Tīrtha. It was created by Mahādeva and gives all desired things.

It was there at that Tīrtha that Mahādeva celebrated the marriages of the ten daughters of Brahmā endowed with all good qualities. Ever since then that became well-known as Daśakanyā Tīrtha. It is meritorious and destructive of all sins. The benefit thereof is glorified as everlasting.

A person should make a gift of his daughter fully adorned in accordance with his capacity. O king, the devotees become meritorious-souled due to the Puṇya arising from the gift. They stay in the proximity of Śiva for as many years as there are hair (on the body).

6-10. After a long time, O Lord of men, they attain human birth usually very difficult to get. They shall be possessors of crores of coins.

One who devoutly takes his holy bath there in that Tīrtha and offers to a quiescent Brāhmaṇa a piece of gold attains great happiness.

O descendant of Bharata, due to the gift of gold all the sins incurred earlier such as verbal, mental, and physical perish entirely.

One who offers gold even as little as the tip of a hair, goes to heaven on death. There is no doubt about this.

There he occupies an excellent aerial chariot and is worshipped by Siddhas and Vidyādharas. He shall stay there until the annihilation of all living beings.

CHAPTER TWO HUNDRED SEVEN

The Greatness of Suvarṇabindu Tīrtha

Śrī Mārkaṇḍeya said:

1-9. In front of it is the sacred Tīrtha well known as Svarṇabindu. People who take their holy bath there go to heaven. On death they do not get a rebirth.

O Lord of the earth, listen to the benefit that is cited as arising from the gift of a piece of gold to a Brāhmaṇa after taking holy bath there in the Tīrtha.

Of all jewels, gold is the excellent jewel. It is born of the fiery brilliance of Agni. Hence it is the greatest on the earth.

If a person, therefore, gives a piece of gold, it is as though the entire earth including the cities and towns, mountains, forests and parks has been given.

O descendant of Bharata, by the gift of gold all the sins incurred earlier, whether mental, verbal or physical, perish entirely.

Even if the devotee gives only a piece of gold as little as the tip of a hair, there in the Tīrtha, he goes to heaven on death. There is no doubt about it.

There he occupies an excellent aerial chariot and is worshipped by Vidyādharas and Siddhas. He should stay there until the annihilation of all living beings.

When his period (of stay in heaven) comes to an end, he attains human birth. He is reborn as a Brāhmaṇa in a family possessing crores of gold pieces.

He shall be free from all the ailments. He shall be honoured in all the worlds. He shall live for more than a hundred years and be well known in royal assemblies.

CHAPTER TWO HUNDRED EIGHT

The Greatness of Ṛṇamocana Tīrtha

Śrī Mārkaṇḍeya said:

1-9. O protector of the earth, thereafter one should go to the highly splendid Tīrtha well known in all the three worlds as 'that which discharges the debts due to the manes.'

A man who takes his holy bath in accordance with the injunctions, offers libation to Pitṛs and Devas and gives gifts, O excellent king, becomes free from indebtedness.

All the Pitṛs (ancestors) wish for a son for their own purpose, because they say "This son shall redeem us from the hell named *Put.*"

Offer of balls of rice and water libation is called the first indebtedness. It is mentioned as the debt of the Pitṛs.

Hereafter I shall mention the *Daiva Ṛṇa* ('indebtedness to Devas'). Agnihotra, Yajñas, tying (for sacrifice) a sacrificial animal and the Iṣṭis should be performed. Thus the indebtedness to the Devas has been mentioned.

Thereafter listen to the human indebtedness. What is promised and then given to Brāhmaṇas during the rites performed at Tīrthas and shrines is the human indebtedness.

O son of Dharma, these three together are called *Ṛṇatrayam* ('threefold indebtedness') of the sons. Good sons are those who take their holy bath in the Ṛṇamocanatīrtha. Therein those with or without sons are redeemed from threefold indebtedness.

Hence, a son of fully controlled self should go to this excellent Tīrtha and offer libations and balls of rice to the Pitṛs.

What is given and consigned to fire (Homa) is of everlasting benefit. If the preceptors are pleased, the devotee derives benefit for seven births.

CHAPTER TWO HUNDRED NINE

The Greatness of Bhārabhūti Tīrtha

Śrī Mārkaṇḍeya said:

1-9. Next to it, O son of Kuntī, is the excellent Puṣkalī Tīrtha. A man who takes his holy bath there in that Tīrtha shall get the benefit of a horse-sacrifice.

O Lord of the earth, thereafter a person should go to the Tīrtha well- known in all the three worlds. It is resorted to by Devas, Dānavas, Gandharvas and celestial damsels.

There stays directly Rudra, the great Lord of Devas. He is remembered as Bhārabhūti because he manifested himself with a great burden.

Yudhiṣṭhira said:

I wish to hear about the Tīrtha well -known as Bhārabhūti. It is endowed with all good features. O leading Brāhmaṇa, my eagerness is very great.

Śrī Mārkaṇḍeya said:

O most excellent one among the sons of Pāṇḍu, listen to the origin of (the name) Bhārabhūti the way it was explained earlier by Lord Śaṁbhu in detail.

In Kṛtayuga, there was a Brāhmaṇa who had mastered the Vedas and Vedāṅgas. He was well - known by the name Viṣṇuśarman. He was perfectly conversant with the topics of all the scriptural texts.

He had the full complement of all good qualities such as forbearance, self-control, compassion, munificence, truthfulness, cleanliness, fortitude, learning, perfect knowledge and piousness.

O excellent king, only those Brāhmaṇas who have qualities of this type redeem the Pitṛs fallen into terrible Narakas.

Those Brāhmaṇas who ardently long for the pleasures of senses are deluded through sins, O excellent king. They fall into terrible Raurava Naraka.

10-15. Those Brāhmaṇas who have forbearance and self-control, whose ears are filled with Śruti sounds, who have conquered the sense-organs, who desist from killing living beings and the finger ends of whose hands shrink from accepting gifts, are capable of redeeming (others).

A Brāhmaṇa, endowed with such sterling qualities stayed on the banks of Narmadā along with other Brāhmaṇas. The means of his sustenance was gleaning of the ears of corns.

On coming to know of such a Brāhmaṇa, Maheśvara, the Lord of Devas, assumed the form of a Brāhmaṇa and personally went direct to his hermitage.

On meeting the Brāhmaṇa reciting the Vedic Mantras in the Pāṭha called *Pada* and *Krama* along with the other Brāhmaṇas, he made obeisance to the Brāhmaṇa. He was also honoured with due formalities of reception.

After a short while, the Brāhmaṇa who was taken by surprise asked: "O Brāhmaṇa boy, what is it you desire that I can do for you?"

The *Baṭu* (Brāhmaṇa boy) said: "O excellent Brāhmaṇa, take me to be a disciple having come to you. If you impart instruction, I shall stay in your house."

The Brāhmaṇa said:

16-26. O Baṭu, you hail from the most excellent Gotra of all Brāhmaṇas. The greatest of all *Dānas* is the *Dāna* of *Vidyā*. How can it be given? By service rendered to the preceptor or by ample fee paid. Or *Vidyā* can be fruitful by another *Vidyā* (in return)?

The Baṭu replied:

Just as other boys who are duly initiated serve you day and night, similarly I too shall serve you along with other boys.

The eminent Brāhmaṇa said, "So it shall be" and began teaching him everyday along with the other disciples. He too (i.e. the Baṭu) regularly brought the gleanings of the ears of corn.

After a few days Īśvara (the Lord in the form of the Baṭu) was told by the other pupils: "O Baṭu, it is your turn now. Do the work of cooking etc."

After saying "So it shall be" the Lord of Devas went off to

Bhāragrāma village. Meditating on all vegetables (and their presiding deities) he spoke these words:

"By the time the Brāhmaṇa returns to the abode along with the disciples, the cooked food should be kept ready by you all remaining invisible."

After saying thus to all of them, the Cosmic-formed Maheśvara took the guise of the Baṭu separately and went there to play.

On seeing him come in the guise of a Baṭu separately, they censured him in harsh words in the presence of the Giri (*Guru*: probable reading):

"Fie upon you! The throats of all of us are parched with hunger. We thought that going to our abode we shall get satisfaction by the food cooked by you. O Brāhmaṇa, by your coming here (to play) you have frustrated our expectations. O Brāhmaṇa, you have come away after making a false promise. You have committed a foul act."

The Baṭu said:

27-39. O bulls among Brāhmaṇas, you need not have any exasperation or regret in the matter of food. You will be going back to the abode where you will find the food ready.

The other Baṭus said:

Everyday while we cook food, it does or does not become ready in the remaining part of the day. Here it is completely uncooked (you have not cooked at all). But what is not ready is being cited by you as ready. After going there and proving your lie, we will bind you and cast you into the waters.

The Baṭu said:

O excellent Brāhmaṇas including the preceptor, listen ye all to my solemn, irrefutable declaration. On hearing it you may perhaps be dismayed. If every item of food you find ready and cooked in the hermitage of our preceptor, all of you will be bound and should be hurled by me into the waters of Narmadā. Or if the food is not ready I should be bound firmly by you all and hurled into the whirlpool of Narmadā even as the preceptor is watching us.

They all assented to this stipulation in the presence of the preceptor. They concluded their holy bath, Japa etc., in accordance with the injunctions and went back to the Bhūtagrāma village.

On seeing an elaborate presentation of the articles of food, they were surprised agreeably. O excellent king, they ate all the items with six tastes severally. Then the delighted and well-nourished excellent Brāhmaṇa spoke these words: "O dear child, I am ready to grant you any boon whatever may appeal to you. All the Vedas with their Aṅgas and Upāṅgas and the different scriptural texts will manifest themselves to you. They will manifest of their own accord to you. Let this be my boon unto you." The boy bowed down and went about playing happily with the other Baṭus.

The next day, O Yudhiṣṭhira, all of them went to the waters of Narmadā for sporting about. Then recollecting the wager and cautioning all of them the Lord (in the form of the Baṭu) bowed down to the preceptor and said with palms joined in reverence: "O holy Lord, I shall hurl into water all the Baṭus who have lost the wager."

40-52. On hearing the words of the Lord, O king, even as the preceptor was watching the other Baṭus dispersed running in all the directions.

The Lord rushed at them with the speed of wind all round and caught hold of them. Tying them up into a weighty bundle the Lord who both curses and blesses, hurled them into the water as though within the house.

The preceptor saw them in the waters of Narmadā and told the Baṭu: "Why did you commit this rash deed? If their parents or the other women in the houses of these boys were to ask me, shall what I tell them? Where have they gone? This being the case, O fair Sir, if any one dies, you will have to make it up with your own life. If those Brāhmaṇa children die, it is certain that I too will die. When I die, many sins of Brāhmaṇa-slaughter will assail you. Even if a single Brāhmaṇa is bound, the assailant will certainly fall into Naraka. O base Brāhmaṇa, I do not know what you will face after death."

On being told thus, Maheśvara, the Lord of Devas smiled and raised up the Brāhmaṇas from the Bhārabhūteśvara Tīrtha.

The weights attached were taken away. A Liṅga called Bhārabhūta was installed there.

Seeing the dead ones coming back as the former Brāhmaṇas, the sin of Brāhmaṇa-slaughter was removed. All the five hundred Brahmahatyās disappeared.

On seeing those boys, the preceptor became amazed. He came to know that except for the great Lord Īśvara, no one else can have such a power.

Realizing that it was the Lord of chiefs of Devas, the Brāhmaṇa bowed down to him and said: "O Parameśvara, whatever has been said by me displeasing you, was due to my ignorance and whatever has been done by me which was not to your liking should be forgiven, O Lord."

The Deva said:

53-57. O holy Sir, you are my preceptor. You are my Lord. You are my grandfather, O Vedagarbha ('one who has mastered the Vedas by heart'), obeisance to you. There is nothing out of the way.

The progenitor, the priest who invests with the sacred thread, the preceptor who imparts learning, he who gives food and he who provides succour from fear — these five are remembered as Fathers (Protectors).

After saying thus to Viṣṇuśarman, the Lord of the universe bowed down to him there in that Tīrtha and quickly went away to the Kailāsa mountain.

Ever since then, that Tīrtha is famous as Bhārabhūti. It is reputed in all the worlds as destructive of great sins.

I shall tell you another event that happened there in the Tīrtha. It is a great legendary event that is divine and destructive of all sins. Listen to it with an attentive mind.

58-68. Formerly, at the beginning of Kṛta Yuga, there was a high-minded Vaiśya well known as Sukeśa. That large-eyed Vaiśya passed away. His son well- known as Somaśarmā was highly pious and righteous. He formed friendship with one poverty-stricken son of a Vaiśya known as Sahadeva. He was very efficient in all activities.

Once he thought of a partnership deal with him. "Friend, with my money as the capital we shall buy and take with us much merchandise. We shall go on voyage in a ship with auspicious embarkation. We shall go to the other shore (country). The profit will be equal between us."

Thus they took counsel together in regard to what they planned. Taking all the requisites for the voyage, they rode (set sail) on the salt sea.

They went to the other shore and sold their wares in a city there. Much gold and different kinds of jewels were acquired by them.

The boat was made fit for the voyage and they got into it.

It was midnight. Sahadeva observed that the boat fully laden with gold was sailing on the high sea and that Somaśarmā, with full trust in him was sleeping with his head placed on his lap. He thought thus: 'This fellow has gone to sleep with his very life in my hand. The entire proceeds (gold etc.) are in his possession. It is not sure that he will give me half the profit after going there. He may or he may not.'

On coming to this conclusion, the sinful wretch hurled Somaśarmā into the salt sea.

69-79. Taking the entire wealth, he crossed the ocean by means of that boat. After a few days, he met with his death.

He was seized by the servants of Yama and taken to the terrible city of Yama. He was taken along that path where the Sun had grown twelve-fold and was blazing as though at the time of the ultimate dissolution of the universe. There were many extremely sharp thorns, hideous dogs, great serpents with sharp fangs, tigers, and huge wolves. There the sands were excessively hot. There was hunger, thirst and pitch darkness. There was no talk (i.e. trace, or drop) of water, no shade or hermitage anywhere. Any food along with water, turns into poison.

If people request for shade, the fire burned all the more hot. The wretched inhabitants who were burned lamented again and again.

They cried, "Alas, mother! Alas, brother! Alas, son!" and fell into swoon on the way. That (Sahadeva) was led through the path of such nature by the servants of Yama.

The servants of Yama left (produced) him at the door of the palace where Lord Yama, the controller of the subjects, was staying. After tying tightly a rope round the neck of the betrayer of his friend they reported: "Listen, O Lord of Devas. You know what should be done thereafter."

Yama said:

The face of those who commit breach of trust has never been seen by me. There are clever and efficient sages appointed here for the purpose of deliberating and deciding what punishment should be meted out to the sinners perpetrating breach of trust to their friends. Cast this fellow over there where they order you to cast him. You need not think about it further.

80-92. Ordered thus the servants of Yama hastened to the great sages along with him. Producing him before them as per order of Yama, they reported with reference to him:

"By this fellow, out of greed for wealth, his own friend who trusted him and was asleep at night was murdered. What should be the punishment for this crime?"

The sages said:

The face of the murderer of friends has never been seen by us before. Keep him hooded with a screen. You can hear later what his punishment shall be.

Those sages pored over the scriptural texts and discussed mutually. The leading Brāhmaṇas then summoned the messengers of Yama and told them:

"The scriptural texts were gone through; the Vedas with their Aṅgas, the Smṛti texts, the Purāṇas, and Mīmāṁsā texts have been consulted by us.

Means of expiation have been laid down in the scriptures in regard to Brāhmaṇa-slaughter, imbibing liquor, theft and carnal approach to the wife of preceptor but there is no way of atonement for the ungrateful (one who kills his friend).

Means of expiation have been prescribed in regard to those who kill women, preceptors, Brāhmaṇas and children. But there is nothing by way of expiation for the ungrateful. Means of expiation have been enjoined in regard to those sinners who demolish tanks, wells and lakes, to those wicked people who cut off and demolish gardens and parks, to those who burn forests, to those who injure lives, to those who administer poison, who deceive their masters, who forsake parents and preceptors, who find fault with others, to a woman who is disloyal to her husband, to a woman who destroys foetus, to a woman bereft of discrimination, who takes food without taking bath, who takes two meals on the *Vaiṣṇavavāsara* (on the eleventh lunar day) etc. A way of acquittal by expiation is seen in regard to all those women but not to those who betray trust and to men who are inimical to their friends. They have no salvation (expiation) according to the Vedas. What need one say of the Purāṇas! In the case of such sinners there is no way of expiation.

93-103. No other way of salvation has been heard by us for killers of friends and of those who have trusted.

O messengers of Yama, take this betrayer of trust from this place. Let him be cast into all the Narakas numbering thirty crores severally and by turns, for a period of hundred crores of Kalpas. You need not hesitate in this respect.

On hearing these words, the servants bound him and took him to cast him into the terrible Narakas. At the outset they took him to the terrible hell named Raurava.

They hurled the great sinner there. As soon as he was put there, a great uproar of protest was heard from the creatures suffering in that Naraka: "This sinner should not be left here. Merely by touching him, our pain increases hundred-fold as though we are cut with swords or burned with well-kindled fuel. What dirty thing did he commit? Just as a good man is reduced to a low status due to association with an evil one, so is the case with the proximity of this fellow. It is like sprinkling acid on a wound. May this favour be done. Let him be taken to another Naraka."

On being requested thus by them, they went towards *Aśuci*. The residents of that hell shouted like those in the previous ones. All those servants wandered from hell to hell. Thus that evil-minded sinner had no place of rest even in Naraka. The situation being such, all of them took him to the presence of Yama. They told him whatever was voiced by the residents of those hells and asked him: "Tell us. What should be done with that fellow who has no place even in hell?"

Yama said:

104-109. Let this foulest sinner fall into brutish wombs for periods of time as mentioned by the sages. Let him be forced into the wombs of brutish creatures.

When these words were uttered by the Controller of subjects (i.e. Yama), the fellow attained birth successively as worms living in feces. Thereafter he became a fly, mosquito, ant, louse, bug etc., by turns and then a bird.

Thereafter, he became an immobile being (like a tree) and then he attained the state of a rock. Then he became a reptile, python, boar, deer, elephant, wolf, dog, mule, camel, pig, domestic animals, ass and buffalo and other similar wombs of brutish creatures successively. At the end he became a beast of burden in the abode of a righteous king of great fame.

110-117. Once that excellent king noted that Kārttikī (the full-moon day in the month of Kārttika) was imminent. He summoned his priest and many other Brāhmaṇas and said: "This I have heard often that Kārttikī festival should not be celebrated at home. Tell me, O excellent Brāhmaṇas, where we all shall go in a body. It is the injunction of the Śruti. 'He who spends the Kārttikī day without holy bath, Dāna and other rites loses the Puṇya performed in the course of a year.' Hence we shall assiduously go in a body to a Tīrtha with all good features in order to take the holy bath and make gifts in accordance with our capacity."

When these words were uttered by the king, the excellent Brāhmaṇas said: "O excellent king, on the northern bank of Revā, there is a Tīrtha yielding salvation, well-known as Bhāreśvara Tīrtha. We shall all go there. It is capable of wiping off all sins."

On being told so, the king took with him plenty of money and filled a cart with all this. That beast of burden was Sahadeva who after committing the murder of his friend, had now reached the species of a bull. He was yoked to the cart.

118-127. Thus he reached the excellent Tīrtha on the banks of Narmadā. After going there, he waited patiently for the fast on the fourteenth lunar day.

The procedure of worship (vv 119-145)

On that day, he went to the banks of Narmadā uttering the name of Rudra many times attentively. Thereafter, uttering the following Mantra he took some mud from a clean place: "You were lifted up by the Boar and the hundred-armed Rudra. I shall also lift (you) up along with the progeny and the binding."

After taking the mud and casting it down on the northern bank, he looked at the Sun. Then with the following Mantra he applied the mud over the body: "O Earth trodden over by horses, traversed over by chariot, walked over by Viṣṇu, O Earth, dispel my sin acquired in the course of hundred crores of births."

Afterwards entering into the water he uttered the following Mantra: "O Narmadā of meritorious waters, your water has originated from Śaṅkara. May it dispel the sins incurred by me even as I take my holy bath."

After performing the holy ablution as per this procedure, he offered libations to Pitṛs and Devas, went to the shrine taking with him the requisite offerings.

In his presence he devoutly meditated upon Śaṅkara, the benefactor of the world.

In accordance with the injunctions laid down in the Purāṇas, he began the worship. Fourfold worship of the Lord during Śivarātri is being prescribed.

In the first Yāma (Watch) (a period of 3 hours) the king bathed Śaṅkara with Pañcagavya. The filling-up was afterwards performed with ghee by the excellent king.

128-138. At the outset incense and lights were offered with due Saṅkalpa (ritualistic utterance of what is proposed to be done). *Arghya* was offered to the Lord of Devas, Śaṅkara, with the Mantra recited as:

"Obeisance to you, O Lord of the chiefs of Devas, O Śaṁbhu the ultimate cause. O Lord, accept this *Arghya* and remove the sin in the form of Saṁsāra (mundane existence). Gold consecrated with Mantras has been given according to the financial capacity. Agni alone represents all the Devas and gold is (obtained) from fire. Hence all Devas may become pleased by the gift of gold. May Śaṅkara be always pleased with the person offering *Arghya*."

According to this procedure Śiva was worshipped by him in the first Yāma.

The procedure at the outset is the same for the second Yāma.

(The king) bathed the Slayer of Tripuras with cow's milk. The filling-up of the Liṅga of the Trident-bearing Lord was later performed with raw rice grains.

Following the procedure mentioned earlier a pair of white cloth was given because a pair of white cloth is very dear to Śaṅkara. Śaṁbhu becomes pleased when white cloth is offered.

On observing that the third Yāma had arrived, the excellent king bathed the Lord with honey and filling-up was done by means of gingelly seeds.

Uttering the following Mantra, a Droṇa (a measure) of gingelly seeds should be offered: "Whether the gingelly seeds are white or black, they dispel all sins. May my bond be cut off by this gift of a *Droṇa* of gingelly seeds."

According to this procedure the king concluded the worship of that Yāma of the night. Then he performed the rite of *Jāgaraṇa* along with entertainments and the chanting of the Vedic passages. The adoration of Śaṁbhu, which is a source of acquiring much merit, was done.

139-147. O son of Kuntī, even Yajvins (those who perform Yajñas) do not get the goal which those persons get, the persons who auspiciously abide by the Jāgaraṇa (keeping awake) rite of the Three-eyed Lord, during Śivarātri in a shrine of Bhava (Śiva). Whatever may be the sins, sins acquired in the course of crores of births, if Jāgaraṇa of Hara and Keśava is performed and the devotees take holy bath, those sins perish.

O king, the devotees derive the benefit of an Aśvamedha for each of the moments spent during the night in the rite of Jāgaraṇa. No one shall obtain the same goal even if people are engaged in the observance of fasts, staying in the shrines, listening to pious narratives, meditating on Hara and Keśava or in performing *Kratu* (sacrifice) with much gold (given as gift). The Tithi (lunar day) of Śivarātri is meritorious and Kārttikī is specially so; the northern bank of Revā and Bhāreśvara Tīrtha too are so.

How can then the sin of one who keeps awake not perish? Thus that Lord of men kept awake during Śivarātri. When it dawned bright, he went to the excellent banks of Narmadā and thought: 'It was through the help of these animals that pulled the carts etc., that I could come to the Tīrtha and have my holy bath. I shall, therefore, make them also have the (benefit of) the bath.'

Then all the vehicles, elephants etc., were thus bathed by him. The merchant who passed through the various births of creatures etc. and was standing in the middle was also bathed.

148-159. With these in view, he made some gifts in accordance with his capacity. By means of this rite, a man becomes rid of the defects (sins) brought about through (riding) the vehicles. Otherwise the profit (benefit) acquired solely goes to them.

After bathing them, the king himself took his holy bath in accordance with the injunctions; offered libations to Pitṛs and Devas, performed the Śrāddha rite duly, offered balls of rice to Pitṛs, ritualistically released a bull endowed with all good characteristics, went to the holy shrine, bathed Lord Śaṅkara successively with the waters of the Tīrtha, Pañcagavya, Pañcāmṛta, waters containing all medicinal herbs and finally with pure water.

Then Śaṅkara was smeared with sweet-smelling sandalpaste. The fourth filling-up of the Liṅga was performed with saffron, camphor, diverse kinds of scents and clusters of fragrant flowers by the excellent king who followed the previous procedure.

Afterwards gift of a cow was made in accordance with the rites laid down in the scriptural injunctions (uttering the following Mantra): "O cow, you are of the form of Rudra. You have been created by Rudra. Redeem me from falling into unfathomable ocean of mundane existence."

A well-adorned cow should be gifted with this procedure. After requesting the Lord of the chiefs of Devas for pardon, the devotee should feed many Brāhmaṇas with six types of foodstuff. They should be honoured with clothes. After adoring them with diverse kinds of monetary gifts, the devotee requests them for forgiveness.

The Lord of the Earth did everything and took food himself later along with his attendants. He stayed there for that night. Even as he spent the night there thus, he heard the utterance of a divine voice in the sky at mid-night.

The Voice said:

160-168. O king, the benefit will accrue to the world all round now. Wicked souls that had fallen into the ocean of mundane existence derive benefit merely by their being present (in the Tīrtha). How it is so is being described, if it can be cause of elation to one born in the family of Śantanu (Dharmaputra).

Now in your house there is a beast of burden. By this fellow the sin of killing a friend and committing breach of trust was incurred in a previous birth, with more than a thousand other rebirths intervening. He was stationed in Narakas due to the sin. Then he was born and reborn into thousands of wombs of creatures. That wicked fellow finally was born as a bull in your abode. In the course of the present religious festival, he was bathed in the Tīrtha by you. He witnessed the worship performed by you and also kept awake. Thereby he has become rid of sins. In front of you, O king, he will cast off his body and go to heaven seated in an aerial chariot.

Śrī Mārkaṇḍeya said:

As soon as this was uttered, the bull, the beast of burden, fell dead. Instantly he was seen seated in an aerial chariot. He bowed down to the leading king and said smilingly:

The Vṛṣa (Bull) said:

169-179. O most excellent one among eminent kings, indeed the efficacy of the Tīrtha is very great, since a man like me is rid of all sins. I have realized completely. There is no other sinner like me, on a par with me.

Henceforth what more shall I do except glorifying the Tīrtha? You are my mother. You are my brother. You are also my grandfather. I should be excused. I am bowing down to you. It is such a splendid Tīrtha where people like me attain a bright status. I do not know what your fate would be.

You have propitiated Maheśāna after adoring him duly. What would be the fate in your case! O Lord, grant me permission to go. These groups of divine beings stationed in heaven are prompting me to hurry up. Hail unto you! I shall go.

After saying this, he vanished in a moment.

Śrī Mārkaṇḍeya said:

When the bull vanished there the king was amazed. He went to his city extolling the incomparable greatness of the Tīrtha.

Such is that Tīrtha situated on Narmadā, destructive of all sins, excellent, dispelling all miseries.

Minor sins perish merely on account of holy bath, O descendant of Bharata. On the fourteenth lunar day in the month of Kārttika, a devotee should observe fast and fill the Liṅga in four ways. Listen to the benefit of that merit.

By the power of these four the great sins perish, viz. those of Brāhmaṇa-slaughter, imbibing liquor, stealing and carnally approaching the wife of preceptor. He gets the excellent benefit of an Aśvamedha Yajña.

One who has observed fast on the fourteenth lunar day in the bright half of the month of Kārttika should make the gift of gold in that Tīrtha. He gets the benefit of Yajña.

180-186. On the eighth and fourteenth days of the month of Vaiśākha too (observe) as before. By making a lamp of flourcake the devotee causes salvation to Pitṛs.

Whatever is given as Dāna there, even if it be as little as the tip of a hair, shall have everlasting benefit. So says Maheśvara.

O king, men who die in Bhārabhūti become purified in their souls. They will reach the goal of Śivaloka from where there is no return.

Or for the sake of the growth in avocation of the world, he will desire to conquer the mortal world. He is reborn in a pure family of Brāhmaṇas who have mastered the Vedas with their Aṅgas. He will live for a hundred years rich with wealth and foodgrain and possessing Vedic lore. He will be free from all ailments.

Again he will come to that Tīrtha and attain the eternal region. Thus, O descendant of Bharata, O excellent king, the meritorious story destructive of sins has been recounted to you. Next to it listen to another great narrative.

CHAPTER TWO HUNDRED TEN

The Greatness of Puṅkhila Tīrtha

Śrī Mārkaṇḍeya said:

1-8. Next, O dear one, is the excellent Puṅkhila Tīrtha. O son of Kuntī, it was there in that Tīrtha that Puṅkha attained Siddhi.

A holy sage, the son of Jamadagni, the highly refulgent destroyer of Kṣatriyas, performed an elaborate penance there on the northern bank of Narmadā.

Ever since then, O Lord of men, the Puṅkha Tīrtha became well-known. He who takes his holy bath there in that Tīrtha and propitiates Parameśvara, becomes endowed with extraordinary strength in this world and attains salvation in the other world. He who adores Devas and Pitṛs becomes free from indebtedness to Pitṛs.

If a man casts off his life there in the Tīrtha, he will undoubtedly proceed to Rudraloka from where he will have no return.

A man who takes his holy bath there in that Tīrtha, shall obtain the merit of a horse-sacrifice. If a man feeds a single Brāhmaṇa there in that Tīrtha, it is as good as a crore of Brāhmaṇas are fed.

Whoever worships the Bull-emblemed Lord there in the Tīrtha undoubtedly obtains the merit of a Vājapeya Yajña.

CHAPTER TWO HUNDRED ELEVEN

The Greatness of Muṇḍi Tīrtha

Śrī Mārkaṇḍeya said:

1-9. What was done by the Lord of Devas in regard to those residing on the banks of Narmadā, was something very surprising to the entire world. I shall recount it to you fully. The Lord assumed the form of a leper and begged of some miserly Brāhmaṇas at the time of Śrāddha. He had smeared himself with red sandalpaste as unguent.

There were bubbles of exudation from his limbs. He was fully covered with worms and flies. He had a foul face and his skin was sorely infested. He was stinking and he faltered at every step.

He went to the abode of a Brāhmaṇa and stumbling at the door said thus: "O householder, I wish to take well-cooked and consecrated food today at your house along with these Brāhmaṇas."

On seeing the Brāhmaṇa with foul effusions all over the body, the Brāhmaṇas in the company of the householder said: "Fie upon you! Fie upon you! O stinking fellow, get out. O base Brāhmaṇa, get away from this house quickly. Since you looked at it, this consecrated foodstuff has become unworthy of being eaten by everyone.

"That is so", said Maheśvara, the Lord of Devas. Even as he was being watched by the excellent Brāhmaṇas, he rose into the clear sky. When the Lord later vanished, the Brāhmaṇas took bath and sprinkled themselves with water all around.

When they were about to take their food separately in the different platters, they saw worms and worms wherever they looked.

10-17. On seeing it, all of them were amazed and said: "What is this?" Then one of them said: "This Brāhmaṇa is Brahmā himself; he has many good qualities."

Another said: "He had come here before in the assembly of many Brāhmaṇas somewhat hesitatingly. He is Parameśvara, the great Yogin.

This transformation of foods is his playful practical joke, the result of our rebuking him, not of anybody else. It is declared by the scriptures that a guest should be honoured. If not, the result would be unpleasant. He is worthy of adoration, being the supreme Soul and a guest in particular. If anyone does not honour a guest who comes at the time of Śrāddha, Piśācas and Rākṣasas spoil it undoubtedly.

In regard to a guest, we should not considered whether he is handsome or ugly, dirty or wearing dirty clothes, Yogīndra or a Cāṇḍāla."

On hearing these words, the Brāhmaṇas with the householder as their leader, rushed to all the directions in search of the Brāhmaṇa guest.

Somehow someone saw him hidden in a thick forest and shouted: "He is seen." All of them came there and saw the Brāhmaṇa standing steady like a post.

18-22. He did not flicker or move, shout or see. Some of them lamented piteously; others began to pray with pleasing words. Thus the Three-eyed Lord was eulogized. Then they requested: "O Lord of Devas, the cooked food of the hungry Brāhmaṇas is utterly spoiled. It behoves you to make it good."

O Yudhiṣṭhira, on hearing the words of those Brāhmaṇas, the Lord became pleased and said to them with great compassion:

"O highly esteemed ones, I have become pleased. So I have made that same food of yours pure like nectar. May the Brāhmaṇas eat it along with their kinsmen and servants. Let them worship my Maṇḍala (mystical circle) everyday.

Thereat, O son of Kuntī, that shrine became famous by the name Muṇḍi. On the day of the Kārttikī festival it is particularly on a par with Gayātīrtha.

CHAPTER TWO HUNDRED TWELVE

The Greatness of Ekaśāla Ḍiṇḍimeśvara Tīrtha

Śrī Mārkaṇḍeya said:

1-10. Henceforth I shall recount another superb act of the Lord. Merely on hearing it, one is rid of all sins.

Assuming the exact disguise of a begging mendicant, Maheśvara, the Lord of Devas, went to village Ekaśālā seeking alms. He was hungry and thirsty.

He had smeared himself with holy ash and had a rosary displayed in his hand. The Lord of the universe had his matted hair and earrings for his ornaments. The trident shone in his hand.

Clad in elephant hide, the Lord of huge physical form was embellished with the great serpents. He was playing on his splendid Ḍamaruka (hand-drum) resembling a Ḍiṇḍima.

The Lord had a skull in his hand. He was surrounded by

many boys. Dancing and singing, laughing and playing at times, he moved on.

The Lord sportingly placed down the Ḍiṇḍima on some houses. Wherever he placed it down, the house collapsed by its weight.

Moving thus the Lord was surrounded by many men. The Lord was sometimes visible and sometimes not visible. Thus the Lord came out of the crowd. He began to run about here and there. Whenever he became invisible, the men stood perplexed. They thought that it should be Śaṁbhu himself. Then they eulogized him.

Even as they devoutly eulogized Śaṅkara, the Lord of the worlds was seen stationed in the form of Ḍiṇḍi (ma). Ever since then, the Lord of Devas is called Ḍiṇḍimeśvara. By seeing and touching him, one is rid of all sins.

CHAPTER TWO HUNDRED THIRTEEN

The Greatness of Āmaleśvara Tīrtha

Śrī Mārkaṇḍeya said:

1-6. Further I shall recount another superb (miraculous) act of the Lord. Merely by listening to it, one is rid of all sins.

Though not a boy, Śaṁbhu himself in the form of a boy was playing along with rustic boys. He was playing with the fruits of embylic myrobalan. I shall narrate it to you, O descendant of Bharata.

The fruits, O son of Pāṇḍu, thrown by the Lord were brought back immediately by them and Hara threw them thereafter.

By the time the Āmalaka fruits went to the various quarters and came back therefrom, they saw the fruits in the form of a Bhūta (ghost) of huge size.

The third act of the Lord took place in the greatest of the holy spots, the excellent Āmaleśvara. Merely by adoring it, one attains the greatest region (Mokṣa).

CHAPTER TWO HUNDRED FOURTEEN

The Greatness of Śrī Kapāla Tīrtha

Śrī Mārkaṇḍeya said:

1-11. I shall recount the fourth great act of the Lord. Merely by listening to it, one is rid of all sins.

The lord wandered over the earth as a Kapālin (holder of a skull) wearing patched garments. He was surrounded by Piśācas, Rākṣasas, Ḍākinīs, and Yoginīs.

He assumed the form of a Bhairava and resorted to a cremation ground where he performed an elaborate penance causing freedom from fear to all the three worlds. He spent the Āṣāḍha month there. Hence his name Āṣāḍhī became well-known.

In another place, the *Kanthā* (patched garment) was left by Lord Parameṣṭhin. Ever since then, O great king, he is called Kantheśvara. By visiting him, one obtains the merit of a horse-sacrifice.

Then the Deva continued his spontaneous wanderings. He met a Balākāra (vendor of gum myrrh or the shoot of the plant). He was told by Hara: "O fair one, if you do not become angry with me now (I have a request). Fill (cover up) the Liṅga with Balā. I shall give you plenty of money."

On being told thus by the Lord, the pedlar was deluded by covetousness. He fitted Balā to the Liṅgas. They were of high and medium quality. He went on filling till his stock was exhausted. On seeing the Liṅga still standing erect, he became worried.

On seeing him thus agitated, Parameśvara broke it into pieces and said laughingly: "My Liṅga was not filled. I shall go away if you consider it to be necessary (if you allow me). I shall give you the money if the Liṅga is filled-up."

The Vaṇik (Pedlar) said:

12-18. I have not performed meritorious deeds. I am not blessed. O Parameśvara, I have to be bound over. Unable to do something pleasing to you, I will regret it for a long time.

On hearing these words of the son of a Vaṇīk, O descendant of Bharata, Maheśvara gave him inexhaustible wealth and stationed himself there.

Ever since then, O great king, the Liṅga stood there with a desire to bless the worlds. It appeared as though adorned with Balākās (Cranes) in order to give credence.

The path made by the Lord and well-established sportingly became well-known in all the three worlds as "Devamārga". He who views this and worships it, is rid of all sins.

He who goes to Devamārga and worships Balākeśvara, reaches Pañcāyatana and goes to Rudraloka.

Men who die in Devamārga become purified souls. They do not come back again from Rudraloka.

O most excellent one among men, by listening devoutly to the greatness of Devamārga, one is rid of all sins. No hesitation need be felt in believing this.

CHAPTER TWO HUNDRED FIFTEEN

The Greatness of Śṛṅgī Tīrtha

Śrī Mārkaṇḍeya said:

1-2. Thereafter, one should go to the Śṛṅgī Tīrtha that accords salvation unto all embodied beings. O great king, there is no doubt about the attainment of salvation by those who die there.

There itself one should offer balls of rice. Thereby one becomes free from indebtedness to Pitṛs. Becoming a purified soul by that merit, he attains the goal of Gaṇeśvaras.

CHAPTER TWO HUNDRED SIXTEEN

The Greatness of Āṣāḍhī

Śrī Mārkaṇḍeya said:

1-3. Thereafter, O prince, a person should go to Āṣāḍhī Tīrtha where Maheśvara has stationed himself after assuming a lovely form. This Tīrtha pertains to all the four Yugas. It is the most excellent one among all the Tīrthas. By taking his holy bath there, O king, a man shall become an attendant of Rudra.

If anyone casts his life into that Tīrtha there, his departure to Rudraloka will certainly be one without any return.

CHAPTER TWO HUNDRED SEVENTEEN

The Greatness of Eraṇḍī Tīrtha

Śrī Mārkaṇḍeya said:

1-3. Then one should go to the confluence of Eraṇḍī (with Revā) which is bowed to by Suras and Asuras. That Tīrtha is highly meritorious and destructive of great sins.

A devotee should observe fast with perfect restraint of the sense-organs and mind. Then he takes his holy bath in accordance with the injunctions; he is rid of the sin of Brāhmaṇa-slaughter.

If anyone devoutly puts an end to his life there in that Tīrtha, he will undoubtedly go to Rudraloka without any return therefrom.

CHAPTER TWO HUNDRED EIGHTEEN

The Greatness of Jāmadagnya Tīrtha

Śrī Mārkaṇḍeya said:

1-10. Thereafter, O Lord of the Earth, a person should go to the highly splendid Tīrtha well-known as Jamadagni Tīrtha where Janārdana became a Siddha.

Yudhiṣṭhira said:

O excellent Brāhmaṇa, how did Vāsudeva, the preceptor of the universe, become a Siddha? Is it by assuming human form with a desire for the welfare of all the worlds?

I wish to hear the full story of the Discus-bearing Lord of Devas properly. O sinless one, may it be recounted by you.

Śrī Mārkaṇḍeya said:

O great king, formerly there was a great ruler of the Haihaya clan. He was known as Kārttavīrya, a king with a thousand arms.

He was richly equipped with elephants, horses and chariots. He was the most excellent one among all warriors wielding weapons. He was also a master of the Vedic lore. He granted freedom from fear to all living beings. He was the Lord of the city of Māhiṣmatī. He was a glorious king, owner of an Akṣauhiṇī.

Once that mighty king set out for hunting deer. After many days, he reached the excellent Bhṛgukaccha where Jamadagni, the highly refulgent ascetic, was staying.

The glorious sage was in the company of Reṇukā. He was the bestower of freedom from fear on all living beings. Lord Nārāyaṇa himself was born as his son Rāma.

He (Rāma) was a knower of Brahman, an excellent Brāhmaṇa but possessing all the qualities of a Kṣatriya. With his genuine devotion, he indeed delighted his parents.

Jamadagni of great refulgence met Arjuna who was out hunting deer and invited him as his guest.

11-20. Saying 'yes', the king went into the meritorious hermitage along with his attendants, army and vehicles. The hermitage of the noble-souled sage instantly became richly equipped and enveloped in great glory.

Seeing this amazing transformation, the king entered it and was promptly served (fed) with his attendants and army.

Casually he (Kārttavīrya) asked the cause thereof (of this transformation). After coming to know that the power of Kāmadhenu was the cause, he said to the Brāhmaṇa:

"O Brāhmaṇa, give me this excellent cow of variegated colour as a donation. In return I shall give you hundred, a hundred thousand or even millions of embellished cows."

Jamadagni said:

I will not give away this excellent Kāmadhenu in lieu of ten thousands, hundred thousands and even crores of other cows. You may go.

On being told thus by that Brāhmaṇa, O descendant of Bharata, the eminent king spoke these words with his eyes turned red: "O base Brāhmaṇa, even in regard to me you have such self-willedness. Hence even as you are watching, I will take away the divine cow from your house."

The Brāhmaṇa said:

Who dares to play with a great angry serpent? One who dares to take away my cow will be sure to he met by the god of Death on the way.

After saying this the furious Jamadagni seized a huge staff, like another Brahmadaṇḍa (the staff of Brahmā) and uttered thus:

21-31. "Whoever has the power or brilliance of a Kṣatriya, O base one in the (Kṣatriya) family, let him take away my cow immediately. His life along with that of his followers will be reduced and crippled."

On hearing these cruel words, Haihaya accompanied by hundreds rushed in but when struck by the Brahmadaṇḍa, he fell down on the ground.

The cow produced a gruff "*Huṁ*" sound and from that cow of variegated colour thousands were seen issuing forth (from her nostrils) with swords, nooses and other weapons. The Kirātas came out from her nostrils and tips of the hair. The Māgadhas came out of the anus. Hundreds and thousands of other warriors issued forth from the other pores.[1] They killed each other. Haihaya (King Arjuna) burned them. All those perished along with the Brāhmaṇas due to that refulgence of Arjuna.

After gaining victory in the battle and killing the excellent Brāhmaṇa, Kārttavīrya joyously went to his city. Evidently the king was deluded by the prompting of the god of Death.

Only when the enemy had gone away did Rāma hurrying homewards came there. He saw his mother piteously lamenting near his father.

---

1. Here a few verses are missing, apparently of the following import: 'They fought against the army of Haihaya. The mutual fight was very tumultuous.'

Rāma said:

By whom has this rash act been committed, only to invite self-destruction? He who has thought of killing my father has been prompted by the desire to meet Death.

On hearing the words of Rāma, she lost all her strength and got agitated. Beating her belly with both the hands, she spoke to him:

"The ruthless Arjuna accompanied with other Kṣatriyas came here. By that king endowed with (a thousand) arms (Jamadagni) was killed. See your father senseless and bereft of life on being killed. Cremate him duly, dear son, and perform the requisite libations."

32-40. On hearing these words, Rāma paid obeisance to her and took this vow. O king, hear what it is: "I will exterminate the entire race of Kṣatriyas twenty-one times. I will take my holy bath then and offer libations to your husband with their blood.

With my axe I will cut off the arms of that wicked Kārttavīrya and will drink the blood thereof. Listen to this truthful vow of mine."

After taking this solemn vow, the valorous son of Jamadagni performed the cremation of his father. At the height of his fury, Rāma went to the city of Māhiṣmatī, cut off the forest of arms of that base Kṣatriya and killed him.

Then for the annihilation of Kṣatriyas he surveyed the whole earth consisting of seven continents, oceans, mountains and forests and parks.

He dug five deep pits in Samantapañcaka in the Kuru land in the four directions of east, west, south and north (as well as the centre).

It has been heard by us that he, being extremely furious offered libations to his Pitṛs with blood in the eddy-like pits filled with (Kṣatriya) blood.

Thereupon, Ṛcīka and other Pitṛs approached the bull among Brāhmaṇas and told him to forgive him. So he stopped (the bloody revenge).

41-48. The area around those eddy-like pits filled with blood is glorified as the meritorious Samantapañcaka.

After desisting from that activity, O son of Pāṇḍu, the highly righteous Rāma spoke to the Pitṛs: "Let this blood poured into the five pits by me become an excellent Tīrtha." Saying "So it shall be" all the Pitṛs vanished.

Thus the contact of Rāma in Devamārga by perception and touch is destructive of all sins of men, O Yudhiṣṭhira.

In order to convince Reṇukā the Pitṛs as deities are seen even today, stationed in Devamārga. They are destructive of all sins.

O great king, by taking a holy bath at the confluence of Narmadā and the ocean as per injunctions in the Tīrtha, men are rid of sins.

O son of Kuntī, the great ocean should not be touched even by the tip of a blade of Kuśa. O excellent king, one should take bath there reciting this Mantra:

"Obeisance to you, the Lord of waters, in the form of Viṣṇu. O Lord of Devas, be present in the briny ocean." This is the *Sparśana Mantra* (Mantra for touch).

49-57. O Pāṇḍava, one should dive into the Lord of rivers uttering this truthful sentence: "Agni is the lustre in the body with forgiveness and graciousness. It is the Retas in the body. It is the navel of Nectar."

Then the devotee should offer *Arghya* to the great ocean with five jewels, fruits, flowers and raw rice grain. O great king, the Mantra thereof is as follows:

"O Lord and chieftain of all immortal ones, you are the storehouse of all jewels. You are the receptacle of all Ratnākaras (oceans containing jewels). Accept my *Arghya.* Obeisance to you."

The Mantra for bidding good-bye is as follows:

"O great Ocean, redeem me from the sins incurred ever since my birth. O storehouse of jewels, you have been worshipped. Do go now to the mountains, O foremost among Pārvaṇas (those who go on increasing at *Parva* time). O Lord, you are the powerful one getting the portals to heaven opened. Who else can be better than Lord Ocean!"

There the excellent great Tīrtha extended upto the ocean.

There the Lord was installed by Rāma, the son of Jamadagni. There Devas, Gandharvas, sages, Siddhas, and Cāraṇas perform the Upāsanā of the Three-eyed Lord and the excellent sage Jamadagni. Men who see Goddess Reṇukā also there, remain in the pleasing Śivaloka for as much time as they desire.

A man who takes his holy bath there and offers libations to Pitṛs and Devas, shall redeem more than a hundred generations of his family from terrible Naraka. They should take the holy bath, offer Dāna and listen with devotion (to the narratives).

CHAPTER TWO HUNDRED NINETEEN

The Greatness of Koṭi Tīrtha

Śrī Mārkaṇḍeya said:

1-6. On the southern bank of Narmadā is the great Tīrtha called Koṭīśvara. Here the holy bath and Dāna etc., yield a crore times the benefit.

Devas, Gandharvas and sages free from sin attained great Siddhi here at the Koṭitīrtha, a rare thing to be achieved on the earth.

Mahādeva called Koṭīśvara is installed there. By visiting him one attains excellent Siddhi.

O excellent king, whatever is performed there, auspicious or inauspicious, shall have a crore times the benefit (or result). This is the statement of the scriptural texts: Those excellent sages who are on the southern path (i.e. stay on the southern bank of the river) become Siddhas on death and certainly they attain Pitṛloka and those excellent sages who are the residents of the northern bank have already gone to Devaloka.

CHAPTER TWO HUNDRED TWENTY

The Greatness of Loṭaṇeśvara Tīrtha

Śrī Mārkaṇḍeya said:

1-7. Thereafter, O Lord of the earth, a person should go to the excellent Loṭaṇeśvara Tīrtha on the northern bank of Narmadā. It is destructive of all sins.

The sins accumulated in the course of seven births are destroyed at the very instant of visiting the Lord of Devas.

The sins incurred since childhood, the sins committed during youth all perish by visiting the Lord of Devas.

Yudhiṣṭhira said:

The great (sanctifying) activity (efficacy) of Narmadā is amazing to all the three worlds and has been entirely narrated by you, O Brāhmaṇa. It is destructive of all sins.

I wish to hear about one great Tīrtha that yields the benefit of all the Tīrthas taken together. Have pity on me and describe it quickly.

Many questions of very rare (solutions) in all the worlds, O excellent one, have been heard (as clarified by you) by me along with my kinsmen.

O foremost one among those conversant with all the questions, after hearing this sole question, with your favour, I shall go (to it) along with kinsmen.

Śrī Mārkaṇḍeya said:

8-18. Excellent! Excellent! O highly intelligent one! There is nothing difficult to attain in all the three worlds to a person like you whose mental power is like this.

O leader of the descendants of Bharata, one who knows Dharma (piety), Artha (wealth), Kāma (love) and Mokṣa (liberation) at the proper times, is an intelligent one and this is his duty. Hence I shall tell you the splendid answer to this question. On hearing it, men on the earth are liberated from all sins.

Narmadā is the most excellent one among all the rivers. She is auspicious and identical with all the Tīrthas. A special efficacy thereof is said to be in the confluence of Revā with the Ocean.

On seeing Revā coming on, O excellent king, the great Ocean bowed down to her. On being united with Revā he thought, 'Who is this excellent river coming into contact with me?'

After reflection he realized that it was the great Revā originating from a Liṅga. (To express his deep reverence) the great Ocean went on rolling (itself before her) when he approached face to face. Where the great river Narmadā entered the Ocean, a Liṅga of the chief Lord of Devas arose there.

The highly esteemed Narmadā, the most excellent one among the rivers, that had originated from a Liṅga, got merged into the Liṅga. Hence she is the most meritorious.

One who stays near Narmadā always and drinks her waters, is on a par with one initiated in all the *Yajñas* and drinks Soma juice everyday.

A man who takes his holy bath at the confluence there and worships Loṭaṇeśvara attains the benefit of (the performance of) a horse-sacrifice.

O king, all the sins committed verbally, mentally or physically, become dissolved on approaching Loṭaṇeśvara.

19-27. A special rite has been prescribed for Kārttikī by Śaṅkara. O excellent king, listen to it, as it is destructive of all sins.

On coming to know of the approaching Kārttikī (full-moon day of Kārttika), one should observe fast on the fourteenth lunar day and then take his holy bath in the waters of Narmadā.

Then he should offer libations to Pitṛs and Devas and perform Śrāddha duly. He should worship Loṭaṇeśvara and keep awake at night. His life is fruitful. All his activities are fruitful.

If Loṭaṇeśvara is not seen with full concentration of the mind, those persons are no better than lame ones. Their life is futile.

In the family of a true devotee none will attain ghosthood and none will be reborn in a base womb.

One should go to the confluence and duly perform the rite of ablution. The rite of keeping awake (at night) should be observed with a provision for meritorious songs and dances.

After the night turns into dawn, the devotee bows to and invokes the Great Ocean and takes the holy bath in accordance with the injunctions laid down.

The Mantra for Āmantraṇa (Invocation)

"Om, obeisance to you, the Lord of the Tīrtha in the form of Viṣṇu. O Lord, be present in the briny Ocean while I take bath."

The Snāna Mantra:

"Agni is the depositor of the semen virile in the body. It is lustrous. Viṣṇu is the navel of Amṛta."

Uttering thus the truthful statement, O son of Pāṇḍu, the devotee takes bath in the Lord of rivers.

28-38. A man might have committed many sins in the course of hundreds and thousands of births, but he dispels all the clusters of sins by taking a bath once in the briny ocean.

O leading member of Kuru family, this all-pervading great Ocean is of divine origin. Hence, otherwise (without Mantra) the Ocean should not be touched by learned men even with the tip of a blade of Darbha grass.

Argha Mantra:

"O receptacle of the store-house of all jewels, you are the most important of all jewels. O chief Lord of all immortal ones, accept the *Argha.* Obeisance to you."

Thereafter the devotee offers libation to the Pitṛs, Devas and human beings. The devotee comes out of the river and gets the Śrāddha performed by eminent five Brāhmaṇas resembling the Guardians of the worlds.

The Lokapālas are to be installed duly and duly worshipped (by worshipping those Brāhmaṇas alone). Then the devotee should confess his good and evil acts to them.

The devotee confesses to them whatever sin has been committed ever since childhood, in the course of youth and old age and then submits the same to the Guardians of the worlds.

The devotee utters it as follows: "Whatever inauspicious act has been perpetrated ever since childhood, in the course of various births (or ever since birth) has been entirely confessed to the Brāhmaṇas. Their presence is in all my situations."

After uttering so the devotee shall roll in front of them. After getting their permission the devotee has to perform the holy bath.

O excellent king, the Śrāddha too has to be performed duly to the Pitṛs. If this is performed, O excellent king, all the sins shall perish.

If anyone is curious to know about himself, analysing his auspicious and inauspicious activities, then listen to his procedure as follows:

39-49. After taking the holy bath in the great Tīrtha, the man goes ahead rolling. A man of righteous actions goes towards the river and a man of evil actions to the opposite side.

Thereby the evil-doer shall realize his previously accumulated sins. After taking the holy bath in the excellent Tīrtha he should duly make Dāna.

After worshipping Loṭaṇeśvara, he is rid of all sins. After adopting a non-crooked way of life, he is rid of all sins.

Hence, O excellent king, after becoming aware of this by means of all efforts, all men should bathe at the place where Hara is present.

After taking the holy bath in accordance with the injunctions, O protector of the earth, he should adore and honour Brāhmaṇas who have mastered the Vedas for the purpose of quelling all the sins.

O excellent king, that Tīrtha has all these good features. Listen attentively to the greatness of that Tīrtha.

A man who takes his holy bath there in that Tīrtha, offers libations to Pitṛs and Devas, devoutly performs Śrāddha to Pitṛs there and makes Dāna (gifts) of cows, plots of land, gingelly seeds and gold to Brāhmaṇas is honoured in Svargaloka for a hundred crore and sixty thousand years. He goes to Svarga seated in an excellent aerial chariot.

At the confluence of Revā and the ocean one gets the same benefit as one derives through holy bath taken in all the Tīrthas on Narmadā.

By giving gold, silver, copper, jewels, pearls, cows and bulls, plots of land and good grain as charity (*Dāna*), one obtains everlasting benefit.

Undoubtedly all auspicious and inauspicious actions bear their fruits.

50-55. Listen to the meritorious benefit of one, whoever be that man, O Yudhiṣṭhira, who casts off his life there in the Tīrtha with devotion.

After sporting about in the Palace of Śiva for crores of years, he is reborn as a Brāhmaṇa conversant with the Vedas and Vedāṅgas in a pure family. He will live for a hundred years richly endowed with sons and grandsons, wealth and foodgrain. He shall be free from all ailments.

One attains by worshipping Loṭaṇeśvara in the month of Kārttika when the constellation Kṛttikā is present, the same benefit as acquired by worshipping Somanātha in the course of twelve pilgrimages.

O son of Kuntī, by visiting Loṭaṇeśvara one gets the same benefit as at Gayā, Gaṅgā, Kurukṣetra, Naimiṣa and Puṣkara. A man who devoutly listens to this auspicious text being read shall go to Rudraloka after being rid of all sins.

CHAPTER TWO HUNDRED TWENTYONE

The Greatness of Haṁseśvara Tīrtha[1]

Śrī Mārkaṇḍeya said:

1-6. Thereafter, O great king, a person should go to an excellent Tīrtha named Haṁseśvara on the southern bank of Revā within two Krośas (4 miles=6 kms.) from Mātṛtīrtha. It is meritorious and destructive of mental depression.

Formerly, Haṁsa, son of one of Dakṣa's daughters born in the family of Kaśyapa, performed a great penance and became the vehicle of Brahmā.

Once, without any direction from Brahmā, he became too impetuous. O Yudhiṣṭhira, he was attacked by Śivagaṇas. He fled away in the course of the destruction of Dakṣa's Yajña. Without bearing Vidhi (Brahmā) he became a deserter and ran away. Even when remembered by Brahmā, the bird did not come to him. So Brahmā cursed him and dismissed him from his office.

Knowing himself to be cursed, Haṁsa (Swan) hurriedly approached Brahmā, the grandfather, bowed down to him and requested:

Haṁsa said:

7-16. It does not behove you to curse me born of brutish womb. It is but natural in the case of brutes that the mind is devoid of discrimination. Still, O Lord, granting that I am a sinner, that I deserted you, the master, O Pitāmaha, I shall tell

1. In order to explain the name *Haṁseśvara* the legend of the curse of Brahmā to his vehicle swan for his desertion and Brahmā's guidance to expiate sin of desertion by installing a Liṅga on the bank of Revā, is narrated.

you how it happened. I became frightened when the fierce attendants of Śarva rushed at me suddenly. In my fright, I left you and fled. Even now, O Lord, I see the cause of fear before me. That was why, even on being remembered by you, I did not come to you.

Śrī Mārkaṇḍeya said:

Saying this to the Creator, Haṁsa heaved sighs in a wretched manner worshipping him through the eyes (reverential glance): "O Lord, save, save me, the sinning brute of deluded mind fallen in front of you. You are the only Lord, the author of the creation. All these objects of diverse types have been created by you. Indeed if I have been created by you in this manner, O Creator, it is verily your own fault.

None other than you is capable of cursing and blessing. Whom shall I then seek for refuge? I have been a slave but now dismissed from the service. O dear one, I deserve to be slapped with the palm of your hand. But save me, your devotee.

Vidyā and *Avidyā* (knowledge and ignorance) manifested themselves from you. So also Dharma and Adharma (piety and impiety), *Sat* and *Asat* (good and bad, existent and non-existent), *Dyu* and *Niśā* (day and night). You create the different aspects of the universe. Such a unique one I seek as refuge.

In view of your single and multifarious activities, you are single and also have many forms. You are devoid of activity as well as engaged in all activities. Hence I seek refuge in you.

Obeisance, obeisance to the most excellent one! Obeisance, obeisance to the bestower of boons! Obeisance to the creator and dispense! Obeisance, obeisance to one who is worthy of being the refuge!

O Lord, what can this speech of mine bereft of the essence of letters and learning offer by way of eulogy? What is my power? What is my knowledge? Forgive this utterance of mine."

Śrī Mārkaṇḍeya said:

17-27. Even as Haṁsa was submitting this Brahmā, delighted in his mind, said: "You have been granted learning (knowledge), O bird, do not be sorry. Purify yourself through penance so that you will attain the end of the curse. By taking the holy bath render service unto Revā. After installing Maheśvara, you will attain your original status ere long.

The benefit of installing Śiva is the same as is attained after performing many Yajñas with the full complement of excellent monetary gifts and Dāna of crores of cows and gold.

By installing Śiva on the banks of Revā, one is rid of all sins whether he be slayer of a Brāhmaṇa, imbiber of liquor, thief of gold or defiler of the bed of preceptor.

Hence, by installing the Three-eyed Lord on the banks of Bharga-sarit (Revā) you shall be rid of all faults and attain the excellent office."

On being told thus by Brahmā, the excellent bird became delighted and contented. Saying "Yes, so be it" he hurried to the excellent banks of Narmadā.

After performing austerities for some time, he installed Śaṅkara after his own name, the excellent Haṁseśvara, O excellent descendant of Bharata. By adoring this deity, the most excellent bird attained the greatest position.

O Yudhiṣṭhira, one should go to the Haṁseśvara Tīrtha, take the holy bath and worship Parameśāna. He is rid of sins.

By eulogizing the Lord with thorough concentration of mind, one can avert wretchedness.

O excellent descendant of Bharata, by performing Śrāddha, offering a lamp and feeding Brāhmaṇas to the extent of one's capacity, one is honoured in Svargaloka.

O son of Kuntī, a person should adore Śiva once or thrice a day and make gift of a recently calved cow to an excellent Brāhmaṇa. He is honoured in Śivaloka for sixty thousand years.

CHAPTER TWO HUNDRED TWENTYTWO

The Greatness of Tilādeśvara Tīrtha

Śrī Mārkaṇḍeya said:

1-10. Next to it within a Krośa (3 Kms.) is the excellent Tilāda Tīrtha where a devotee should go thereafter. It was there that Jābāli gained purity by eating gingelly seeds.

He was full of defects and faults. He had abandoned his father and mother. He coveted the wife of his brother. He was a sinful seller of his son. He deceived his preceptor. Being full of such sinful faults, wherever he went he was insulted and rejected by good people, O descendant of Bharata. No one cared to associate with him even in the assemblies.

Thus the Brāhmaṇa became excessively ashamed, O king. He worried over this for a long time because he was not aware of any means of attaining sanctity.

He performed pilgrimages to all the Tīrthas. He took his bath in Revā, after reaching *Arṇavopānta* (the vicinity of the sea) on the southern bank of Narmadā. There, O son of Kuntī, Jābāli stayed and began eating gingelly seeds.

He started by eating gingelly seeds once a day; then on alternate days; and gradually once in three days, six days, twelve days, fifteen days and a month.

He observed the vows of Kṛcchra, Cāndrāyaṇa etc. with gingelly seeds. Thus a regular gingelly seed eater, he reached the seventy-second year.

As time passed on Īśvara became pleased with him and granted him purity here and hereafter and also *Sālokya* salvation (the state of being present in the same world as the Lord).

That Lord was installed, O foremost one among the descendants of Bharata, by him. The deity was called after his own name. The deity got the name Tilādeśvara all over the world.

11-16. Ever since then, this Tīrtha became very famous as being destructive of sins. A person should take his holy bath there in that Tīrtha on the eighth and fourteenth lunar days. He should observe fast on Harivāsara (i.e. eleventh day). He must perform Homa with *Tila* (gingelly seeds). He shall smear himself with gingelly seeds instead of unguents. He must use gingelly seeds for bath and offer gingelly seeds with water. He must give gingelly seeds as gifts and eat gingelly seeds. (Thus) he is rid of different kinds of sins.

He must fill the Liṅga with gingelly seeds. He must offer lamps with the gingelly oil. He attains Rudra Loka. He sanctifies his family till the seventh generation.

O excellent king, by offering the balls of gingelly seeds at the time of Śrāddha all the ancestors who had committed prohibited actions (*Vikarmasthas*) attain the desired goal.

Those who are staying in Svargaloka derive everlasting satisfaction and rejoice as a result of the Śrāddhas and Brāhmaṇa-feeding. They rejoice for many years.

The man takes the members of the three families viz. that of father, that of mother and that of wife, to heaven after redeeming them.

CHAPTER TWO HUNDRED TWENTYTHREE

The Greatness of Vāsaveśvara Tīrtha

Śrī Mārkaṇḍeya said:

1-11. Within a Krośa therefrom, O son of Kuntī, is the excellent Vāsava Tīrtha. There the Vasus stayed for twelve years and installed the deity.

The eight Vasus are: Dhara, Dhruva, Soma, Āpa, Anila, Anala, Pratyūṣa and Prabhāsa.

Formerly, O descendant of Bharata, they were distressed due to the curse of Pitṛ (father, ancestor) that condemned them to stay within womb. They came to the Tīrtha on Narmadā and performed penance with the sense-organs fully controlled.

They propitiated the great immutable Lord of Bhavānī for twelve years. O great king, Maheśvara was delighted thereby.

He became visible to them and granted them excellent desired boons. Thereupon the Vasus installed Maheśvara called after their own name. Śaṅkara being (then) pleased, they went away passing through the firmament.

Ever since then that Tīrtha became well-known after the name of Vasus. O great king, a devotee should worship Śiva with easily available offerings. Lights should be offered assiduously on the eighth day in the bright half of a month. The devotee should offer the same everyday as per his capacity. He should stay in the vicinity of Śiva for eight thousand years. Then he enters Śiva's abode. He never resides in a womb.

A devotee who worships Lord Īśāna with flowers, tender sprouts, fruits and foodgrain shall never meet with wretchedness. Freed from all griefs, he is honoured in Svargaloka.

O son of Kuntī, one who is able to stay at least one day in the Vāsaveśvara Tīrtha shall shake off heaps of sins and rejoice in heaven like the Sun. He should devoutly feed Brāhmaṇas and give clothes and monetary gifts.

CHAPTER TWO HUNDRED TWENTYFOUR

The Greatness of Koṭīśvara Tīrtha

Śrī Mārkaṇḍeya said:

1-6. Thereafter, O son of Kuntī, there is the great Koṭīśvara Tīrtha within a Krośa therefrom. If the holy bath, *Dāna*, *Japa*, *Homa*, adoration etc. are performed devoutly by men, they will have a crore-fold more benefit.

There Devas, Gandharvas, Sages, Siddhas, Cāraṇas etc., go towards the ocean to see Narmadā. They gathered there in crores, O king, at the confluence of Revā and the ocean. They experienced unparalleled joy on visiting the confluence of Revā and the sea.

They took their holy bath. They installed Śiva, the great Īśvara named Koṭīśvara and adored him in accordance with the injunctions, with their respective devotion.

Thus by propitiating Śarva in Koṭitīrtha they attained great Siddhi. Hence that Tīrtha is unparalleled among all the Tīrthas, meritorious and the most excellent. Whatever is performed there, auspicious or inauspicious, O tiger among kings, shall give crore-fold fruit.

7-12. There in the Tīrtha, the excellent sages who are stationed on the southern bank go to the eternal state of Siddhas and also to the excellent Pitṛloka. Those who stay on the northern bank of Narmadā go to Devaloka. This is my firm opinion.

A devotee should worship Maheśvara with the flowers of Bilva, Arka, Dhattūra, Kuśa and Kāśa as well as other seasonal flowers, make offerings of various nature duly and with utterance of Mantras as per injunctions, O Yudhiṣṭhira, and propitiate Dhūrjaṭi with incense, lamps, *Arghya* and *Naivedya*. Thereby he attains Śivaloka and remains there for the duration of the reign of fourteen Indras.

Adoration performed on the eighth day in the dark half of the month of Pauṣa is remembered as of special significance.

O excellent king, the eighth and fourteenth days of all months also are good. On those days, a devotee should adore Śiva and honour Brāhmaṇas of excellent nature by feeding them devoutly.

CHAPTER TWO HUNDRED TWENTYFIVE

The Greatness of Alikeśvara Tīrtha

Śrī Mārkaṇḍeya said:

1-5. Thereafter, a devotee should go to the excellent Alikā Tīrtha within a distance of a Krośa (3 Kms.) therefrom.

There was a Gandharva female named Alikā. Her habits were foul and her mind crooked. She was granddaughter (daughter's daughter) of Citrasena. She went to Sage Vidyānanda, wooed him and was accepted by him. She resorted to him for ten years.

For some reason, she killed her husband while he was asleep. She then went to her father Ratnavallabha and told him this.

Hence she was abandoned by her father and mother, O king, and rebuked by many: "You are the murderess of foetus and of husband. So do not show us your face. O murderess of a Brāhmaṇa, O sinful woman, go away. You have been abandoned. Go away from the house."

Śrī Mārkaṇḍeya said:

6-13. Thus the deluded woman, on being sternly rebuked by both of them, felt inclined to cast off her body after resorting to some Tīrtha somewhere.

O Yudhiṣṭhira, she went on enquiring about various Tīrthas from Brāhmaṇas and heard that the Tīrtha at the confluence of Revā and the ocean was destructive of sins.

O son of Kuntī, she performed penance there and observed expiatory fasts such as Kṛcchra, Atikṛcchra, Pārāka, Mahāsāntapana etc.

Through the vows of Cāndrāyaṇa and Brahmakūrca she got her body emaciated. Thus, O king, a hundred and fifty years passed off in penance including meditations, adorations etc., of Śiva, since she desired (self-) purification.

After a few days, Śiva came to know of her ardent resolution. On being induced by Pārvatī, the delighted Śiva spoke to her:

Īśvara said:

O daughter, do not be rash. Now you are pure in your body. I am pleased now with your penance. Choose your desired boon.

Alikā said:

O Lord of Devas, if you are pleased, (and) if I am considered to be worthy of boons, do grant me perfect purity. I have already been awfully scorched by diverse kinds of fiery sins. I am helpless and you are my Lord. You alone are the preceptor of the worlds, the redeemer of the wretched and the helpless, the deity worthy of being refuge unto all a embodied beings.

Īśvara said:

14-22. O fair lady, you have become purified in body; do not feel acutely aggrieved. Instal me here designating me after your name. Thereby you will attain heaven.

After saying this, the Lord of chiefs of Devas vanished there itself. Alikā, thereupon, devoutly took her holy bath, installed Śaṅkara and made liberal gifts to Brāhmaṇas. She attained the highly exalted region.

O Yudhiṣṭhira, she went back to her father and mother. She was duly honoured by them as well as by her other kinsmen. Seated on an excellent aerial chariot and wearing divine garlands, O king, she went to the world of Gaurī. Even today she rejoices as the female companion of the goddess.

Ever since then, O son of Kuntī, that Tīrtha became famous as Alikeśvara. O Yudhiṣṭhira, any devotee, man or woman, who takes his holy bath there in the Tīrtha and devoutly worships Mahādeva accompanied by Umā, shall be rid of all sins. He attains the world of Śaṅkara.

By feeding Brāhmaṇas always, one gets rid of all sins, mental, verbal or physical. Whatever sin was committed before, gets dissolved.

By offering lamps to the deity, one can avert attacks of ailments. By offering incense, utensil, ornamental frame, bell and waterpot to the deity, O great king, one shall obtain the world of Śaṅkara.

CHAPTER TWO HUNDRED TWENTYSIX

The Greatness of Vimaleśvara Tīrtha

Śrī Mārkaṇḍeya said:

1-10. Within a distance of a Krośa therefrom is that meritorious Tīrtha Vimaleśvara. By taking holy bath there, offering Dāna, performing Japa, Homa, *Arcana* etc., and by propitiating the deity Vimaleśvara, one will obtain whatever one desires, whether it be the acquisition of heavenly pleasures or petty worldly things.

Formerly, it was due to the great power of this Tīrtha that Śatakratu (Indra) attained perfect purity after killing Triśiras, the son of Tvaṣṭṛ.

It was there that a Brāhmaṇa, Vedanidhi, performed a very great penance formerly and became pure like the Sun, even as the diverse impurities of Karma became feeble. Due to the favour of Mahādeva, he became pleasing to the eyes like the Moon.

Formerly Bhānu (Sun) became tormented by the arrows of Smara (Cupid) and coveted Bhānumatī, his own daughter. Due to that sin he became afflicted with Kuṣṭharoga (leprosy). He too performed a penance here and attained purity. By the grace of Mahādeva who was pleased, he regained his position and rejoiced.

Similar, O son of Kuntī, is the case of the saintly son of Vibhāṇḍaka. He had been associating with Yogins in forest but came into contact with the king. He considered himself extremely defiled due to the defect of the contact with the king.

Along with Śāntā, his wife, he approached the confluence of Revā and the ocean. He performed penance for twelve years. Through Kṛcchra and Cāndrāyaṇa, the sage propitiated the Three-eyed Lord. By the grace of Mahādeva who was pleased he regained his purity.

11-18. Formerly, O king, Śarva was instigated by Śarvāṇī to infatuate the wives of sages in Dāruvana. Thereupon he saw himself *Samala* (defiled by impurity) and considered the confluence of Narmadā and the ocean as the greatest holy spot. O great king, he stayed there with Umā and performed penance. Since he became *Vimala* (free from impurity), the deity is called Vimaleśvara. He himself stayed there by that name with a desire for the welfare of all the worlds.

Then there is the story of Brahmā. The grandfather of the worlds created Tilottamā. After creating her and seeing the charming lady in front, he was overpowered by *Bhāvi-yoga-bala,* the force of inevitability of the future (course of events). Though Lord of all the subjects, he became her lover.

Thereby he felt himself guilty and sinful. He resorted to the banks of Revā. Observing the vow of silence he visited the Tīrthas. He took bath thrice a day remembering Śiva. He then took his holy bath at the confluence of Revā and the ocean and worshipped Śaṅkara. In a short time, O saintly king, Brahmā too became free from impurities.

Thus many other excellent Devas, sages and kings eschewed the impurities of sins and became pure.

Similarly, O leading king, by taking the holy bath and adoring Śiva there, you too shall attain excellent purity, although you are already pure.

19-23. A person whether a man or a woman should take the holy bath there and worship Maheśvara. Thereby he shall be rid of sins and defects and become honoured in Brahmaloka.

He who observes fast and visits Vimaleśvara, O king, on the eighth and fourteenth lunar day and on all festive occasions, gets rid of the sins committed in the course of seven births and goes to Śivālaya. The person should perform Śrāddha in accordance with the injunctions and be free from the indebtedness to the Pitṛs.

He should feed Brāhmaṇas in accordance with his capacity and offer them monetary gifts.

Whatever one likes most in the world, whatever is beneficial to him in the house should be given to a person of good qualities, if the donor desires everlasting benefit. By offering gold, foodgrain, clothes, umbrellas, shoes, waterpot etc., and constructing temples according to his capacity, one shall become a king on the earth. He should propitiate Parameśvara through songs, dances and tales (about the deity).

CHAPTER TWO HUNDRED TWENTYSEVEN

Special Injunctions regarding the Pilgrimage

Śrī Mārkaṇḍeya said:

1-10. Thus, succinctly and in accordance with their importance these Tīrthas have been recounted to you. O son of Pāṇḍu, no one is competent to enumerate in detail all the Tīrthas.

This river Narmadā is sacred and pure. It is well-known in all the three worlds. She is the most excellent of all the rivers, and a favourite of Mahādeva.

If anyone always remembers mentally and reflects on Narmadā, O king, he obtains quickly the excellent benefit of a hundred Cāṇḍrayaṇas.

Persons who have no faith, those who are atheists fall into the terrible Naraka. So said Parameśvara.

Lord Maheśvara himself resorts to Narmadā always. Hence the river should be known as meritorious and destroyer of the sin of Brāhmaṇa-slaughter.

This river born from the person of Maheśvara is mentioned as Māheśvarī Gaṅgā (Gaṅgā of Maheśvara); O Yudhiṣṭhira, she is called the Southern Gaṅgā of Bhārata.

Jāhnavī is the Vaiṣṇavī Gaṅgā, Sarasvatī is Brāhmī Gaṅgā. There is no doubt about this that Revā is Māheśvarī Gaṅgā.

Just as in the form of the Supreme Puruṣa (Being) the Lord has adopted Traimūrtatva (trinityhood, being three gods) i.e. Brahmā, Viṣṇu and Maheśa in one and there is no difference among them, so also, O son of Kuntī, do not think that there is any difference among the three rivers.

On the two banks of Revā, there are Tīrthas in thousands, hundred thousands and crores, O descendant of Bharata.

The Tīrthas are situated in water, on ground and in firmament and among trees. Who is competent to decisively fix their number, be he the Lord of Speech or Maheśvara?

11-19. By remembering Revā, sins committed in the course of a single birth perish. By visiting it the sins of three births perish. By taking the holy plunge into Revā, the sins committed in the course of seven births perish.

If a devotee takes his bath in Revā, it is as good as a task of Devas performed by him, Homa in the sacrificial fires duly performed and as the four Vedas fully studied by him.

The Tīrthas have been recounted to you succinctly and in accordance with their importance.

O son of Kuntī, the details can neither be recounted by me nor heard by you.

Yudhiṣṭhira said:

Tell me the procedure, the *Yamas* (restrictions) and *Niyamas* (regulations). Tell me further how to understand the meaning of expiation.

Śrī Mārkaṇḍeya said:

You have asked pertinently, O great king, regarding what is conducive to welfare in the other world. Listen attentively. I shall tell you everything as I know.

One should perform acts of a permanent nature by means of the body that is non-permanent. The Prāṇas (vital airs) shall surely go away like guests. One should extract the essential from the inessential viz. *Dāna* from wealth, truth from the word (speech), piety and glory from life and benevolence from the body (through physical activity).

It is heard that Kāla (Eternal Time, god of Death) cooks living beings in this big cauldron of deep-rooted illusion by means of fire in the form of the sun, where night and day serve the purpose of fuel, tossing and stirring with the ladle in the form of months and seasons.

It behoves you to carry on your duties hereafter completely knowing what is prescribed by the injunctions of the scriptural texts. Neither this world nor the other one can bring in happiness to a person of suspicious, hesitating nature.

20-29a. The achievement of result from the following is correlated with the faith of the person concerned: Mantra, Tīrtha, Brāhmaṇa, godhead, astrologer, medicine and preceptor.

If a Homa is performed without faith (and scrupulous care) gift is made, penance is performed and pious act is done similarly, without faith, O son of Kuntī, it is called *Asat* (false). It has no value either here or hereafter.

He who disregards the procedure laid down in the scriptural texts and acts capriciously, does not achieve fulfilment, nor happiness nor the greatest goal.

Of course, there are diverse means for the purification of the bodies of men. But no means of purifying one's body can be on a par with resorting to Tīrthas.

Purification is possible (firstly) through Kṛcchra, Cāndrāyaṇa and other observances or secondly by resorting to Tīrthas.

When a person proceeds towards a Tīrtha, O king, Devas and Pitṛs too follow him moving in the sky. They follow him with great delight.

The devotee performs all these rites: Śrāddha for the purpose of prosperity, taking leave of the deity and beloved kinsmen, the adoration of Viṣṇu and Śaṅkara and of the Lord of the Gaṇas etc.

After being formally permitted by Brāhmaṇas he should take up the regulations of the vows and proceed ahead. Only one who practises these restraints can attain the benefit of Tīrtha, O excellent king: eating food once a day, celibacy, lying down on the ground, truthful speech, avoidance of food from other people, abstention from accepting monetary gifts, avoidance of hatred, deception etc.

He shall adopt the guise of a saintly person; he should be modest and free from hypocrisy and arrogance.

29b-38a. He whose hands, feet and mind are under control, and possesses learning, austerity and fame attains the benefit of the Tīrtha.

O eminent king, one who is free from anger, addicted to

truth, steadfast in vows and regards himself equal with other living beings attains the benefit of the Tīrtha.

Except in the case of Kurukṣetra, Viśālā, Virajā and Gayā, tonsuring of the head and observance of fast is universally applicable in all the Tīrthas.

Holy bath, adoration of the deity, offering of balls of rice during Śrāddha and feeding Brāhmaṇas in accordance with one's capacity is the general practice in all the Tīrthas.

Listen attentively, O son of Kuntī, I shall recount the procedure in regard to one who sets out on pilgrimage for the sake of expiation with the mind fully restrained.

He shall take food only once a day. He shall be celibate. His food shall be without salt. After taking bath (elsewhere) he should proceed towards the Tīrtha (for another bath). His sole food should be Haviṣya (sacrificial food cooked in ghee). He should avoid conversation with a fallen person. He shall not indulge in talking too much.

He should eschew calumny, association with base ones and food from others. He should wear two cloths but be barefooted. He should be clean.

He should make the Saṁkalpa (ritualistic affirmation of intention) mentally and set out after formal permission. After going to the Tīrtha and taking the bath he should perform the adoration of the deity. If he is in a mood to repent and regret he shall be rid of all evil actions.

38b-49. The achievement of results and fulfilment in regard to the following is in accordance with the faith: Vedas, Tīrthas, Deities, astrologers, medicine and preceptor.

In Purāṇas and Smṛtis, the benefits of visiting a Tīrtha have been stated, O leading descendant of Bharata. A devotee should not suspect that such statements are Arthavādas (euphemistic utterances). He shall then reflect upon what is stated in the scriptural texts and come to a proper decision.

In regard to persons incapable of performing Kṛcchra rites physically the procedure for purification is as follows: He shall perform expiation after knowing the (efficacy of) a particular Tīrtha.

Listen, O great king, to that inasmuch as it is relevant to Narmadā. If the man sets out from a distance of twenty-four Yojanas, he shall obtain the auspicious benefit of twenty-four Kṛcchras.

In regard to the Yojanas beyond this Pādakṛcchra (one-fourth of the Kṛcchra) is proclaimed for one who sets out with a desire for purity (sanctity) as to the place within this range, the expiation occurs at every Yojana space according to learned men.

O great king, in the Tīrtha named after Praṇava i.e. Oṁkāreśvara Tīrtha, in the confluence of Revā and Urī and in Bhṛgukṣetra the benefit is remembered as double the previous one. In the confluence of the celestial river, in Śūlabheda as well as in the confluence of Karajā, O excellent king, it is a quarter less than the double.

Some say that it is thrice in the confluence of Eraṇḍī, the confluence of Kapilā and also in the confluence of Kubjā and Revā.

O great king, in Oṁkāra also that shall be proper and relevant. Similar is the case in the confluences of other rivers also with Revā.

O Yudhiṣṭhira, they say that the previous benefit is (on a par) with two Kṛcchras. In the confluence of Revā and the ocean, he attains (the benefit of) thrice the Kṛcchra.

50-59. O Yudhiṣṭhira, the Kṛcchra in the Śuklatīrtha is mentioned as four times (in benefit). Going by the stages of a Yojana, a devotee should stay there for some time, O excellent king. Thus he shall cover twenty-four Yojanas. Thus continuing the service unto Revā, perfectly united in the Yogic state, the devotee should be devoid of hypocrisy and arrogance and equipped with pure intellect for the purpose of sanctity. He shall be liberated.

Thus, O son of Kuntī, the characteristics of the topic of expiation have been recounted to you. The procedure regarding the pilgrimage to Revā should be guarded as a secret.

Yudhiṣṭhira said:

O sage, tell me the measure of Yojana. By understanding it, it will certainly cause the purification of my mind.

Śrī Mārkaṇḍeya said:

Listen, O son of Pāṇḍu, I shall describe the extent of the measure of a Yojana. So also I shall describe the special features regarding the Kṛcchra with reference to the concerned pilgrimage.

They say that the measure of an *Aṅgula* is the length of eight Yava-grain or more placed obliquely or three Vrīhis (rice-grain). Twelve Aṅgulas make one *Vitasti.* Two *Vitastis* make one *Hasta* (Hand, about 18 Inches). Four *Hastas* constitute one *Dhanus* (bow). The same is called *Daṇḍa* by those conversant with the specialities of measurements. Two thousand *Dhaṇūs* constitute one *Krośa.* Four *Krośas* make one *Yojana.* Thus, O bull among the descendants of Bharata, the measure of Yojana has been recounted to you.

Thereby the devotee making his pilgrimage understands the measure of the benefit too acquired by him.

O Excellent king, the benefit of Kṛcchra has already been recounted in respect to the Tīrtha in the form of water. As and when special features crop up I shall mention them in those contexts. Even as it is being mentioned to you who have faith, O king, listen to it.

60-67. The benefit of Kṛcchra etc., has been mentioned in the Tīrtha. There too the devotee attains the benefit of Kṛcchra through Upoṣaṇa (fast) also. One obtains the benefit of Kṛcchra through *Dinajāpya* (uttering of the names of the deity in the day time) also within one's capacity.

After taking the holy bath in the Tīrtha and visiting, worshipping and bowing down to the Lord of Devas well-known there, a man obtains the benefit of the Kṛcchra, O son of Kuntī.

The main benefit of a Tīrtha is through the holy bath. The second benefit is through fasts. The third benefit is through the visit, adoration etc. of the well known deity cited. The fourth benefit is through Japa day and night within one's physical capacity. The fifth benefit in regard to all the Tīrthas has to be reckoned on the basis of the distance.

One who has come within a range of a Yojana from the banks obtains a tenth of the benefit accruing from the Tīrtha concerned. No hesitation need be felt in this regard.

Taking a plunge in a Mahānadī (big river) together with observance of fast (even if) within a range of a Yojana, shall accord the benefit of Kṛcchra to men, O son of Kuntī.

Kulyā is a stream flowing to a distance of six Yojanas. Those that flow twelve Yojanas are called *Alpanadīs* (small rivers). Those that flow twenty-four Yojanas are *Nadīs. Mahānadīs* are rivers that flow to a greater distance.

CHAPTER TWO HUNDRED TWENTYEIGHT

The Benefit of Pilgrimage by Proxy

Yudhiṣṭhira said:

1-9. O excellent sage, O storehouse of mercy, if one undertakes pilgrimage for the sake of another, what is the extent of benefit? Who gets the benefit?

Śrī Mārkaṇḍeya said:

Listen, O king, to what I say in regard to the pilgrimage on behalf of others. How much shall be the benefit accrued? How should it be performed?[1]

Resorting to Tīrthas should never be undertaken in this world on behalf of a baser one by a person of superior caste through greed for money etc.

O great king, a learned man should perform a pious action himself. If there is no physical strength or another pressing matter intervenes, one should get the pious activity usually done through a person of one's own caste. A pious rite got done through sons, grandsons etc., or kinsmen of the same Gotra is the ideal things, they say, O Yudhiṣṭhira. Hence it is better that one gets them alone to do the work. Neither through one of a higher caste nor through one of a lower caste (should it be got done).

It is my opinion that a rite performed through a baser man is not proper. A superior one performing the rite on behalf of an inferior one may result in wretchedness.

One should not give knowledge, leavings of food or *Havis* to a Śūdra. He should not be taught righteous and pious rites nor should he be initiated in *Vratas.*

The following six things cause downfall of women and Śūdras: Japa, penance, pilgrimage, renunciation of the world, practice of Mantras and initiation for the adoration of a deity.

10-18. A woman with husband (alive) meets with downfall (if she undertakes any of these). A widow can perform everything. If the husband cannot perform, the wife should perform with his permission.

If one goes on pilgrimage for the sake of another, he will get one-sixteenth of the benefit. If one goes to a Tīrtha incidentally, one gets half of the benefit.

If one undertakes pilgrimage accompanying another and takes the holy bath, he gets the benefit of the bath but not the benefit of the pilgrimage, as mentioned in the scriptural texts, namely destruction of sins.

A man who takes the holy bath on behalf of the following, gets one-eighth of the benefit: father, paternal uncle, mother, maternal grandfather, maternal uncle, brother, father-in-law, son, patron, grandmother, preceptor, sister, mother's sister, granddaughter, instructor and others.

One doing directly so on behalf of parents shall attain one-fourth of the benefit. Learned men say that the benefit is half in the case of mutual service (of husband and wife). A man obtains a sixth, a third, a fifth and a fourth of the benefit, if he performs a rite on behalf of a sister's son, disciple, brother's son or own son.

Thus, O son of Kuntī, the performance of sacred rites on behalf of others should be undertaken by kinsmen as traditionally practised. The procedure thereof has been recounted to you.

At the advent of rainy season, all the rivers are *Rajasvalās* (like women in their monthly courses) excepting Gaṅgā, Yamunā, Sarasvatī and Narmadā.

CHAPTER TWO HUNDRED TWENTYNINE

The Benefit of Listening to this Purāṇa

Śrī Mārkaṇḍeya said:

1-8. Thus, O king, the Purāṇa, the scriptural text of piety and holy rites has been recounted to you as narrated by Vāyu in the celestial assembly, thanks to the pleasure of Śiva.

There are sixty crore sixty thousand Tīrthas in the beginning, middle and the end of Narmadā at every step.

The Saṁhitā consisting of twelve thousand verses[1] was heard by me even as the Lord of Devas narrated it. It has now been recounted to you.

1. VV 3-4 state that this Purāṇa (*Revā Khaṇḍa*) consists of 12,000 verses and was narrated on Mt. Amanrakaṇṭaka.

While I was staying on Mountain Amarakaṇṭaka, O king, I was asked by you. Everything has been succinctly recounted to you now.

Listen to the meritorious activity of Narmadā. It gives the same benefit as listening to the recitation of all the Vedas along with the six Aṅgas in the *Pada* and *Krama* manner.

It may even be more. When the narrative of the divine river is heard, one attains the same benefit as is gained by a person by performing a twelve-year Satra (sacrifice lasting twelve years).

By taking the holy bath once in Narmadā, one attains the same benefit as is obtained by the holy bath taken in all the Tīrthas including the ocean. The narrative of the activity of Narmadā is auspicious at the beginning, middle and end.

9-15. Listen to the meritorious benefit accruing unto a man who hears the splendid story of Narmadā. He attains Śiva's holy region and becomes an attendant of Rudra and rejoices along with him surrounded by Rudrakanyās.

If the pious text of the narrative, the most excellent one among all scriptural texts, is kept in the house of anyone belonging to any of the four castes,[1] O descendant of Bharata, whether he is in a city or a village, country, rural area or in a big land, he is Brahmā, Śiva himself and Lord Janārdana.

There are three good causes in the world, of which the path of Dharma is the most excellent. It is the weighty scriptural text of Devas too. It is the great cause of Siddhi. O son of Kuntī, I heard it directly from the mouth of Īśvara and recounted to you.

All the meritorious Tīrthas situated on the southern or northern bank (of Narmadā) have been particularly described according to their importance. One who visits, touches, glorifies and listens to them, is liberated from all sins and goes to Rudraloka.

16-24. If this Purāṇa uttered by Śiva is listened to always, a Brāhmaṇa becomes a knower of the Vedic lore, a Kṣatriya becomes victorious, a Vaiśya earns much wealth and a Śūdra becomes righteous.

On hearing this a woman attains conjugal felicity, progeny, wealth and heavenly pleasures.

A Brāhmaṇa-slayer. a drink-addict, a thief and a defiler of

1. This generous ourlook is noteworthy.

preceptor's bed etc., become rid of sins on listening to the greatness of Narmadā.

A sinner creating dissension, an ungrateful one, a servant guilty of the breach of master's trust, a cow-slayer, one who administers poison and one who sells his daughter—all these undoubtedly are rid of sins after listening to it.

O king, those devotees of purified souls, who always listen to it and adore it, are blessed. It is as though Devas, preceptors, Narmadā and Lord Maheśvara—all these are adored by them.

Hence this scripture becomes a bestower of benefits, when assiduously adored with great devotion through sweet scents, flowers and ornaments.

One who gets the entire auspicious story of Narmadā written and makes a gift of it to a Brāhmaṇa attains that benefit which accrues from holy baths and Dāna performed in all the Tīrthas of Narmadā. There is no doubt about it.

25-28. This Purāṇa narrated by Rudra is a bestower of great meritorious benefits, heavenly pleasures, progeny, wealth, fame and glory. It is destructive of all sins, O son of Kuntī, and dispels misery and evil dreams.

It is a bestower of all Siddhis of cherished desires and wealth on those who read and listen.

May there be peace! May there be welfare! May all the people be free from ailments! Hail unto cows and Brāhmaṇas! May piety be our resort, O son of Dharma!

Revā is the destroyer of Narakas. It sanctifies the whole universe through the Tīrthas thereof. O son of Kuntī, may Narmadā be a bestower of piety and all-round welfare on you always!

CHAPTER TWO HUNDRED THIRTY

The Series of Tīrthas Enumerated[1]

Sūta said:

1-10. After saying this to the son of Pāṇḍu, the saintly son of Mṛkaṇḍa, the wise sage who remembered the events of seven Kalpas, stopped.

Everything connected with the excellent greatness of Revā has been recounted to you, O excellent ones, in the way it was recounted to the son of Kuntī by Sage Mārkaṇḍa.

This meritorious, excellent river Revā, the sole sanctifier of the universe, was born of the body of Rudra. It accords freedom from fear unto all living beings.

To the son of Dharma who had requested him (to narrate), the scion of the family of Bhṛgu narrated the different confluences and Tīrthas from Oṁkara to Jaladhi (from the shrine of Oṁkāreśvara to the ocean).

O sages, I shall briefly tell you. How can all the sixty crore sixty seven thousand Tīrthas be recounted by any one? Even in the course of hundreds of years it is not possible.

Yet, O excellent sages, in the manner it was narrated to the son of Kuntī, I shall enumerate the auspicious series of Tīrthas beginning with the holy place Oṁkāra. Even as it is being enumerated briefly, O great sages, be pleased to listen.

After bowing to Maheśāna along with Umā, after bowing down to both Brahmā and Acyuta, Sarasvatī, Gaṇeśāna, the lotus-like feet of Vedavyāsa, all the preceptors of yore, the knowers of seen and unseen objects, after bowing down to the divine river Narmadā, I shall enumerate this series of holy spots.

Oṁ obeisance to Oṁkāreśvara, the omniformed one, the immanent soul of all, beginning with whom, O Brāhmaṇas, I shall enumerate the series of Revā Tīrthas.

11-20. In this splendid and auspicious series of Revā Tīrthas enumerated by Mārkaṇḍa the following are dealt with one by one: the chapters on Purāṇasaṁhitās: The description of the hermitage of Mārkaṇḍa; then the Praśnādhikāra (the section

1. This is an old way of presenting 'Table of Contents'.

of questions asked); then the praise of Narmadā; the glorification of the fifteen flowing currents;

The clarification of the names; the origins of the Kalpas; the enumeration of the names of twenty-one Kalpas;

The characteristic features of the seven Kalpas experienced by Mārkaṇḍeya; the greatness of Revā as well as that of Śiva and Viṣṇu;

Characteristics of Saṁhāra (Annihilation) and the origin of Oṁkāra; the greatness of Oṁkāra; the glorification of Amaraṅkaṭa;

Amareśvara Tīrtha; the great Dāruvana; Dārukeśvara Tīrtha and Carukeśvara Tīrtha;

Carukāsaṅgama confluence; Vyatīpāteśvara; Pātāleśvara Tīrtha and that (Tīrtha) which is called Koṭiyajña;

Varuṇeśvara Tīrtha and the hundred eight Liṅgas; Siddheśvara; Yameśa and Brahmeśvara thereafter;

Sārasvata; Aṣṭarudra; Sāvitra; that which is called Soma; the great Tīrtha Śivakhāta and Rudrāvarta, O excellent Brāhmaṇas;

The great Brahmāvarta Tīrtha; then Sūryāvarta; Pippalāvarta Tīrtha and the confluence of Pippalī;

21-30. The greatness of Amarakaṇṭa; the confluence of Kapilā (with Revā); the origin of Viśalyā; the glorification of Bhṛgutuṅga Mountain;

The meritorious confluence of Viśalyā; the confluence of Karamardā; Karamardeśvara Tīrtha; the excellent Cakratīrtha;

The confluence of Nīlagaṅgā; the annihilation of Tripuras; the glorification of Tīrthas and Dāna; the Madhūka Tṛtīyā Vrata;

Apsareśvara Tīrtha; the injunction regarding hurling of the body; the Tīrtha named Jvāleśvara Tīrtha the confluence of Jvālā;

Śakratīrtha; Kuśāvarta; Haṁsatīrtha; Aṁbarīṣa's Tīrtha and Mahākāleśvara;

Matṛkeśvara Tīrtha; description of Bhṛgu Tuṅga; the greatness of Bhairava there; glorification of Capaleśvara;

The greatness of Caṇḍapāṇi, the confluence of Kāverī; Kubereśvara Tīrtha and the confluence of Vārāhī;

The confluence of Caṇḍavegā; Caṇḍeśvara Tīrtha; the meritorious confluence of Eraṇḍī; the excellent Eraṇḍeśvara Tīrtha;

Pitṛtīrtha there itself and the origin of Oṁkāra there; the greatness of the five Liṅgas of Oṁkāra, O leading sages;

The greatness of Koṭi Tīrtha; and Kākahrada Tīrtha; Jaṁbukeśvara Tīrtha; and Sārasvata Tīrtha thereafter;

31-40. The confluence of Kapilā and Kapileśvara Tīrtha; Daitya-Sūdana Tīrtha and Cakra Tīrtha; Vāmana Tīrtha;

They know of a hundred thousand Tīrthas in the eastern confluence of Kapilā; then the characteristics of Svarga and Naraka as described by the sage;

The structure and internal arrangement of the human body; the description of the gift of a cow; Aśokavanikā Tīrtha and the description of Mataṅga's hermitage;

Aśokeśvara Tīrtha; the excellent Mataṅgeśvara; the meritorious forest of deer; Manoratha Tīrtha there;

The confluence of Aṅgāragartā; the excellent Aṅgāreśvara; Meghavana Tīrtha; the enumeration of the names of the goddess;

The confluence of Kubjā; Kubjeśvara Tīrtha; Bilvāmraka Tīrtha; the Pūrṇadvīpa Tīrtha thereafter;

The confluence of Hiraṇyagarbhā of meritorious glorification; the Tīrtha named Dvīpeśvara;, the meritorious Yajñeśvara;

Māṇḍavyāśrama Tīrtha; the confluence of Viśokā; the Tīrtha named Vagīśvara; the meritorious confluence of Vāgu;

Sahasrāvartaka Tīrtha there; Saugandhika; the confluence of Sarasvatī; the excellent Īśāna Tīrtha;

Devatātraya Tīrtha; Śūlakhāta thereafter; Brahmoda; Śāṅkara; Saumya; and Sārasvata thereafter.

41-50. Sahasrayajña Tīrtha; Kapālamocana; Āgneya; Aditīśa; the excellent Vārāha Tīrtha;

Devapatha Tīrtha; Yajñasahasraka Tīrtha; Śukla Tīrtha; Dīptikeśa; Viṣṇu Tīrtha; Yodhana;

Narmadeśvara Tīrtha; Varuṇeśa; Māruta; Yogeśa; Rohiṇī Tīrtha; and Dārutīrtha, O excellent ones;

Brahmāvarta; Patreśa; Vāhna; Saura glorified: Meghanāda; Dārutīrtha; Devatīrtha; Guhāśraya;

The Tīrtha called Narmadeśvara; the excellent Kapilātīrtha; Karañjeśa; Kuṇḍaleśa; Pippalāda thereafter;

Vimaleśvara Tīrtha; the confluence of Puṣkariṇī; the praise of Śūlabheda; there itself the exploit of Andhaka;

The offer of solace unto the Devas; and the complete subjugation of Andhaka; the origin of Śūlabheda; the testing of the deserving ones; the praise of *Dānadharma* (munificence and piety); the glorification of Ṛṣiśṛṅga; the attainment of Svarga by Dīrghatapas; the inclination of Bhānumatī;

The departure of Śabara to heaven; the greatness of Śūlabheda; Kapileśvara Tīrtha; Mokṣatīrtha thereafter;

The confluence of Mokṣanadī river; Vimaleśvara Tīrtha; Ulūka Tīrtha; the confluence of Puṣkariṇī;

51-60. Ādityeśvara Tīrtha; Saṅgameśvara Tīrtha; the confluence of Bhīmakulyā; the auspicious Bhīmeśvara Tīrtha;

Mārkaṇḍeśvara Tīrtha; Pippaleśvara; Karoṭīśvara Tīrtha; auspicious Indreśvara Tīrtha;

Agastyeśa; Kumāreśa; the excellent Vyāseśvara; Vaidyanātha; Kedāra; the Tīrtha named Ānandeśvara;

Mātṛtīrtha; Muṇḍeśa; Caura; Kāmeśvara; the confluence of Anudhūhī; the two Tīrthas viz. Bhīma Tīrtha and Arjuna Tīrtha; the Tīrtha named Dharmeśvara; Luṅkeśvara thereafter;

Then Dhanadatīrtha; Jaṭeśa; Maṅgaleśvara; Kapileśvara Tīrtha; the excellent Gopāreśvara;

The Tīrtha named Maṇināgeśvara; the confluence of Maṇinadī; Tilakeśvara Tīrtha; Gautameśa thereafter;

The Mātṛtīrtha there itself was described by the sage, O leading sages; Śaṅkhacūḍa; Kedāra; Pārāśara thereafter.

Bhīmeśvara; Candreśa; the confluence of Aśvavatī; Bahvīśvara; Nāradeśa; Vaidyanātha; Kapīśvara;

Kuṁbheśvara; Markaṇḍa; Rāmeśa; Lakṣmaṇeśvara; Megheśvara; Matsyakeśa; what is called Apsarā Hrada;

Dadhiskanda; Madhuskanda; Nandikeśa; Vāruṇa; Pāvakeśvara Tīrtha; Kapileśvara;

61-70. The Tīrtha called Nārāyaṇa; the excellent Cakratīrtha; the great Caṇḍāditya Tīrtha; the excellent Caṇḍikā Tīrtha;

The Tīrtha called Yamahāsa; the auspicious Gaṅgeśvara, what is called Nandikeśvara; what is named Naranārāyaṇa;

Naleśvara; Mārkaṇḍa; Śukla Tīrtha thereafter; the great Vyāseśvara Tīrtha there and Siddheśvara;

Koṭitīrtha; Prabhā Tīrtha; the excellent Vāsukīśvara; the confluence of Karañja; the excellent Mārkaṇḍeśvara;

The Tīrthas named Koṭīśvara, and Saṅkarṣaṇa; Kanakeśa; Manmatheśa; the Anasūyaka Tīrtha;

The meritorious confluence of Eraṇḍī; the splendid Mātṛtīrtha; the Tīrtha called Svarṇaśalākā; Aṁbikeśvara;

Karañjeśa; Bhārateśa; Nāgeśa; Mukuṭeśvara; Saubhāgyasundarī Tīrtha; the excellent Dhanadeśvara;

Rohiṇya; Cakratīrtha; what is called Uttareśvara; Bhogeśvara; Kedāra; Niṣkalaṅka thereafter;

Mārkaṇḍa; Dhautapāpa; Āṅgiraseśvara Tīrtha; the confluence of Kotavī; the meritorious Koṭitīrtha there;

The great Ayonija Tīrtha; the excellent Aṅgāreśvara; Skānda; Nārmada; Brāhma; what is called Vālmīkeśvara;

71-80. Koṭitīrtha; Kapāleśa; Pāṇḍutīrtha; Trilocana Tīrtha, Kapileśa; Kambukeśa; Prabhāsa; Kohaneśvara;

Indreśa; Vālukeśa; Deveśa; Śākra; Nāgeśvara; Gautameśa; the excellent Ahalyātīrtha;

Rāmeśvara; Mokṣatīrtha; Kuśeśvara and Laveśvara, Narmadeśa; Kapardīśa; Sāgareśa thereafter; the great Ghaurāditya Tīrtha; Aparayonija Tīrtha; Piṅgaleśvara Tīrtha, the excellent Bhṛgvīśvara;

Daśāśvamedhika Tīrtha; Koṭitīrtha, O excellent ones; Mārkaṇḍa; Brahmatīrtha; the excellent Ādivarāha;

The Tīrtha named Āśāpūra; Kaubera; Māruta; Varuṇeśa Yameśa; Rāmeśa; Karkaṭeśvara;

Śakreśa; Somatīrtha; the excellent Nandāhrada; the Vaiṣṇavacakra Tīrtha; the ones called after Rāma and Keśava;

Rukmiṇī Tīrtha; the excellent Śiva Tīrtha; Jayavārāha Tīrtha; the Tīrtha called Asmāhaka;

Aṅgāreśa; Siddheśa; Tāpeśvara thereafter; again the Tīrtha named Siddheśvara; Varuṇeśvara;

The meritorious Parāśareśvara; the excellent Kusumeśa; Kuṇḍaleśvara Tīrtha and Kalakaleśvara;

81-90. What is called Nyaṅkuvārāha; the excellent Aṅkola Tīrtha; Śvetavārāha Tīrtha; Bhargala; the excellent Saura Tīrtha;

Huṁkārasvāmi Tīrtha; the splendid Śukla Tīrtha; the confluence of Madhumatī; Saṅgameśvara Tīrtha;

Narmadeśvara; the confluence of three rivers; Anekeśvara Tīrtha; Śarbheśa named after Mokṣa;

The meritorious confluence of Kāverī; the Tīrtha called Gopeśvara; Mārkaṇḍeśa; Nāgeśa; the confluence of Udaṁbarī;

The Tīrtha called Sāṁbāditya and the confluence of Udambarī; Siddheśvara (Mārkaṇḍa) as well as that created by Siddheśvarī;

Gopeśa; Kapileśa; the excellent Vaidyanātha; Piṅgaleśvara Tīrtha; the great Saindhavāyatana;

The Tīrtha called Bhūtīśvara; thereafter Gaṅgāvāha; Gautameśvara Tīrtha and Daśāśvamedhika;

The meritorious Bhṛgutīrtha and the well known Saubhāgyasundarī; Vṛṣakhāta there itself; Kedāra; Dhūtapātaka;

Dhūteśvarī Tīrtha; Eraṇḍī Saṅgama; Kanakeśvarī Tīrtha, Jvāleśvara Tīrtha thereafter;

The Tīrtha named Śālagrāma; the excellent Somanātha; Udīrṇavārāha Tīrtha; Candraprabhāsaka;

91-100. Dvādaśāditya Tīrtha; the Tīrtha that is named Siddheśvara; Kapileśvara Tīrtha, the auspicious Traivikarma Tīrtha;

The Tīrtha called Viśvarūpa; that which is created by Nārāyaṇa; Mūlaśrīpati Tīrtha; what is called Caulaśrīpati;

Devatīrtha; Haṁsatīrtha; the excellent Prabhāsa Tīrtha; Mūlasthāna; Kaṇtheśa; the Aṭṭahāsa Tīrtha thereafter;

Bhūrbhuveśvara Tīrtha; the well known Śūlesvarī; Sārasvata; Dārukeśa; the excellent Tīrtha of Aśvins;

The unparalleled Sāvitrī Tīrtha; Vālakhilyeśvara; Narmadeśa; Mātṛtīrtha; the excellent Devatīrtha;

Macchakeśvara Tīrtha, the splendid Śikhitīrtha; O excellent sage, Koṭitīrtha and Mṛḍā named Koṭīśvarī;

The Tīrtha named Paitāmaha; (Tīrtha) called Māṇḍavyeśvara; Nārāyaṇeśa there; Akrūreśa thereafter;

Devakhāta; Siddharudra; the excellent Vaidyanātha; Matṛtīrtha; Uttareśa thereafter;

Narmadeśa; Mātṛtīrtha again; Kurarī Tīrtha; Ḍhauṇḍheśa; Daśakanyaka;

Suvarṇabindutīrtha; Ṛṇapāpapramocana; Bhārabhūteśvara Tīrtha; Muṇḍīśvara;

101-110. Ekaśāla; Ḍiṇḍipāṇi; the great Āpsarasa Tīrtha; Munyālaya; Mārkaṇḍa Tīrtha named Gaṇitā-Devatā;

Amaleśvara Tīrtha; Kantheśvara Tīrtha; Āṣaḍhı Tırtha; Śṛṅgī Tīrtha;

Bakeśvara Tīrtha; Kapāleśa; Mārkaṇḍa; Kapileśa; the confluence of Eraṇḍī;

Eraṇḍi Devatā Tīrtha; Rāmatīrtha thereafter; the great Tīrtha of Jamadagni, the confluence of Revā and the ocean;

Loṭaṇeśvara Tīrtha; Tīrtha named Luṅkeśa; Vṛṣakhāta Kuṇḍa also, O excellent sages;

Haṁseśvara; Tilāda; Vāsaveśvara; Koṭīśvara Tīrtha; the excellent Alikā Tīrtha; Vimaleśvara Tīrtha in the confluence of Revā and the ocean.

Thus the highly meritorious series of the Tīrthas has been

described by me, O great sages. The meritorious pearl necklace of the Tīrthas has been wreathed through the string in the form of the banks.

It is purified by the waters of Narmadā. It has been made by Mārkaṇḍeya for embellishing good people and for the welfare of all the worlds.

It suppresses the darkness of sins. It should always be worn by the seekers of piety. By repeating this once, sin committed in the course of a day and night is destroyed.

By repeating this three times, the sin arising in the course of a month is destroyed. By repeating it before Śiva, sin committed in the course of three months is destroyed. By repeating it for a month, sin of a year is destroyed and by repeating it for a year, sin of a hundred years is destroyed.

111-113. If a devotee recites the meritorious series of the Tīrthas, standing before Brāhmaṇas taking food at the time of Śrāddha, he would be on a par with one who performs Gayāśrāddha.

If he recites this with faith in front of the deities at the time of worship, he will delight all the Devas and sanctify the entire family.

Thus the meritorious series of Tīrthas situated on the banks of Revā has been recounted by me, O sinless excellent sages. Listen further.

CHAPTER TWO HUNDRED THIRTYONE

The Number of Tīrthas Enumerated

Sūta said:

1-6. Similarly, O excellent sages, I shall enumerate the Tīrthastabakas (bunches of flowers in the form of the Tīrthas) wherewith the wreath of Tīrtha series has been strung together and divided (into separate units) for the increase of devotees' delight.

I shall mention the bunches (groups) of the Tīrthas in the same manner as mentioned by the son of Mṛkaṇḍa earlier in response to the queries made by the son of Kuntī.

Indeed the meritorious Revā is the *Kalpalatā* (wish-yielding creeper) that originated by drinking the water of Śiva. It is splendidly blossomed through the flowers of the Tīrthas situated on both the banks. The three worlds have been rendered fragrant by the glorious sweet scents.

Sage Mārkaṇḍa, the most excellent one among intelligent persons is, indeed the bee capable of knowing best the taste of the honey of those flowers.

The sage, a leading scion of the family of Bhṛgu, always wears in his heart that sacred garland of flowers rendered decorative by the bunches of Tīrthas. O excellent sages, I shall explain the situation of the bunches thereof.

7-18. Beginning with Oṁkāra Tīrtha and ending with the western ocean, there are thirty-five confluences of rivers. They are destructive of sins.

They are eleven on the northern bank and twenty-three on the southern bank. The thirty-fifth one, the most excellent one, is the confluence of Revā and the ocean.

Thus along with the confluences on the two banks of Revā, there are four hundred famous Tīrthas, O excellent Brāhmaṇas.

There are three hundred thirty-three Śiva Tīrthas. I shall mention these too individually, which you listen to, O excellent ones.

O leading sages, among them there are ten Mārkaṇḍeśvara Tīrthas, ten originating from Āditya (i.e. Āditya Kṣetras), nine Kapileśvaras, eight installed by Soma, an equal number of Narmadeśvaras, eight Koṭitīrthas, and seven Siddheśvaras.

Nāgeśvaras are seven on both the banks of Revā. Seven indeed are created (installed) by Vahni (Fire-god). There are seven Āvartas there.

Kedāreśvara Tīrthas are five and five Indra Tīrthas. Varuṇeśas are five and five indeed are Dhanadeśvaras. There are five Devatīrthas and four Yameśvaras;

Vaidyanāthas are four and four are Vānareśvara Tīrthas. O leading sages, Aṅgāreśvara Tīrthas also are as many. Sārasvata Tīrthas are four and there are four Dārukeśvaras.

Gautameśvara Tīrthas are three and Rāmeśvara Tīrthas are also three. Kapāleśvara Tīrthas and Haṁsatīrthas are three each.

Mokṣatīrthas are three and Vimaleśvaras too are three. The sage stated that there are three Sahasra-yajña Tīrthas.

19-27. Three Bhīmeśvaras are enumerated and there are three Svarṇatīrthas. Two Dhautapāpakṣetras have been mentioned. So also two Karañjeśas.

There are two Ṛṇamocana Tīrthas and two Skandeśvaras. O Brāhmaṇas, there are two Daśāśvamedha Tīrthas and two Nandī Tīrthas.

There are two Manmatheśas and two Bhṛgutīrthas. There are two Parāśareśvaras and two Ayonīsaṁbhavas.

There are two Vyāseśvaras and two Pitṛtīrthas have been mentioned. There are two Nandikeśvara Tīrthas and two Gopeśvaras have been remembered.

So also two Māruteśas and two Jvāleśvaras are remembered. There are two meritorious Śuklatīrthas and two Apsareśatīrthas.

There are two Pippaleśvara Tīrthas and two Tīrthas named Māṇḍavyeśvara. Similarly the scion of the family of Bhṛgu enumerated two Dvīpeśvaras. There are two Uttareśvara Tīrthas and two Aśokeśas, two Yodhanapuras and two Rohiṇī Tīrthas.

Two Luṅkeśvaras have been enumerated by the sage. O Brāhmaṇas, there are one hundred nineteen Tīrthas mentioned one by one. Two hundred fourteen Tīrthas have been grouped in the *Stabakas* (bunches).

These Tīrthas are Śaivas (pertaining to Śiva). O excellent ones, listen to the Vaiṣṇava, Brāhma and Śākta Tīrthas enumerated in order.

28-38. The sage enumerated twenty-eight Vaiṣṇava Tīrthas. O excellent sages; among them six are Vārāha Tīrthas.

Four are Cakratīrthas. The remaining eighteen alone are praised by Viṣṇu. Thus the son of Mṛkaṇḍu said earlier.

Seven Tīrthas have been enumerated where Brahmā achieved *Siddhi*. In three of them there is the adoration performed by Brahmā and the other four have Brahmā as the Lord. Thus twenty-eight Tīrthas have been enumerated in due order and number.

This is unparalleled in sanctity; this is excessively destructive of sins. The greatness of the meritorious story of Narmadā has been declared by the sage.

Sūta said:

Thus the series of Tīrthas on Revā have been generally briefly mentioned by me in the same way as Sage Mārkaṇḍa recounted to the son of Kuntī.

Many subsidiary Tīrthas are concealed therein. O sinless ones, listen to the details as to where and how many lie embedded there.

All round Oṁkāra Tīrtha in all directions within two Krośas from Mountain Amarakaṇṭaka the number of Tīrthas whether hidden or manifest, O excellent Brāhmaṇa, is three and a half crore.

In the confluence of Kapilā, there are a crore of Tīrthas.

In Aśokavanikā Tīrtha there are a hundred thousand shrines.

O excellent sages, in the confluence of Aṅgāragartā, there are a hundred Tīrthas.

There are ten thousand Tīrthas in the confluence of Kubjā. A hundred Tīrthas are stationed in the confluence of Hiraṇyagarbhā.

There are sixty-eight Tīrthas in the confluence of Viśokā and a thousand Tīrthas in the confluence of Vāgu.

39-45. There are a hundred Tīrthas in the confluence of Sarasvatī, two hundred in Śukla Tīrtha, a thousand in Viṣṇutīrthas and ten thousand in Māhiṣmatī.

O Brāhmaṇas, more than a hundred thousand Tīrthas are present in Śūlabheda. The sage has mentioned that there are more than a thousand Tīrthas in Devagrāma.

More than seven hundred Tīrthas are present in Luṅkeśvara and one hundred eight Tīrthas in the confluence of Maṇinadī . They know of more than one hundred eight Tīrthas in Vaidyanātha.

O Brāhmaṇas, in Kuṁbheśvara Tīrtha there are as many. More than a hundred thousand Tīrthas are situated in the confluence of Revā and Urī.

It is the statement of Mārkaṇḍa that there may be more than that. Eighty-eight thousand Tīrthas are present in Vyāsadvīpa.

There are ten thousand eight Tīrthas in the confluence of Karañjā. Similarly there are one hundred eight Tīrthas in the confluence of Eraṇḍī. There are sixty-eight Tīrthas in Dhūtapāpā. The sage has spoken of a hundred meritorious Tīrthas in the Skānda Tīrtha.

46-54. Sixty-eight Tīrthas are present in Kohaneśa and one crore and a half Tīrthas are present in Koriḷāpura.

He has mentioned more than a thousand in Rāmakeśava Tīrtha. Indeed a thousand Tīrthas are present in Asmāhaka.

O excellent Brāhmaṇas, there are eight hundred two thousand Tīrthas in Śuklatīrtha as mentioned to the son of Kuntī by the scion of the family of Bhṛgu formerly.

In the case of the remaining rivers, except in the case of the confluence of Kāverī, he has mentioned one hundred eight Tīrthas in each confluence.

O Brāhmaṇas, there are five hundred Tīrthas in the confluence of Kāverī. As said, special efficacy exists in the Tīrthas during Parvans (festival days).

They say that Mokṣatīrtha is excellent and supported by the Purāṇapuruṣa (Ancient Being). One crore Tīrthas are present in the holy spot of Bhṛgu. O excellent sages, who is competent to speak more about the Tīrthas? It is mentioned as the resort of all immortal ones and all Tīrthas. It is well-known in all the three worlds and is honoured. It is the means of achievement of miraculous powers. In Bhārabhūti one hundred eight Tīrthas are present.

One hundred fifty Tīrthas are present in Akrūreśvara Tīrtha. The sage has mentioned that there are more than a hundred thousand Tīrthas in Vimaleśvara Tīrtha at the confluence of Revā and the ocean.

CHAPTER TWO HUNDRED THIRTYTWO

The Finale of the Revā Khaṇḍa

Sūta said:

1-7. Thus, O Brāhmaṇas, the excellent greatness of Revā has been recounted to you as imparted to the son of Kuntī formerly by Mārkaṇḍeya.

So also the groups of the Tīrthas with special characteristics in some have been recounted by me in the proper order and the due number.

This is unparalleled in sanctity. This is highly destructive of sins. The story of Narmadā and the greatness spoken by the sage is meritorious.

O leading sages, the intelligent son of Mṛkaṇḍa, the Brāhmaṇa who survived seven Kalpas on Narmadā was the most excellent one among those who know the Highest Reality.

Formerly after resorting to all the Tīrthas and all the rivers, he sought refuge in Revā whom he saw as one who remembers many Kalpas, one born of the physical form of Śiva and one about whom Śarva said, "This is my Kalā (digit)." She is a divine river without old age and death, the great destroyer of Daityas. She is endowed with great power, is a destroyer of worldly existence, the very Jāhnavī (Gaṅgā) of Bhava.

He (i.e. Mārkaṇḍeya) had great and excellent devotion towards her and he became free from old age and mortality.

8-18. O excellent ones, sixty crore sixty thousand Tīrthas are established on both the banks together step by step.

All round there are thousands of rivers with Tīrthas therein. But, O leading sages, I think they never come on a par with Revā.

O Brāhmaṇas, thus everything that was asked by you has been recounted to you, which originally the Wind-god told the sages after having himself heard directly from the mouth of Maheśa.

Similarly the son of Mṛkaṇḍa too after seeing the sacred river along with the Tīrthas step by step narrated it to the son of Pāṇḍu.

Thus, O excellent Brāhmaṇas, the meritorious story of Narmadā, very rare in all the three worlds, has been narrated to you.

Of what avail is the water of the thousands of other rivers, if the water of Revā that destroys sins is resorted to?

A person who resorts to the water of Mekalā attains permanent salvation.

Even as a man resorts to it always with faith or without it and undertakes pilgrimage to the Tīrthas, he will invariably obtain whatever he wishes.

This water of Narmadā is directly Brahmā, Hari and the great Hara. This is the Brahman without form, the *Kaivalya* (state of being the Absolute).

The Tīrthas and the rivers that bestow pleasing benefits may roar only as long as Revā and the eager service thereto is not remembered by men during Kali Age.

Certainly, for the sake of the welfare of the world, this Revā, a power in the form of a river, has been caused to issue forth from his own body by Śiva.

Yajñās, forests and holy shrines etc., roar much only as long as the glorification of the name of Narmadā is not carried out in the Kali Age.

19-30. The weight of austerities, Dānas, Vratas and other things is reckoned only so long as the river born of Bharga is not resorted to by men on the earth.

Those who stay on the northern bank are the followers of Rudra (and go to Rudra's region). Those who stay on the southern bank attain the Vaiṣṇava Loka.

They are blessed, they are the excellent ones who reside in the lands where this Narmadā flows continuously, this Narmadā that is capable of destroying Narakas. It is created by Śiva himself.

Those who drink the meritorious water originating from the river of the Consort of Pārvatī, are really meritorious. They never meet with grief.

O Brāhmaṇas, one who listens to or glorifies this unparalleled sacred story of Revā, is rid of all sins.

The benefit thereof is eight times more than the benefit obtained when all the Vedas along with the six Aṅgas recited in the *Pada* and *Krama* order are listened to.

By listening once to the story of Revā one obtains that benefit which a performer of Sattra lasting twelve years obtains.

By listening once to the greatness of Revā, one gets the benefit of plunging into all the Tīrthas, Oceans etc. This narrative is conducive to piety. It is most excellent of all scriptures. If it is written(copied) and kept in the house by any person of any caste, in any village, city, rural zone or region of land, that man is Brahmā, that man is Śiva, he is Lord Janārdana himself.

This is the path of piety, wealth, love and salvation, resorted to by Devas. It is the preceptor of preceptors. It is the great scripture causing the achievement of perfection.

31-39. A devotee should always listen to this Purāṇa uttered by the Lord. A Brāhmaṇa shall become well-versed in the Vedas; a Kṣatriya becomes victorious; a Vaiśya becomes wealthy; and a Śūdra becomes pious.

By listening to this a woman obtains conjugal felicity and good progeny and also glory, happiness, heavenly residence and rebirth in a most excellent family.

The following sinners are liberated from sins : a person who discriminates in seating people in rows at the time of meals, the ungrateful, one disloyal to one's master, one who deceives friends, a slayer of cows, an administerer of poison, one who sells one's daughters, a Brāhmaṇa-slayer, an imbiber of liquor, a thief, one who lies on the bed of the preceptor. These and other sinners listening to the story of Narmadā and resorting to the river for a year, shall undoubtedly be liberated from all sins.

One who spoils cooked food, one who cooks wastefully, one who censures Devas and Brāhmaṇas, a slanderer of parents, preceptors, good people and king—all these undoubtedly are liberated from sins.

Those persons of purified souls who listen everyday to this sacred narrative pertaining to Narmadā and worship it with flowers, fruits, sandalpaste etc., diverse kinds of food offerings, do get great benefit. If this sacred story is honoured, it is as though Devas and preceptors are honoured.

40-49. This benefit happens here as well as in the other world. No hesitation need be felt in this respect. Hence by means of all efforts one should worship devoutly this sacred book and a person who reads it must be honoured with scents, garments, ornaments, etc., and also the book, *Revā-Māhātmya.* In regard to the auspicious story of Narmadā, one obtains that benefit which is usually obtained through study of the Vedas and the maintenance of Agnihotras.

By listening to the story of Narmadā one gets that merit entirely which is obtained in Kurukṣetra, Prabhāsa, Puṣkara, Rudrāvarta, Gayā, Varāṇasī in particular, Gaṅgādvāra, Prayāga, the confluence of Gaṅga and the ocean and other similar Tīrthas. The story of Narmadā is auspicious in the beginning, middle and end. Listen to the great benefit that one who devoutly listens to it gets.

After reaching the shrine of Śiva, he will become an attendant of Rudra. He will be surrounded by virgins of Devas. He will rejoice with Śiva.

This is a narrative of reighteousness. It is meritorious. It is the most excellent of all narratives. O excellent ones, it should be read in the house of anyone of the four castes. I consider his house blessed. The householder and the family are also blessed. If any devotee honours the book about Narmadā, it is as though Narmadā too is honoured and also Lord Maheśvara. If the reader is honoured, Devas and sages too are honoured.

50-55. A man who causes the entire excellent story of Narmadā to be written and gifts it to a Brāhmaṇa obtains the benefit of plunging into Narmadā and all other Tīrthas. There is no doubt about it.

This story is an ornament unto all the scriptures. This Purāṇa is narrated by Rudra. It accords the benefit of great merit, heavenly pleasures and sons. It is conducive to wealth, fame and glory.

It augments piety and longevity. It destroys misery and evil dreams. It bestows all the Siddhis and cherished things on those who read and listen to. If this Purāṇa of great merit gifted by one is read by Brāhmaṇas the devotee stays in Śivaloka for as many years as there are letters in the Purāṇa.

Thus this story of Narmadā has been narrated well by the chief sage Sūta. Originally it was obtained by the Wind-god from the mouth of Śarva and narrated to others. It is worthy of being known by all the three worlds. Sūta narrated this in front of the sages and the Kulapati.

:: The End of Revā Khaṇḍa ::

INDEX